# A Brilliant
# Solution

# Carol Berkin

# *A Brilliant Solution*

❦

## Inventing the American Constitution

Harcourt, Inc.

*New York   San Diego   London*

www.HarcourtBooks.com

Library of Congress Cataloging-in-Publication Data
Berkin, Carol.
A brilliant solution: inventing the American Constitution/Carol
Berkin.—1st ed.
p.      cm.
Includes index.
ISBN 0-15-100948-1
1. United States. Constitutional Convention (1787)
2. United States—Politics and government—1783–1789.
3. Statesmen—United States—History—18th century.
4. United States. Constitution—Signers.
5. Constitutional history—United States.   I. Title.
E303 .B47 2002
973.3'18—dc21   2002005648

Text set in Adobe Caslon
Designed by Linda Lockowitz

Printed in the United States of America

First edition
C  E  G  I  K  J  H  F  D  B

*To the "Sunday Morning Dissertation Salon"—*
*Angelo Angelis, Kathy Feeley, and Cindy Lobel*

# Contents

# A Brilliant Solution

# Introduction

THE GENESIS OF THIS BOOK lies in two national crises:
the first, a challenge to the peaceful transition of
power in the White House; the second, a challenge to the
security of our nation. These two crises—the disputed
presidential election of 2000 and the bombing of the Pentagon and the World Trade Center—made me realize
that, after thirty years as a historian, I begin every struggle
to understand the present with a search of the past.

On November 7, 2000, with winter's chill already in
the air, Americans across the country went to the polls to
cast their vote for the new president of the United States.
While the ballot they encountered contained choices on
state or local officials and perhaps referendums on local
issues, these were overshadowed by the choice of a new
occupant of the Oval Office. Whether they went to bed
early or stayed up until the wee hours of the morning,
most voters expected that they would know the name of

their next president on the following day. There was, after all, a vast network of television and radio stations, news services, poll takers and statisticians, computer experts and "number crunchers," not to mention current and former politicians drafted by the media working around the clock to provide commentary and make predictions about the outcome of the election. Albert Gore or George W. Bush—Americans would learn the name of the victor over their morning coffee.

It was not so. For weeks, indeed months, what will surely become the most celebrated disputed election in presidential history dragged on. Accusations and counteraccusations of fraud, deception, mechanical error, and human error raged around the votes cast in the state of Florida, and a new term—"the chad"—entered the American vocabulary. The battle was waged in the courts and in the media rather than in the military or the streets, reflecting perfectly the political culture of the nation. In the end, the Supreme Court played a role in settling the dispute. The true victory, most commentators and political figures agreed, was the fact that the American Constitution had come through yet another trial by fire and a peaceful transition of power had been achieved. But the true lesson seemed to be that the presidency was the only prize worth winning.

ON SEPTEMBER 11, 2001, on a beautiful sunny day in New York City, two planes, commandeered by terrorists, struck and destroyed the World Trade Center. To the south, in Washington, D.C., a third plane crashed into the Pentagon, sending smoke billowing into the sky within sight of the White House. To many Americans, this attack on their own soil seemed like a dream, or, more properly, a nightmare—the reality of it took days, perhaps weeks to sink in.

We, as a nation, were dazed and shaken—but we looked with considerable confidence to the national government, and especially to the president, to direct our response to the crisis. That response came quickly. Military jet fighters raced to provide protection for the president of the United States. The vice president was taken to safety as well. At the same time, diplomats moved to secure cooperation from other nations, wielding the great influence and power of the United States to prompt this cooperation, even before any policy regarding the terrorists was firmly in place. Congress members and senators took up critical issues, debating and passing emergency relief funding for New York City, aid packages for domestic industries, and changes in law enforcement restrictions, and sending them to the president for his approval. Government officials quickly took advantage of the media that brought news, commentary, and discussion into the homes of virtually every American. President Bush soon appeared on television, speaking directly to the nation and the world. And over the ensuing days and weeks, the president, as the leader of the national government, set out the official policy that would be pursued in dealing with the terrorist threat at home and abroad. Within days billions of dollars worth of military equipment and thousands of military personnel were deployed for a war against the terrorists responsible for the attacks and those who harbored them. In the simple caption "America Strikes Back," the dominance of the United States in world affairs was affirmed.

FOR A HISTORIAN, the need to put current events in historical perspective is an occupational hazard. But these two crises seemed to provoke a similar need in others. Since November 2000 scores of network anchormen and –women, radio talk show hosts, my own college and graduate students, and neighbors I have encountered in the supermarket have asked me the same question that I have asked myself: What would the founding fathers think of these events? Any answer, no matter how expert the historian, could only be conjecture. But the question prompted me to set down answers to other questions that might help Americans gain the historical perspective they seemed to be seeking. What political crises had the founding fathers faced, and how did they react to them? What problems did they hope to solve when they met and drafted a new constitution in the summer of 1787? What role did they envision for the president and for other branches of the government in times of calm or crisis? What dangers did they think lay ahead for their nation?

The image of the United States, and of its government, projected in the election crisis and the terrorist attacks makes the leap across the centuries to 1787 a difficult one. It takes a conscious act of imagination to see America through the eyes of its founding fathers—and to share their perspective may be disturbing. These men inhabited a world alien to modern Americans, a world in which the United States was a fragile, uncertain experiment, a newcomer, and to some degree a beggar at the gates of power and prestige among nations. In 1787 our treasury was empty. Debts to foreign governments and debts to our own citizens could not be paid, and this was a blow to the nation's honor as well as to its future credit. Everywhere these men looked, anarchy seemed to threaten, for the Revolution had unleashed new expectations and a new rhetoric of equality and political participation. These new ideas threatened a social revolution that would destroy not only their own fortunes but also the rule of law. All around them civil strife seemed to be erupting unchecked, and news of uprisings in western Pennsylvania, Virginia, and Massachusetts during the previous year shook the confidence not only of these wealthy men but also of Americans of all social classes. With no police force of any sort, military or civil, the restoration of law and order was in doubt. Even worse, a political disorder on the highest levels had reached critical proportions. The cooperation among the states, forged in the 1770s and sustained during the war, had vanished with independence. Competition and exploitation reigned, and the revival of a fierce localism pitted Virginian against Marylander, New Yorker against New Jerseyite, Georgian against South Carolinian. And while state governments vied with one another, the "league of friendship" called the Confederation that Americans had established as their first national government grew more impotent, more lethargic, and more incompetent with every passing day. The nation was on the verge of self-destruction—or, worse, of simply fading away. Not a few French and English officials in America predicted that soon enough this upstart experiment in republicanism would come to an end.

Looking back, we might argue that the founding fathers' dire predictions and sense of impending doom were exaggerated. Perhaps the nation's recovery from postwar economic depression was simply slow, not impossible. Perhaps a compromise on providing funds to the Confederation government so that it could honor its debts would have eventually been hammered out. Perhaps the states, weary of bickering and sabotaging one another, would have revived policies of cooperation in matters of trade and commerce. Perhaps backcountry farmers would have abandoned direct action in favor of the slower processes of legislative reform. Such Monday-morning quarterbacking is a hallowed American tradition. Yet historians engage in it at great risk. Our job is to understand the motivations and actions of historical figures, and to do this we must begin with their perceptions of their present circumstances and their future. Reading the correspondence of George Washington, James Madison, William Livingston, and Alexander Hamilton, one cannot doubt that they viewed their circumstances gravely. It was this sense of crisis that led them to Philadelphia in May 1787, where they gathered behind locked doors and bolted windows to overthrow the legitimate government established by the Articles of Confederation and, by writing the Constitution, to stage what can only be called a bloodless coup d'état.

It would be comforting to think that the men who created that constitution believed confidently that they were designing a government for the ages. Many historians have told the story in just this comforting way. Those who take as gospel Thomas Jefferson's exaggerated claims that the founders were "demigods" assure us that the hand of God guided the pens of the convention members. Others tell us that these men convened in order to set America's destiny in a stone as solid as the Ten Commandments. From these historians has come a story of men with a vision and the intellectual and moral means to achieve it. Many scholars who take a more secular view describe the Constitution as an embodiment of a shared political culture, an expression of a widely shared consensus on political and social values. They, too, appear certain that the founding fathers knew what they were about. Even the historians who view the convention as a gathering of socially conservative, self-interested members of a ruling class, prompted by a desire to protect the "haves" from the jealous actions of the "have-nots," portray these counterrevolutionaries as confident manipulators and astute politicians. In short, the majority of historians seem to suggest that the founders knew just what to do—and did it, creating a government that would endure for centuries.

The members of the Constitutional Convention would be amused to read these histories. For the only people not certain of the choices to be made at the convention, and even less certain of the longevity and effectiveness of the government they would eventually produce, were the founders themselves. Before the convention began, betting men were divided over the ability of representatives from the thirteen states to agree on anything at all. George Washington was one of the doubting Thomases. For most of the month of July 1787, the delegates feared the convention would dissolve, broken by intractable disagreements. From September until spring of the following year, men like James Madison anguished over the possibility that the Constitution would be rejected by the ratifying conventions.

If these men doubted that the convention could achieve anything at all, they also doubted how long any of their achievements could last. The congenitally optimistic Benjamin Franklin captured the limited hopes of his fellow delegates when he observed that, with luck and wisdom, they would produce a government that could forestall, for a decade perhaps, the inevitable decline of the Republic into a tyranny of one, a tyranny of a few, or a tyranny of the majority. A noted historian once characterized the men who opposed the Constitution as "men of little faith," implying that the Constitution's authors were optimists about the future of the government they had created. Yet the papers of the founding fathers do not support this interpretation. Madison's remarkable record of the debates in the convention reveal, on virtually every page, a collective anxiety about what they were doing and a near-paranoid fear of conspiracies springing up around them—and among them. If they assumed a set of enduring truths, many of these truths were negative. Chief among them were that men were corruptible and that power always corrupted. Greed and lust for power, as Franklin frequently pointed out in the convention debates, were unquenchable in mortal men.

Anxious and uncertain, the convention delegates nevertheless persevered. They brought to bear their political experience, their sensitivities to legal loopholes, their commitment to representative government, and they focused their energies and attentions on resolving existing conflicts, correcting existing errors, and protecting as best they could against a descent into tyranny. When they were done, they submitted their handiwork to the citizens for ratification rather than attempting to impose it through assassination or military force. In this way, they invited their neighbors to share responsibility for the fate of their experiment in representative government.

It is this story of anxious but determined men who set for themselves the task of saving their nation that I have set out to tell. The structure that resulted from their efforts will seem both comfortingly familiar and strangely alien to modern readers. It was a government in which Congress rather than the president was assigned the responsibility of leading the nation. Indeed, the executive branch emerges in this original constitution as a secondary arm of authority, more restricted than empowered, more a handmaiden to the legislators than their guide. The delegates applied themselves most intensely to crafting the lawmaking branch of government, leaving the judiciary to be fleshed out later on and devising the mechanism by which the executive was chosen more by default than by choice.

I can only imagine the bewilderment and bemusement the convention delegates would feel if they were somehow magically transported to America in the twenty-first century. How would we explain the intense struggle over the election of the president in 2000 while the election of many Congress members was noted only in passing? What would they think of the hybrid of universal suffrage and their older mechanism of an electoral college? How could we reassure them that political parties were not the nightmare of partisanship and faction they had labored so hard to prevent? They would surely marvel at the place of pride the United States held in the family of nations, but they would be puzzled by our unspoken assumption, so evident after September 11, that the president was expected to set our agenda in every aspect of domestic and foreign relations. "Hail to the Chief" would be a tune only Alexander Hamilton might relish hearing played.

Above all, I am certain that they would be amazed— and thankful—that the Republic they gave life to had endured.

# CHAPTER ONE

# The Call for a Convention

## "Our present federal government is a name, a shadow"

THE YEAR WAS 1786. It was the tenth anniversary of the Declaration of Independence and the third year of life in a new nation, but political leaders everywhere feared there was little cause to celebrate. Dark clouds and a suffocating gloom seemed to have settled over the country, and these men understood that something had gone terribly wrong. From his plantation in Virginia, George Washington lamented the steady stream of diplomatic humiliations suffered by the young Republic. Fellow Virginian James Madison talked gravely of mortal diseases afflicting the confederacy. In New Jersey William Livingston confided to a friend his doubt that the Republic could survive another decade. From Massachusetts the bookseller turned Revolutionary strategist, Henry Knox, declared, "Our present federal government is a name, a shadow, without power, or effect." And feisty, outspoken John Adams, serving as the American minister

to Great Britain, observed his nation's circumstances with
more than his usual pessimism. The United States, he
declared, was doing more harm to itself than the British
army had ever done. Alexander Hamilton, John Jay,
James Monroe, Robert Morris—in short, men from
every state—agreed that a serious crisis had settled upon
the nation. The question was could they do anything to
save their country?

It seemed like only yesterday that these same men,
along with Americans everywhere, had greeted the future
brightly. In 1783 Americans had looked forward confidently to reaping the benefits of independence. British
political oppression, with its threat to natural rights and
traditional liberties, had come to an end, and with it the
challenge to America's most dearly held principle, "No
taxation without representation." In every colony turned
state, lawmaking was safely in the hands of a representative assembly, and a guarantee of citizens' rights was
written into most state constitutions. British economic
oppression had ended as well. Free from the restraints
imposed by British navigation, or trade, laws, American
shippers, farmers, and planters looked forward to selling
tobacco and wheat directly to foreign nations, and entrepreneurs looked forward to manufacturing finished products for sale to markets abroad. New Englanders were
equally optimistic, for John Adams's dogged persistence
had won them the right to fish the outer banks of Newfoundland. Independence also meant that the rich farm-
lands west of the Appalachians were at last open to

settlement, good news for ordinary farmers and perhaps even better news for major speculators like George Washington, the Lees of Virginia, and even Benjamin Franklin, who owned shares in large land companies.

Unfortunately, each of these blessings soon proved to have a darker side. True, the restrictions and injustices suffered in the colonial era had been eliminated but so, too, had many of the advantages of membership in the British empire. An independent American merchant marine was free to carry American products to the ports of their choosing, but they no longer enjoyed the protection of the British navy on the high seas. New England fishermen had won the right to fish off Newfoundland, but they had lost the guaranteed British Caribbean markets for their catch. Chesapeake tobacco planters had renounced their debts to Scottish merchants and English consignment agents when they declared independence, but in the process they had lost their most reliable sources of credit. And settlers faced no barriers to westward migration, but they could no longer rely on a well-trained and well-equipped army when Indians attacked. Slowly, Americans realized their new dilemma: Who would provide the protection colonists once found in the sheltering arms of their mother country?

The pessimism slowly engulfing men from Maine to Georgia was intensified by the lingering postwar depression in the South and in New England. Two major British military campaigns had left the Carolinas in shambles, with scores of homeless and penniless still to be cared for.

Rice planters had to replace much of their labor force as hundreds of slaves had run away or found refuge in British army camps. Farther north peace, not war, had dealt the crushing blow to New England's economy. Despairing, idle fishermen could be seen in every seaport town, helpless in the face of British trade restrictions against them in the West Indies. Local agriculture fared no better. Far from the battlefield during most of the Revolution, New England farmers had expanded their production to meet the demands for food in other regions. Now that farming had resumed in every state, New Englanders were scrambling to meet mortgage payments for land they had cleared and planted during the Revolution. A wave of foreclosures and evictions swept across the western counties of Massachusetts, and local prisons soon overflowed with debtors. In Berkshire and Hampshire Counties, the busiest workers were local carpenters, called upon to construct larger jails.

These nagging economic problems had not brought Americans closer together. Wherever one looked, the competing interests of creditors and debtors, rural farmers and urban merchants, artisans and importers, acted as centrifugal forces, dividing the nation. While state governments debated what to do, private citizens took matters into their own hands. Disgruntled Vermont farmers, who had declared their independence from New York in 1777, demanded that the new American government, the Confederation Congress, recognize their statehood. More disturbing was the news that in New Jersey, South Car-

olina, Pennsylvania, Virginia, and Maryland, backcountry farmers were rising up in armed rebellion and had to
be controlled by militia units.

Relationships among the states were no better. In the
aftermath of the Revolution, real political power resided
in these state governments. Animated by a heartfelt ill
will and rivalry, state legislators missed no opportunity to
exploit the weakness of their neighbors. They rushed to
enact tariffs and trade barriers, replacing the hated British
restrictions with restrictions of their own. New Jersey had
gone so far as to create its own customs service, an ironic
tribute to the regulatory system of its former British
rulers. Virginia's penalties for avoiding its interstate import duties would have impressed even the most venal
British customs men. With duties to pay at every state
border, even the most intrepid merchant or shipper found
interstate commerce a nightmare. States with natural advantages made every effort to abuse those without them.
Virginia and South Carolina cheerfully squeezed what
they could out of hapless North Carolina. Meanwhile,
New York and Pennsylvania, both blessed with major
ports, imposed steep duties on all goods destined for
neighboring states. James Madison described New Jersey,
trapped between the two states, as "a cask tapped at both
ends." Connecticut also fell victim to New York's greed.
Tired of being victimized, Connecticut and New Jersey
were rumored to be planning a joint assault on New York.

Other sovereign rights claimed by the states hurt
domestic trade. Each state insisted on issuing its own

currency, and, thus, a New Yorker sending goods to South Carolina ran a gauntlet of ever-fluctuating exchange rates before his wares reached their final destination. By 1785 the conflict and chaos created by thirteen independent mercantile systems was obvious, yet calls for commercial cooperation that year and the following year were met with suspicion, resistance—and a decided lack of interest.

The solution to these problems, and others, would seem to modern Americans to be the task of the national government. But in 1786 the national government was ill equipped to handle even the smallest crisis. Many of the men who created that government now realized how badly flawed it was. Indeed, it was this faltering, floundering government that threatened, in Washington's view, to condemn America to appear as a "humiliating and contemptible figure...in the annals of mankind."

America's first constitution, the Articles of Confederation, had been written by the Second Continental Congress soon after the Declaration of Independence was signed. Pennsylvania lawyer John Dickinson was called upon to produce the first draft of the document, but the conservative Dickinson's inclination toward a strong central government did not sit well with his fellow Revolutionaries. Congress made short shrift of the document Dickinson presented, systematically editing out any suggestion that the Confederation would enjoy any real power over the states. Where Dickinson's version began with a firm declaration that the "Colonies unite themselves so as never to be divided by any Act whatever," the amended version began with the equally firm declaration that "each state retains its sovereignty, freedom, and independence."

It was not hard to understand why a congress sitting in 1776 preferred a "firm league of friendship" rather than a potent central government. What, after all, was the country waging war against but the tyranny of centralized power? And what were they fighting for but to secure the absolute sovereignty of their local representative assemblies? For these Revolutionaries, the rallying cry of "No taxation without representation" had meaning only in the context of their local colonial assemblies, now free from the oppression of the British Parliament and the British king. The Revolution was not one battle for independence but thirteen—proof that a profound localism still trumped any embryonic identity as "Americans." These identities were, after all, relational: Patrick Henry, John Adams, and Richard Henry Lee were Americans when they contrasted themselves with the citizens, government officials, and soldiers of England, but at home, when they looked to their own right and left, they were Virginians, New Jerseyites, Connecticut men. Thus, when Patrick Henry declared in 1774 that he was no longer a Virginian but an American, his countrymen took this for the rhetoric that it was. Despairing of this localism sooner than most, General Washington's brash and brilliant young aide-de-camp, Alexander Hamilton, bemoaned the fact that so few Americans "thought continentally." His mentor and friend, General Washington, was forced to agree. When, as commander in chief, he asked a New Jersey militia troop to swear loyalty to the United States, they refused. "New Jersey," they said, "is our country."

The Continental Congress showed little inclination to "think continentally" as they wrote the Articles of Confederation. As sensible men about to wage a war, they were willing to concede the power to declare war and make peace to the Confederation. Their "common defense... and their mutual general welfare" depended upon central coordination in war and a unified voice in treaty negotiations. In all other areas, however, they took pains to create a government incapable of the political or economic abuses suffered under king and Parliament. In 1776 the wounds inflicted by corrupt royal governors and royal judges were still raw. So, too, was the memory of upper houses or councils in their colonial governments that often betrayed local interests in exchange for patronage and social status. Thus, the Confederation would have no separate executive branch, no independent judiciary, and no upper chamber in the legislature. To create any of these was to risk carrying the worst of the colonial past into the present. Instead, the Articles called for a unicameral representative assembly or congress that would conduct all the government's business.

The distribution of power within this Confederation Congress was in perfect harmony with the goals of the Revolution, for each state had a single vote, regardless of its size or population or the number of delegates it chose to send as its representatives. Intercolonial suspicions and competition were as much a legacy of the past as parliamentary high-handedness—and no state, reveling in its independence from British control, wanted to submit itself to the collective control of its neighbors. Tellingly, disputes between the states over claims to western lands delayed the ratification of the Articles for almost five years.

The Articles also reflected the ardent desire of the Revolutionary leaders to prevent the rise of a new tyranny from the ashes of an older one. To insure that the government they created would not, could not, become oppressive, they did more than drastically limit the scope of its authority. They denied it the one basic power that they knew tyranny required. Eighteenth-century men and women called it "the power of the purse"; modern Americans know it as the right to tax. The Confederation would have no independent source of income, and this, the Revolutionaries were sure, meant it could never present a danger to American liberty.

Handicapped as it was, the Confederation government did manage to wage the war successfully, wrest loans from foreign governments, and, to everyone's surprise, win major concessions at the peace table in 1783. But the Confederation's inadequacies soon became apparent as it switched from winning independence to overseeing an independent nation. Its diplomatic record was appalling. After the surprising success of the nation's Paris peace commissioners, America suffered a series of rebuffs, embarrassments, and downright humiliations from foreign nations, large and small. Every effort to protect American interests ended in failure. When Spain closed the port of New Orleans to American shipping in order to slow the influx of Americans into territory adjoining and overlapping Louisiana, the Confederation recognized the crisis that would follow. Without a gateway to the ocean, settlers coming to Kentucky and Tennessee would be cut off from much-needed supplies and deprived of any access to markets for their crops. Yet American ambassadors could make no headway in persuading Spain to reopen the port for they had no leverage in the negotiations. As westerners' confidence in the Confederation faded, they devised their own solutions. One frontier entrepreneur went so far as to sign a loyalty oath to the Spanish government in exchange for trade concessions.

At the same time, the British openly defied the terms of the Paris peace treaty by refusing to evacuate their Ohio Valley forts. Their continued presence was an affront to American sovereignty, but it was also a real threat to peace on the frontier. Commanders in these forts operated as agents provocateurs, providing Ohio Valley Indians with encouragement, arms, and ammunition as they mounted organized resistance to American settlement. The Spanish offered the same encouragement and aid to the Choctaw, Creek, and Cherokee along the southern frontier. The Confederation could do little to force the British out or to prevent either foreign nation from abetting the Indians. Britain's firm quid pro quo for giving up the western forts was the repayment by American planters and merchants of personal debts to British creditors and the compensation to Loyalists for confiscated property. But Congress had no money to cover these debts and obligations itself, and it had no means to prevent state legislatures from obstructing the collection of prewar debts. The Confederation had no military clout, either. With a peacetime army of fewer than seven hundred poorly equipped soldiers, it could not drive the British out or quell the violence on the frontier. Thus, when southern tribes threatened to mount a full-scale war, Georgia and North Carolina took matters into their own hands. Both states undercut the authority of the national government by negotiating independent treaties with the Indians on their borders.

Grim as these diplomatic failures were, they paled before the humiliation of the American merchant marine in the Mediterranean. Without the protection of the British navy, American vessels carrying wheat and flour to southern European markets became easy prey for Barbary Coast pirates. In 1785 the Dey of Algiers seized an American ship, confiscated its cargo, and imprisoned its crew. When ransom demands arrived, Congress could not meet the captor's price. Crew and captain languished in prison, victims of one government's greed and another's poverty. When the ruler of Tripoli offered to insure safe passage to all American ships—for a price—Congress could not raise the protection money. By 1786 the survival of this valuable trade route was in question.

Perhaps the most telling sign of a failing government was the morale of Congress itself. All too rapidly, the Confederation had sunk into a lassitude bordering on paralysis. By the fall of 1785 attendance at congressional sessions was already embarrassingly low. Throughout the winter and spring of 1786, absences reached crisis proportions, quorums could rarely be met, and the business of Congress—limited though it was—was rapidly coming to a halt. Tired of dealing with problems they could not solve, congressmen from every state preferred to stay home.

Who could blame them? Every day Congress faced a host of angry creditors, foreign and domestic, clamoring for repayment of wartime loans. But the federal treasury was empty, and Congress had no means to fill it. Under the Articles of Confederation, Congress's only source of revenue was the generosity of the states. When the states proved cavalier, if not derelict, in their support, the federal government could do nothing. In Paris, London, Madrid, and Amsterdam, American diplomats found it impossible to negotiate new loans, for no one was willing to lend money to a nation that could not honor its existing debts. Veterans who held government certificates, widows who had lent their small fortunes to the war effort, and wealthy speculators who had gambled on the government retiring its debt were all losing faith in a government that turned out empty pockets to its creditors.

The Confederation devised two creative plans to solve its financial problems. Both failed. First, it placed its hopes in raising revenues through the sale of the Ohio Valley lands that had been ceded, grudgingly, by the states. Congress produced a series of well-thought-out and well-designed plans for the division of these lands, their sale, and their political progression from territorial status to statehood. The Northwest Ordinances that resulted were, without question, the government's finest peacetime accomplishment. But if no one challenged Congress's right to the revenues from the sale of western land, few settlers were willing to buy that land without the promise of military protection. The hoped-for flood of income never grew larger than a trickle. With no funds to arm a military and no military to secure the funds, Congress was forced to look elsewhere for revenue. In 1785 it asked permission to levy a small import tax. The states said no. With that, the Confederation Congress seemed to abandon all hope of solvency.

If men like Henry Knox and James Madison were surprised to find the Articles of Confederation so flawed, there was one political figure ready to say "I told you so." In 1780, long before the American victory in the war was assured, the young immigrant from the West Indies, Alexander Hamilton, sat down to compose his thoughts on a suitable government for a new, independent republic. In a long letter to his friend James Duane, Hamilton called for a strong national government, able to rein in the individualism and localism of the states, with powers to tax and regulate commerce and the military and naval power to win the respect of foreign nations. Perhaps Hamilton found it easier to "think continentally," for, though he had settled in New York, he had no deep family roots in any state. Indeed, several of the men who rallied early to Hamilton's cause were born abroad or had moved from one region to another. For others, their national identity had been forged through long years in the Continental army. But Hamilton's unshakable confidence that the right government could serve as midwife at the birth of a new economic and political challenger in the family of nations cannot be explained by his recent arrival in America. More clearly than most, he saw the potential of the young Republic, and, more quickly than anyone, he dismissed the Confederation as a faulty blueprint for a dynamic nation.

By 1785 Hamilton had begun to sound more like a prophet than a cynic. That spring a group of influential Virginians, including George Washington, James Madison, and Edmund Randolph, took steps that were decidedly Hamiltonian. At their urging, Virginia appointed commissioners to negotiate an agreement with neighboring Maryland on the use of the rivers and bays the two states shared in common. Washington invited the commissioners to hold their meetings at his Mount Vernon estate, perhaps hoping that his presence would inspire real cooperation. So it did. Encouraged by the ability of two states to come to an amicable agreement, Maryland proposed that a meeting on interstate commerce be held, this time including Pennsylvania and Delaware. The project grew spontaneously. When Virginia politicians with nationalist inclinations suggested that all the states be invited, their governor Patrick Henry—no friend to the nationalist agenda—surprised them by agreeing that interstate commerce was a topic in urgent need of discussion. On February 23, 1786, Henry circulated a letter to his fellow governors, recommending that every state send delegates to a commercial convention in Annapolis that September. Enthusiasm rose briefly—and then died. Although the most ornery of states, Rhode Island, pledged to send a delegation, four states refused to act. When the convention met on September 11, only five states were represented. Most of the delegates were ardent supporters of what could best be called a nationalist movement.

These delegates shed no tears over the poor turnout. Free of the need to argue with, persuade, or outvote men who opposed their nationalist views, they were able to devote their energies to drafting a manifesto that they offered as a convention report. Pointedly calling themselves the duly appointed Commissioners to Remedy Defects of the Federal Government, these twelve men from New York, New Jersey, Pennsylvania, Delaware, and Virginia urged their legislatures to call a "general meeting, of the States, in a future Convention, for the same, and such other purposes, as the situation of public affairs, may be found to require." "And such other purposes" opened the way, of course, to far more than recommendations to improve interstate trade. With masterful understatement, the report noted that any effective reform of commerce would require "a correspondent adjustment of other parts of the Federal System." No one should have been surprised to learn that the author of this report was Alexander Hamilton.

Fortune—in the form of hundreds of angry farmers—now seemed to smile on the nationalists. For at the very moment that the Annapolis convention was meeting, six hundred desperate farmers were storming the courthouse at Springfield, Massachusetts. The trouble had been brewing for some time, ever since the return of peace brought with it an economic depression in the western counties of the state. Many of these farmer-rebels, armed with pitchforks and old muskets, were in danger of losing their farms to creditors. Since 1783 they had watched helplessly as their property taxes rose and their profits declined. As the wealthy Bostonians who held the mortgages on their land went to court to begin foreclosure proceedings, the farmers saw their futures slipping away. For months they sought relief through political channels, petitioning the state assembly to issue paper money, to lower taxes, and to approve "stay laws" that would temporarily prevent the courts from acting on the foreclosure demands. The state government, however, turned a deaf ear. Dominated by hard-money men and mortgage holders, it refused to provide any relief to these debtors.

In August 1786 the farmers decided to take matters into their own hands. The government, they said, had turned its back on the people—and the people no longer owed such a government any loyalty. This was a rhetoric familiar to all Americans, torn straight from the pages of John Locke and the Declaration of Independence. The farmers struck their first blow against the new tyranny by blocking the entrance to the court of common pleas at Northampton, preventing lawyers and judges from entering. Within days the farmers' revolt had spread. Reports of court closings came from Worcester, Concord, Taunton, and as far north as Great Barrington. But the heart of the rebellion seemed to be at Springfield, where a thirty-nine-year-old Pelham veteran of the Battle of Saratoga, Daniel Shays, led some fifteen hundred men in an assault on the courthouse. Dressed in their old Continental army uniforms, sporting sprigs of hemlock in their hats just as the Continental soldiers had once done, Shays's makeshift army seized and occupied the courthouse on September 25.

A frightened Massachusetts government took steps to restore law and order. The governor called up an impressive force of over forty-four hundred militiamen, and General Benjamin Lincoln, a veteran like Shays of Saratoga, was appointed to lead this army against the rebels. The end came quickly. On February 3, 1787, Lincoln surprised and routed the farmers. A general amnesty was issued, and although Shays and thirteen of his followers were tried and convicted, Governor John Hancock thought it best to pardon them.

The rebellion sent shock waves across the nation and across the ocean. Thomas Jefferson, serving as American ambassador to France, was one of the few Americans who refused to be alarmed by the uprising. Writing to James Madison from Paris on January 30, Jefferson declared that "a little rebellion now and then is a good thing."

Madison emphatically did not agree. Neither did the chief justice of Massachusetts, William Cushing, who spoke for many of Boston's most prominent former Revolutionaries when he pronounced the leaders of the rebellion to be "evil minded persons," demagogues, and rabble-rousers who were "ignorant, unprincipled, bankrupt, and desperate." Even Samuel Adams, one of the earliest and most devoted champions of revolution, condemned the rebels. There was no moral connection, he insisted, between the American Revolution and their revolt. "Rebellion against a king may be pardoned," he declared, "but the man who dares to rebel against the laws of a republic ought to suffer death." Men more distant from the scene responded to news of Shays's Rebellion with anguish rather than anger. "I am mortified beyond expression," wrote George Washington, calling the revolt "a triumph for the advocates of despotism."

But in truth, the most powerful emotion stirred in the breasts of planters and wealthy merchants by Shays's Rebellion was fear. How many more "evil minded persons" stood ready to stir up the discontent and despair of farmers, slaves, and urban debtors? Only a strong and energetic government could stand in the way of what these men of property labeled anarchy. It was a sobering realization—and it was one that played into the hands of the nationalists as 1787 began.

The Confederation Congress had not yet endorsed the Annapolis report's request for a national convention. But while Shays's Rebels were still at large, both Virginia and New Jersey announced their intention to send delegates to Philadelphia. In January, as General Lincoln bore down on the rebels, Pennsylvania and North Carolina announced that they, too, would attend. Delaware and Georgia soon followed suit. By the time the rebels had surrendered, the Confederation Congress, meeting in New York City, had decided to take up the matter of the Philadelphia convention. Still reeling from the rejection of its impost proposal, and aware of the impact of the Massachusetts uprising, Congress had little choice but to seek help wherever it could find it. On February 21, 1787, the Confederation issued the following resolve: "That in the opinion of Congress, it is expedient, that on the second Monday in May next, a convention of delegates, who shall have been appointed by the several states, be held at Philadelphia...."

Hamilton had every reason to celebrate his victory. But from his beloved Mount Vernon, George Washington struck a more somber note. He wrote to his young friend James Madison: "That the present moment is pregnant of great, and strange events, none who will cast their eyes around them can deny." Stranger events were certain to follow.

~♦~

# CHAPTER TWO

# Making Mr. Madison Wait

## "A small number...had assembled"

THROUGHOUT THE WINTER and early spring of 1787 the remaining states took up the task of selecting delegates to the Philadelphia convention. Yet how much authority the convention really had, and what its agenda would be, remained unclear to almost everyone. The Confederation Congress's charge to the convention had been decidedly—and no doubt purposely—vague. Dark as their future looked, Congress was understandably hesitant to endorse its own demise. The makeup of the convention delegations suggested that Congress was right to worry: men of nationalist inclinations volunteered their services in every state, while men suspicious of the convention's purposes demurred. By April the die, as John Adams was so fond of saying, was cast. How far the convention would go, however, still remained a mystery.

If it were up to James Madison, the convention would make a second revolution. Eager to see the creation of a new government, and with it a radical redistribution of power in the nation, James Madison had made his way to Philadelphia a full eleven days before the convention was to get under way. The young Virginian's arrival went largely unnoticed in the bustling city. Small and somber looking in his habitual black suit, his thin strands of hair combed forward to hide his receding hairline, the thirty-six-year-old Virginia planter and lawyer might have been mistaken for one of the Presbyterian clergy also convening in the city that month. But Madison's bellicose mood made him more a kindred spirit to the Revolutionary War army officers, members of the Society of the Cincinnati, who were the third group gathering in Philadelphia. For although he was more hypochondriac than warrior, James Madison had come to Philadelphia battle-ready, determined to steer the convention away from the limited task of amending and correcting the Articles of Confederation and toward designing an entirely new constitution. Madison's proposal, later streamlined and revised as the Virginia Plan, would earn him, rather than Alexander Hamilton, the title of "Architect of the Constitution."

Madison had devoted great care to the proposals he hoped would serve as a blueprint for this new government. Always the scholar, he was ready to buttress these proposals with references to noted political theorists and philosophers both ancient and modern. But Madison understood practical politics as well as he knew political theory. His instincts told him that the first coherent proposals offered to the convention would set the agenda for the coming debates. And Madison was determined that those proposals would be his. Jemmy, as his friends called him, intended to leave nothing to chance.

Unfortunately, Madison would have to wait several weeks to test his strategy. Although the convention was set to open on May 14, there were few signs that the delegates were even on their way to Philadelphia. Madison's impatience was laced with anxiety, and conditions in Philadelphia did little to lift the gloom surrounding him. After one of the worst winters in local memory, spring had failed to bring the city any of the hoped-for relief. Instead, April unfolded in an endless procession of rainy days, dampening everyone's spirits further. By early May pedestrians on Philadelphia's crowded streets were forced to dodge mud puddles as well as the usual beggars and pickpockets who mingled menacingly among the respectable citizens. By the time Madison arrived, the heat and humidity had soared, yet despite the heavy, still air, most of the windows and shutters on houses, shops, and taverns remained tightly shut. A plague of oversize black flies had descended upon the city. At night the insect population buzzed and swarmed, while inside the sweltering bedrooms Philadelphians tossed and turned in discomfort. The City of Brotherly Love was rapidly turning into the city of muffled curses.

But on Sunday, May 13, it was not curses that roused Madison from his slumber. Instead, he awoke to the sound of chiming bells, cannon fire, and the cheers of a crowd, sounds that penetrated even the tightly shuttered windows of his boardinghouse. There was no need to ask the cause of this commotion, for only one American could bring so many people out in greeting. Alone among the Revolutionary leaders, General George Washington enjoyed a celebrity that reached beyond the borders of his native state. Notable as many other delegates might be, the commander in chief of the Continental army was the only genuinely national figure attending the convention. As Philadelphia's citizens turned out to greet the hero of the Revolution, Madison gave thanks that Washington had decided to serve as a Virginia delegate. He knew that the simple presence of George Washington would go further toward winning the approval of the people for the convention's work than all of Madison's own learned disquisitions on government reform.

Throughout the early months of 1787, Washington's attendance had been uncertain. Despite his concern for the nation's future and his increasing nationalist commitment, the general had been reluctant to commit himself to the Virginia delegation. In part, that reluctance came from family tragedies that winter. In January Washington's favorite brother, John Augustine, had died suddenly of what the general diagnosed as a "fit of gout in the head." The loss of "the intimate companion of my youth, and the friend of my ripened age" had depressed Washington greatly, and the failing health of both his mother and his sister only deepened his sorrow. His own poor health added to his hesitation to make an arduous journey to Philadelphia. In March the grieving Washington suffered a debilitating attack of rheumatism, an attack so severe that "at times," he wrote Virginia's governor, Edmund Randolph, "I am hardly able to rase [*sic*] my hand to my head or turn myself in bed."

But there was more to Washington's reluctance than poor health or family tragedy. Although he was under pressure from friends and political allies to accept, Washington worried that attending the convention carried a risk to his public reputation. Governor Edmund Randolph and the general's old friend David Humphreys might insist that Washington's presence was essential to the success of the convention since the people had "unbounded confidence" in his patriotism and wisdom. From far away in Massachusetts, another old friend, Henry Knox, appealed not only to Washington's sense of duty but also to his ego, assuring Washington that he would be chosen to preside over the convention and promising that, if the delegates produced an "energetic and judicious" new government, Washington would receive the lion's share of credit. Serve at the convention, Knox concluded, and you will be doubly entitled "to the glorious republican epithet—The Father of your Country."

Still, Washington hesitated. Throughout his career he had nurtured his reputation carefully, and he was loath to tarnish it by an association with what might be a highly unpopular cause. Only recently he had faced criticism from friends and political acquaintances who warned that his membership in the Society of the Cincinnati, a hereditary military organization, was casting suspicion on his commitment to republican principles. Although Washington defended the society, declaring that its sole purpose was to sustain the camaraderie born of military service, he took the warning that his reputation was in danger to heart. When the society asked him to serve as its president, Washington declined.

Washington's membership in the Society of the Cincinnati was a delicate matter. But the stakes were different, and far higher, in the matter of the Philadelphia convention—and Washington knew it. His attendance at any political gathering was tantamount to an endorsement of its actions, and the convention's actions were likely to be radical. Were the people ready for a major political change? Privately, Washington had his doubts. In a letter to John Jay that March, he had raised the question bluntly: "Is the public mind matured for such an important change...?" Yet the consequences if he refused to attend seemed even more severe. That same month he voiced the fear to his friend David Humphreys that his absence might be seen as "an implied dereliction to Republicanism." In the end, Washington followed his own conviction that drastic change was necessary and that he was obliged to play a role in seeing that change was made.

Washington's arrival momentarily raised Madison's spirits. But the following day—the day the convention was to begin—the young planter noted with classic understatement that only "a small number...had assembled." It was little consolation to Madison that delays like this were common. In eighteenth-century America, nature and the primitive communication and transportation systems often conspired to make any gathering date more a hope than a reality. Even the shortest journeys and the briefest stays away from home required careful and extensive preparations since communication over even small distances was often difficult, usually unpredictable, and always slow. Because no one knew how long this convention would sit, delegates felt more than the usual pressure to set their affairs in order. That process could be both lengthy and complicated, for although many of the delegates were wealthy, their livelihoods depended upon their active participation in agriculture, in their legal practice, or in their businesses. To protect their interests as best they could, many paused to draft detailed instructions to overseers, sons, wives, or partners before departing home. Even the most meticulous preparations sometimes failed, however. Empty chairs at the convention bore witness to the number of delegates who had to rush home to resolve crises, rescue crops, or appease disgruntled clients.

Like communications, eighteenth-century travel was a challenge. Even the shortest trip was likely to be uncomfortable at best and dangerous at worst. Travel time was unpredictable since unforeseen delays due to bad weather, poor roads, or sudden illness were common. Men who set sail for England, Europe, or the West Indies knew it was prudent to have their wills in order before embarking. Americans who accepted diplomatic posts abroad often left wives and children at home, fearful that the ocean voyage would end in tragedy. Political leaders who journeyed from plantation or rural town to state capitals knew that the miles they put between themselves, their farm, and their family were not easily reversed. Floods could wipe out roads; ice and snow could beach ferryboats; rains could make a speedy return in case of a crisis impossible. Such were the realities of eighteenth-century life in America.

Nature, it turned out, conspired against the convention delegates in the spring of 1787. The winter had been especially hard not only in Pennsylvania, but along much of the eastern seaboard. Roads everywhere were impassable. The nation might be in a deepening crisis, but the simple fact was that the men assigned to deal with that crisis had trouble reaching their destination. It would be late May before the required quorum of seven states could be reached. Until then, there was nothing for Madison to do but wait.

Sensibly, Madison turned his days in Philadelphia to good use. Together with Washington, he established close working ties with several local Pennsylvania delegates. By the time the convention got under way, a solid nationalist coalition of Washington, Madison, Robert Morris, Gouverneur Morris, and the venerable Benjamin Franklin had been created. For Washington, the serious business of coalition building blended easily with the pleasures of socializing. He took pleasure in paying a call on Philadelphia's most distinguished citizen, Dr. Benjamin Franklin, soon after his arrival in town. Now in his eighties, Franklin was in poor health, suffering from crippling gout and painful kidney stones. Despite his aches and pains, Franklin was looking forward to hosting the visiting dignitaries of the convention. He had laid in an ample supply of spirits, he assured Washington, and had expanded his dining room to seat two dozen guests. He was also looking forward to serving as a Pennsylvania delegate to the convention. Washington came away from this first meeting certain that Benjamin Franklin had lost none of his interest in politics or his genius for political strategy. Perhaps as importantly, he came away certain of Franklin's disaffection with the Confederation government.

What Washington may not have known was that the roots of the doctor's disaffection were as much personal as political. In 1780, after serving as one of America's three commissioners to France, the septuagenarian Franklin had accepted an assignment as minister to that country. Over the next four years, his diplomatic success was nothing short of miraculous. He had parlayed his personal popularity among the members of the French court into political influence, gaining access to the king through his chief minister the comte de Vergennes. Playing the "American Original" to the hilt with his fur hat, his witty aphorisms, and his avuncular flirtations, Franklin made himself an essential guest at every aristocratic social gathering. His homespun style belied his political brilliance, and he repeatedly outsmarted the sophisticated Vergennes. He negotiated critical loans of both money and supplies, won French recognition of American independence, and later, as one of the peace commissioners, outfoxed the overconfident English and European diplomats at the Paris talks. On his return to America, all Philadelphia hailed him as a hero. Yet Congress ignored him. He had expected, he would later confess to a friend, that Congress would "at least have been kind enough to have shewn their Approbation of my Conduct by a Grant of some small Tract of Land." Yet no such reward came his way. Indeed, Congress's only action had been to replace him as postmaster general while he was in France. He was astonished to see men of far less distinction receive congressional patronage and could only assume that "one or two envious and malicious Persons" had turned the government against him. Such rejection was, no doubt, as painful as his celebrated gout.

Washington and Madison knew they could count on a second Pennsylvania delegate, Robert Morris, to support radical changes in the government. Morris's nationalist commitment was a matter of record. Like Washington, "Bob" Morris was a war veteran, but his battles had been waged on the financial front rather than the field. As a member of the Continental Congress, he had procured much-needed supplies and funds for Washington's needy army. Later, under the Confederation, Morris had helped the government stave off complete financial collapse during the war. After the war, when the Confederation Congress again called on his expertise, he had seen first-hand the futility of a government without an independent source of income. At his urging, Congress had proposed the impost; when it failed, Morris had retired to private life in ill-disguised disgust.

Morris was a personable, good-humored man, and Washington had gladly accepted his offer of hospitality during the convention. Yet if Morris conveyed to his houseguest every appearance of wealth and self-confidence, his world was actually quietly crumbling. He was already living far beyond his means, and rumors were beginning to spread in the city that he was guilty of unsavory financial activities. For the moment, however, Morris's years in debtors' prison, his desperate flights to avoid arrest, and pauper's death still lay far in the future. And for the moment, he remained a valuable adviser to the nationalist cause.

By mid-May convention delegates began to trickle into town, taking up residence at the Indian Queen on Fourth Street or sharing a room at Mrs. Mary House's boardinghouse on Fifth and Market, not far from Ben Franklin's home. The Virginia delegation had swelled to six of the expected seven by May 15, and they immediately began a round of meetings to refine Madison's proposals for a new government. Working with Edmund Randolph, George Mason, and Washington, Madison managed to distill his plan into fifteen proposals for the convention's consideration.

On Friday, May 18, Alexander Hamilton at last arrived and immediately threw himself into the frenzy of caucusing that now filled the days of most of the delegates. Although still a young man, Hamilton was widely acknowledged by friends and enemies alike as exceptional. He had an agile mind and a remarkable capacity to master new bodies of knowledge, and his critical skills were unparalleled. He could analyze the most complex economic and political problems and provide their solutions with apparent ease. It was, perhaps, this genius for analysis that made Hamilton appear a visionary, able to read future possibilities as clearly as most men read past events. Although his wavy chestnut hair, fair complexion, and surprisingly sensitive mouth suggested Apollo, few men were foolish enough to dismiss Alexander Hamilton as a lady's man or a dandy. Those who had crossed political swords with him knew he was a fierce and cunning fighter. Out of respect or hatred, the men who knew him best called him "Little Mars."

Despite Hamilton's many talents, Madison would not find him to be the much-hoped-for comrade in arms. For one thing, Hamilton was saddled with a New York delegation that strongly opposed any major changes to the Confederation. His two fellow delegates would alternately embarrass and infuriate Hamilton while they attended the convention and leave him a rump delegation when they departed Philadelphia in protest. But the frustrating makeup of the New York delegation was not the major reason for Hamilton's inability to dominate the convention as he had dominated the movement leading to it. The truth was, Alexander Hamilton's views on a new government were out of sync with the views of most of the delegates. These men were ill at ease with his advocacy of life terms for legislators, and their republican principles were offended by his vision of an executive officer who bore too close a resemblance to a benevolent monarch. But the most disturbing Hamiltonian stance was his complete disregard for state sovereignty and his willingness—indeed, his eagerness—to see the states reduced to little more than functional departments in a national political structure. Hamilton, in short, thought far too continentally for his colleagues. On this, Hamilton was surprisingly philosophical. What he wanted, above all, was the establishment of a national government with sufficient powers to serve as a basis for future greatness. As long as the convention produced a government with the power of the purse, Hamilton felt confident that much of what he desired would follow. The details he left to men more attuned to the sentiments of the convention—men like Jemmy Madison.

By the last week in May, Philadelphia's taverns and boardinghouses were overflowing with delegates from Georgia, both Carolinas, Delaware, New Jersey, New York, Massachusetts, Virginia, and Pennsylvania. Connecticut's delegates were rumored to be on their way. The New Hampshire delegation's arrival was unpredictable since the state legislature had not managed to raise their travel expenses. Maryland's presence was delayed since the original appointees had declined to serve and the state legislature was scrambling to find replacements. There was no need to wait for Rhode Island. Alone among the states, "Rogue's Island" had decided to boycott the proceedings.

With well over the required quorum of seven states, the delegates decided to waste no more time. On Friday, May 25, they made their way to the Pennsylvania statehouse, where their sessions would be held. To no one's surprise, the day had dawned gray and overcast, and rain was already falling as they entered the neat two-story statehouse, better known as Independence Hall. The convention would hold most of its sessions on the first floor in the spacious East Room. Normally this room was flooded with light and air, for it had large windows on two of its walls. But this summer the windows were shut tight to keep the insects out, and the blinds were closed to protect the proceedings from prying eyes. The dim light and the sweltering heat did little to foster the delegates' appreciation for their elegant surroundings. As they took their seats around the small, sturdy tables that had been provided for them, the northerners were already wilting in their wool suits. Southern delegates, wiser in the ways of surviving the heat, remained a bit crisper in their linen.

James Madison snared a seat near the front of the room with an unobstructed view of the presiding officer's chair. From this vantage point, he could hear every man who rose to speak and he could observe the reactions of those who listened. In his neat and tiny hand, he would secretly preserve each day's proceedings. It would be decades before this meticulous historical record would be made public.

Madison would have little to record that Friday, for the delegates, many of them old hands at setting up political

bodies, both temporary and permanent, devoted the
opening session to housekeeping chores. The first order
of business was to select a presiding officer. To no one's
surprise and with no one's opposition, the delegates chose
George Washington to serve as their president. With noticeable feeling, Washington thanked the convention for
the honor bestowed upon him and reminded them of the
unique business they were called upon to execute. Madison duly recorded both the unanimous election and
Washington's opening remarks. Once the president had
taken his seat, the convention moved on to the appointment of a secretary. They chose Major William Jackson,
a wartime friend of both Hamilton and Washington, for
this salaried post. Jackson, who had been waiting in anticipation outside the East Room, was ushered in, took
his place beside the presiding officer, and immediately
began to keep the official record of the convention's proceedings. The convention then named a committee to
prepare a set of standing rules and orders.

The next order of business was the formal presentation of delegation credentials. One by one, the state delegations appeared before the presiding officer and read the
charges given them by their legislatures. When charge
after charge began with a firm affirmation of the sovereignty and independence of the state government, the
mood of the nationalists surely darkened. For suddenly,
without intent or warning, one of the major stumbling
blocks facing the convention had surfaced: the states' resistance to shared sovereignty. If the delegates hoped to

create a strong central government, the states' cherished claims to absolute sovereignty would have to be abandoned or rejected. And if it was agreed that sovereignty should be divided between local and national governments, a second struggle would surely follow over which government should get the lion's share.

Every delegate knew that in a tug-of-war between the states and the central government, any power granted to one must, of necessity, diminish the autonomy of the other. In the end, a choice would have to be made about who should enjoy the bulk of these powers. Men like Madison and Hamilton hoped the convention would make the right choice, transferring many critical powers to the national government But if the state legislature of Delaware had its way, the nationalists' dream of an effective central government was doomed. Small and without special economic resources, Delaware clung tenaciously to its sovereignty, fearful that a strong national government would be dominated by the larger, richer states. Delaware's legislators were not ready to cede any of its autonomy to such a central government. Its delegation announced that they were explicitly forbidden to approve any change in the "one state, one vote" clause of the Articles of Confederation. Delaware's rigid stance highlighted another major question the convention would have to answer: If power was to be vested in the central government, who would control its use?

These questions of power and sovereignty hung in the air. No one doubted they must be resolved, but on this rainy Friday afternoon, no one seemed ready to tackle them. Without a single word spoken on the future shape of the nation, the convention adjourned until Monday morning at ten.

Monday's session began with the theatrical entrance of Benjamin Franklin. Still troubled by gout, Franklin traveled the short distance to Independence Hall in his luxurious sedan chair, carried on the shoulders of four prisoners taken from a nearby jail. After carefully lowering the chair, which boasted glass windows as well as elegant upholstery, the four muscular bearers were returned to their cells. Franklin's appearance proved to be one of the few lively moments of the day, for once again the convention managed to pass the entire day without raising any substantive issues. Instead, they debated the report of the Rules Committee.

Madison dutifully recorded the rules that were finally agreed upon. While most dealt with simple procedure, a surprising number suggested the convention's concern with preserving a gentlemanly civility once serious debate began. The terms of respect "whilst [a member] shall be speaking" were carefully spelled out: "None shall pass between them, or hold discourse with another, or read a book, pamphlet or paper, printed or manuscript...." If two men rose to speak at the same time, the presiding officer, George Washington, would determine the order in which they were to be heard. Taking into account the presence of loquacious and combative personalities among the delegates, the convention wisely agreed that no one should be allowed to speak more than twice on any issue each time it was raised. And when a member behaved badly, he could be "called to order by any other member, as well as by the President; and may be allowed to explain his conduct or expressions supposed to be reprehensible."

More than proper behavior was on the delegates' minds, however. These men had a healthy regard for their own political careers and reputations, and how they looked to their home constituents was thus never far from their minds. In order to have an open, freewheeling discussion of issues, they needed assurances that their image as decisive political leaders would not be jeopardized. Toward that end, they agreed to eliminate the recording of all preliminary votes; this way, they could change their minds, and their votes, without appearing to be either indecisive or unprincipled. This concern with creating an open and safe atmosphere for discussion ran like a leitmotiv throughout the early days of the convention.

With the approval of these and a host of other procedures, the delegates' energies appeared to be spent. As for the question of amending the old government, or creating a new one—once again Mr. Madison would have to wait.

# CHAPTER THREE

&~9)

# A Gathering of Demigods

## Men of "Ability, Weight, and Experience"

FROM HIS VANTAGE POINT near Washington's high-backed presidential chair, James Madison could survey the delegates gathering each morning in the East Room. Some were friends of long-standing; others, recent acquaintances; many were known to him only by name or reputation. What mattered most to Madison, of course, was who would stand firm for radical changes in the nation's government—and who would oppose those changes. Much depended upon which men would emerge as the key players, the dominant voices in the debates that were about to begin.

Although John Adams had described the convention members as men of "Ability, Weight, and Experience" and Thomas Jefferson had, in a moment of reckless exaggeration, pronounced them "demi-gods," neither judgment captured the true character of the gathering. Indeed, the fifty-five delegates who would eventually make up the convention were more interesting than Jefferson's mantle of divinity allowed and more diverse in their abilities and talents than Adams's praise suggested. As the weeks stretched into months, these political leaders would come to know one another for the imperfect, exasperating, but often admirable men that they were.

Although many of the men were strangers to one another, they could see quickly that they shared much in common. They were men of wealth and comfort— landowners, slaveholders, lawyers, merchants, land and securities speculators, and an occasional doctor or clergy- man—men with a near monopoly on formal education and professional training in a predominantly agrarian so- ciety. The majority were lawyers or men who had studied law, and thus they brought to Philadelphia a familiarity with political forms and political forums born of experi- ence and training. This preponderance of lawyers may ex- plain the often exhausting verbosity on the convention floor; it certainly explains that unfaltering attention to procedure and form already revealed in the opening days of the convention. Lawyers or not, most were born to property and fortune, although a minority had risen from obscurity to wealth by virtue of some combination of tal- ent, luck, and well-made marriages. A few of these self- made men still bore traces of their humble beginnings, revealing their origins in their carriage, their calluses, or their plain speech. Yet there was no one in the room who might properly be called a man of ordinary means, a yeo- man farmer, a shopkeeper, a sailor, or a laborer.

The delegates also shared certain attitudes and took certain privileges for granted that would make modern Americans uncomfortable. As free, property-holding white men, they were the only group to enjoy full citizenship and a political voice in the new Republic. Few if any of the delegates questioned the class, gender, or racial bases of their privileged status, and they showed little or no discomfort when they spoke of "equality" or "unalienable rights" as if these were universal in a society that sustained slavery and female subordination. Yet if they assumed their participation in government and political decision making as a right, they also saw it as an obligation. During the Revolution most of the delegates old enough to participate had risked their lives as military officers or their fortunes as contributors to the American war chest. Virtually all of the delegates had served, or were serving now, as state legislators, members of the Continental or Confederation Congresses, judges, mayors, or governors—positions that carried more responsibility than financial benefits.

Thus, the East Room was filled with middle-aged men of wealth, education, and political experience. But this collective profile hides as much as it reveals. For in personality and character, the delegates were as varied as any elite group might be. A number were self-sacrificing, honorable to a fault, above reproach in personal and public matters. Others were vain, ambitious, even unscrupulous in their political and private relationships. Some were profligate; some were puritan. A few were, indeed, worthy of the title "demigod," while most were men of ordinary intelligence whose years of experience compensated for limited abilities. As Madison's notes would reveal, the convention had its share of windbags and fiery orators. And as the character sketches made by William Pierce would show, it also had its share of eccentric dressers and dandies, alcoholics and snuff addicts, mediocrities and boors.

Even in this gathering of men accustomed to being heard and heeded, some voices and opinions came to dominate others. These were the men whom Madison would need to rely on—or be prepared to combat. A dozen men emerged as the critical participants in the convention, shaping the debates, igniting the controversies, and proposing the compromises that made a new constitution possible. Madison was, of course, one of them. Hamilton, restricted as he was by the makeup of his delegation and his own outspoken extreme views, was another. Benjamin Franklin, as the grand old man of the Revolution, was a third, although the convention gave the doctor more respect than actual authority that summer. The remaining leaders were Roger Sherman, Gouverneur Morris, James Wilson, Elbridge Gerry, William Paterson, John Dickinson, Charles Pinckney, Edmund Randolph, and George Mason. In temperament, appearance, morals, and manners, these leaders were a study in contrasts, and as the convention progressed, political and ideological differences among them would emerge.

Tall and ungainly, Connecticut's Roger Sherman stood out among the elegantly dressed, often bewigged gentlemen on the convention floor. His appearance was both uncouth and uncompromising, his thin, sharp features framed by graying hair cut straight across his forehead. At sixty-six, the man they called the "Old Puritan" had lost none of the marks of his humble beginnings as a shoemaker. His plain, poorly tailored coat sat uncomfortably on his massive shoulders, and below his sleeves, his large hands were marked by calluses. Sherman, a man of big, awkward gestures, was so odd looking that people were known to laugh as he passed by. Despite his appearance and his early poverty, Sherman was now a well-regarded lawyer and judge. He was also a cunning politician. A man of few words when he was winning a political battle and a crafty debater when he was not, Sherman would speak a remarkable 138 times at the convention. Only James Madison, James Wilson, and Gouverneur Morris would rise to their feet more often. John Adams described Sherman as a "solid, sensible man," high praise indeed from a man not given to compliments, and Thomas Jefferson declared that Sherman had never said a foolish thing in his life. A small-state man, protective of Connecticut's interests, Sherman would lock horns with Madison over key issues of representation despite the shared nationalism of the two men.

With eight delegates, Pennsylvania boasted one of the largest delegations. It was also one of the most star-studded. In addition to the guidance provided by Bob Morris, the nationalists had the support, oratorical and strategic, of three other Pennsylvanians: Benjamin Franklin, Gouverneur Morris, and James Wilson. If the good doctor was larger-than-life, his fellow delegate Gouverneur Morris was almost as impressive. Born into the charmed circle of New York's Hudson Valley landed gentry, the brilliant, urbane thirty-five-year-old Morris was deserving of a place in Jefferson's pantheon of demigods. Imposing in stature, genial in the company of his peers, fluent in several languages, and possessed of a natural sophistication, "the Tall Boy" was as much a hedonist as an intellectual. He scandalized the convention's proper New Englanders by his open philandering, although he won the admiration of the more worldly New Yorkers and South Carolinians, who marveled at the success in the boudoir of this fleshy middle-aged man hobbled by a wooden leg. Morris's oratorical skills were as remarkable as his sexual appetite. Content and style were perfectly balanced when he spoke. He could capture his audience's attention with a burst of focused, intense emotion—and hold them spellbound as he slowly articulated his ideas. Those ideas were built upon a fundamental contradiction: Morris viewed most men and women as his social and intellectual inferiors, yet he was deeply committed to a republican form of government. Supremely confident in his opinions and of his right to express them, Gouverneur Morris took the floor at the convention 173 times.

James Wilson lacked Gouverneur Morris's flair and his charm, but at forty-five, Wilson was acknowledged as one of the ablest lawyers in the country and a talented political writer. Tall, neatly dressed, with strong facial features but poor vision, the thickly bespectacled Wilson appeared more stern and unapproachable than perhaps he was. His nickname, "James the Caledonian," suggested that he was a man more admired than loved. Like Bob Morris, Wilson suffered from a compulsion to speculate, and he, too, would end his life as a fugitive from creditors, impoverished and shunned. But in 1787 Wilson was in his prime, more influential in shaping the Constitution than any delegate save for James Madison. Wilson's voice was heard more frequently on the floor of the convention than anyone's except for Gouverneur Morris.

Elbridge Gerry was the most striking of the four Massachusetts delegates—and the most troublesome for the nationalists. The forty-three-year-old Gerry was small and thin, with a noticeable squint in his eye, a slight stutter, and a face dominated by a long nose and a perpetually worried, dissatisfied look. Despite his physical appearance, Gerry had a surprising reputation as a ladies' man. Whatever his mysterious charm with the women, men did not take to him. He was touchy, easily offended, stubborn, and displayed a suspicious nature and a constant pessimism that would remind modern readers of Christopher Robin's sorrowful friend, Eeyore. Gerry's stutter made him a poor orator, although his argumentative style did as much harm as his disability. And yet—Gerry was both politically shrewd and politically experienced. He had begun his political career as a radical, a devoted follower of the democratic-minded Samuel Adams. He had been an active patriot and an expert on military and financial matters in the Continental Congress. Although

Gerry never saw active military service, his advocacy of higher pay and better equipment for the Continental troops earned him the nickname "Soldiers' Friend." Gerry began the convention as a reliable member of the nationalist camp. Over the months, however, he came to fear that the solutions proposed by the convention to the nation's problems were worse than the problems themselves. A strong central government, Gerry concluded, would not protect the liberties of the people as well as their state governments could. In the end, he became a thorn in Madison's side, a fierce and vocal opponent of much that the nationalists hoped to accomplish in Philadelphia.

Tiny, mild-mannered, and modest William Paterson shared Roger Sherman's suspicions that the larger states would dominate any new government created in Pennsylvania. Only five feet two inches, the forty-two-year-old lawyer was small even by eighteenth-century standards. His big nose and piercing eyes dominated his face, giving him a somewhat sensuous appearance, but his neat wig suggested the fastidiousness that was central to his character. Paterson's family had left Ireland when he was a small child, and his father became a peddler of tin ware in Connecticut. A move to New Jersey improved the family fortunes and allowed William to attend the College of New Jersey (which later became Princeton University). As a career, Paterson chose the law, and, like many in his profession, he entered government, serving in the provincial congress, the New Jersey state constitutional convention, and the state legislative council. In 1783 he mysteriously and abruptly withdrew from public life. His selection as a delegate to the Philadelphia convention marked an end to his political retirement. Although he left the convention in late July, he was recognized by all the delegates as the most articulate champion of the interests of the smaller states. Paterson was proof, like Sherman, that nationalists could have very different agendas from one another.

Delaware's John Dickinson was a nervous, cautious man whose long battles with illness had left him emaciated and looking far older than his fifty-four years. Dressed always in black, he more closely resembled the Puritan minister of Hawthorne's imagination than a prosperous lawyer living in comfort on a large estate. Conservative by nature and more skilled as a mediator than an activist, Dickinson had taken up his pen in the 1760s to urge colonists to use economic pressure rather than violent resistance against the Stamp Act. In his famous *Letters from a Farmer in Pennsylvania*, Dickinson firmly supported resistance to unjust laws yet called for a peaceful solution to the conflict between mother country and colonies rather than revolution. When the conflict reached its crisis in 1776, the "Penman of the Revolution" voted against the Declaration of Independence—then promptly enlisted in the American military. By his actions, Dickinson showed himself to be that strange hybrid: a moderate revolutionary. From his estate in Delaware, he had watched the growing economic rivalry among the states with dismay and came to the Philadelphia convention ready to support any reasonable proposal for a strong, effective central government. He was ill throughout most of the summer, and his fatigue and discomfort muted his voice in the convention. But before he left for home in late July, Dickinson would manage to broker the critical compromise between the large states and the small states over representation.

On the whole, these central players in the drama of the convention were middle-aged men with long years of political experience. Charles Pinckney was the exception. At twenty-nine, this South Carolina country gentleman appeared not to be intimidated in the company of his elders; indeed, Pinckney displayed a self-assurance that bordered on arrogance. He was a man of undeniable ability, a brilliant conversationalist, and a fiery orator. But he was often superficial, pushy, and so ambitious to make a name for himself that he was willing to lie and cheat if it worked to his advantage. Men like Pinckney made unstable allies but even more dangerous enemies. Fortunately for the nationalists, Charles Pinckney was an ardent supporter of a strong central government, so ardent in fact that he arrived at the convention armed with his own plan for that government. He presented his plan on the floor of the convention soon after it began its deliberations. Although little attention was given to the proposals of this brash young planter, Pinckney would later claim that they served as the real basis for the Constitution. The claim, like much of Pinckney's statements, was grandiose, but his ideas did play a significant role in the debates that summer. Despite all his faults, Pinckney emerged as a leader on the floor of the convention, an effective debater, and a master of the quick retort. He played an equally important role as the member of several key committees appointed in August and September to speed the convention along.

Virginia, like Pennsylvania, had sent its best and brightest to Philadelphia. Along with George Washington and James Madison, this stellar group included two of the state's most respected jurists, George Wythe and John Blair. But the men Madison most relied on to press the nationalist cause at the convention were Edmund Randolph and George Mason. Randolph, the governor of Virginia, was only thirty-four, but his political experience and maturity distinguished him from the other "youngster" in the group, Charles Pinckney. Randolph was a tall, somewhat portly man, with large brown eyes and a handsome face framed by loose dark hair. He carried himself with the confidence of a Virginia planter and his manners were impeccable. Born to wealth and trained in the law, Randolph had taken his place among the political leadership of Virginia at the tender age of twenty-three when he helped secure the adoption of the state's first constitution. The political career that followed was meteoric: he was mayor of Williamsburg and Virginia's attorney general before he turned thirty, and by 1786 he sat in the governor's seat. It was Randolph, eloquent and poised, whom the delegation selected to present Madison's plan for a new government. Although Randolph was a member of the inner circle of the nationalist camp, his commitment faltered as the weeks went by. His identification as a Virginian did battle with his desire to "think continentally"; by September he had joined the opposition, refusing to sign a constitution that established a strong central government. Ironically, his nationalism revived once he returned to Virginia, and he campaigned for ratification of the document he had renounced.

Randolph's colleague George Mason appeared made of sterner stuff. Mason was the master of Gunston Hall plantation and one of the richest men in Virginia. Now in his sixties, Mason was best known and widely admired for drafting the Virginia Declaration of Rights in 1776, a guarantee of basic liberties that quickly became the model for other state constitution writers. In the early 1780s Mason withdrew from the public arena and, like William Paterson, did not return to politics until called to serve at the Philadelphia convention. Mason would speak often at the convention, demonstrating the precision of thought and the intelligence that led James Madison to declare he "had the greatest talents for debate of any man he had ever seen." Like Randolph, Mason came to Philadelphia a committed nationalist, but his support faded as the convention refused to confront issues Mason considered crucial and fundamental. Chief among these issues was slavery, which Mason considered a blight on the republican values of his country. Equally disturbing to this Virginia gentleman was the convention's failure to include a bill of rights in the national Constitution. George Mason's defection was a blow to Madison, both personally and politically.

All these political twists and turns lay in the future, of

course. Although Madison could see the delegates clearly in the earliest days of the convention, nothing had yet been proposed to animate them or to expose the depth of their support or opposition to the serious business Madison hoped would soon be at hand. In the meantime, other delegates continued to trickle in. If these men were far from the demigods Jefferson wished us to envision, a number of them were memorable for their foibles and failings.

At the South Carolina table, the peacock of the convention, Pierce Butler, could be seen, sporting his powdered wig and his coat trimmed lavishly in gold lace. Butler was the only delegate who could lay claim to blue blood, for—as he compulsively reminded everyone—his father was a baronet. Butler had inherited his father's sense of superiority but not a vast estate, and so had been forced to acquire his own fortune. He did this by marrying the daughter of a wealthy South Carolinian. Yet Butler had proved himself more than a dandy when during the Revolution he had risked his marital fortune for the cause of independence. His patriotism earned him the respect of his colleagues that his silk suits could not, and at the convention Butler proved a solid supporter of the nationalist agenda.

Nearby, the most jovial member of the convention filled his seat at the Delaware table. Forty-year-old Gunning Bedford Jr.—tall, social, impetuous—was distinguished as much by his obesity as by his good humor. On his death his epitaph would gently acknowledge his bulk, asserting that "his form was goodly." Without question the largest man at the convention, Bedford would rise on several occasions to lend his considerable weight to the debates.

If Bedford exuded optimism and goodwill toward his fellow men, Maryland's Luther Martin radiated cynicism and hostility toward those around him. Nothing in Martin's career history suggested a difficult life: he had graduated from the College of New Jersey, studied law, and by the age of thirty he had risen to be the attorney general of his state. He had one of the largest and most successful legal practices in the nation. Yet Luther Martin was a troubled man, an alcoholic given to eccentric, often antisocial behavior that disgusted his enemies and saddened his friends. Generous to a fault with needy clients, Martin was often arrogant in dealing with his peers. At the convention his untidy dress provided a dramatic contrast with the elegant Butler and the prim Paterson, but it was the strong smell of liquor on his breath that set the thirty-nine-year-old delegate apart from the rest. Neither his alcoholic haze nor his poorly hidden contempt for his fellow delegates prevented Martin from speaking his mind. He would rise frequently to speak against a new constitution, trying the patience of the delegates with long, rambling harangues that nevertheless contained kernels of insight and moments of lawyer-sharp reasoning. The nationalists were fortunate that Luther Martin did not do battle with them in a sober state.

Several men whom Madison might have wished to see when he looked out at the delegates were not there.

Thomas Jefferson, the author of the Declaration of Independence, was absent, busy with diplomatic duties in France. Fellow diplomat John Jay, the tall, somber Huguenot from New York who had helped negotiate the peace treaty and served as ambassador to Spain, had been barred from the New York delegation by the Clinton faction as too openly nationalist for their tastes. Thomas Paine, the corset maker turned radical propagandist whose plainspoken pamphlet *Common Sense* had helped thousands of Americans break the final bonds of loyalty to England, was away in Europe, soon to be fomenting revolution against another king. Feisty, fretting John Adams was in England, leveling his disapproving puritan eye on George III's court, intent on proving that an ambassador need not master even the most rudimentary social graces to be effective. Whatever his shortcomings as a diplomat, Adams would have been a valuable ally for the nationalists at the convention. He had been the guiding force behind the recently adopted Massachusetts state constitution, a document that incorporated the principle of balance of powers that Madison hoped to see in the national government. Missing, too, were Henry Laurens, one of the leading patriots of South Carolina, and John Hancock, whose intellect was negligible but whose political savvy was on a par with his egotism. Hancock was too busy in the Massachusetts governor's mansion to journey to Philadelphia.

There were some absences that Madison welcomed. Fellow Virginian Richard Henry Lee, the man who had formally proposed that independence be declared, wanted no part in any nationalist discussion nor did Virginia governor Patrick Henry, who had made his opposition to the convention painfully, and publicly, clear. Finally, Samuel Adams, the country's earliest agitator for independence, remained in Massachusetts.

More than anything else, the exclusion of Samuel Adams from the Massachusetts delegation defined the moment as post-Revolutionary. In the 1760s and 1770s, Adams was the reigning master of protest, with a genius for organizing street demonstrations, spreading rumors, and staging confrontations. He alone of the Revolutionary elite was at home in the dockside taverns where workingmen took their ease. It was Adams who galvanized these working-class men with his harangues against British tyranny and his dire warnings of a plot to enslave them, and Adams who choreographed their demonstrations against the Stamp Act and the tea tax. But the nationalists at the Constitutional Convention had no use for Adams's particular talents. They were there to create a strong central government, not to destroy one. Government inefficiency and impotence was what they feared, not tyranny. There was no role for a skilled rabble-rouser in a shabby coat and threadbare stockings when the political agenda was the protection of property, not its destruction. The specter of Shays's Rebellion hung over the elite gathering in the East Room, and Adams's democratic impulse was out of sync with the fear of debtor riots and farmers' revolts that prevailed there. And at a meeting intent on discretion and secrecy, Adams, the irrepressible publicist, would be a liability rather than an asset. In 1787 Samuel Adams was a relic of the past, best appreciated from a distance. The men gathering in Philadelphia were a different breed of revolutionary.

THE FIRST SALVO in this constitutional revolution came on Tuesday, May 29. Even before George Washington called the meeting to order, the East Room was abuzz with rumor and speculation. Although few knew with certainty, many of the delegates were convinced that the Virginia delegation intended to start the debate on the fate of the Confederation that very day.

The first order of business seemed to confirm rather than dispel the whispered speculations. George Wythe, known in his native Virginia as "Wythe the Just," rose to present the Rules Committee's recommendations on secrecy. Wythe's weather-beaten face was almost expressionless as he read off three simple, but hopefully effective, measures to insure absolute confidentiality for the convention proceedings. First, no one was allowed to make a copy of any entry in the convention journal being kept by Major Jackson without the presiding officer's permission. Second, no one but the delegates could have access to that journal. Finally, as Madison put it in his notes, "nothing spoken in the House [could] be printed, or otherwise published or communicated without leave." In short, secrecy was to be complete.

Later, delegates and supporters of the Constitution would produce a variety of explanations for these measures. Secrecy was essential, some said, to insure that foreign diplomats and observers, eager to report home to their governments on the health of the new Republic, would not be privy to the frank discussion of economic, political, and social problems plaguing the Confederation. Others pointed out that secrecy prevented a further blow to the morale of a public already anxious about the future of the nation and deeply divided as to the solution to its problems. But men with political experience had a different explanation. What had weighed most heavily on the minds of the delegates was not so much the dangers to the nation or to its citizens, but the danger to their own reputations and their own political futures. Even the least perceptive delegates knew there were risks in exposure. And even the most respected knew that they must, ultimately, answer to the state legislatures who sent them to Philadelphia. Who, then, wished to be on record supporting measures their local governments opposed? Who would dare to exceed or ignore his instructions if such independent actions were made public? Who would vote "yea" on overthrowing the government if the newspapers carried word of this the next day? No, it was clear that what was said in Independence Hall must not be heard outside the shuttered windows and locked doors. Without secrecy, there would be no honest discussion of the issues. Without honest discussion, there would be no solution to the crisis facing the nation.

If seasoned politicians understood the delegates' desire for secrecy, not all of them approved of it. Thomas Jefferson was appalled by the wall of silence the convention had constructed. He considered the "tying up the tongues of their members" an "abominable precedent."

"Abominable" it might be, but the closed windows, locked doors, and carefully regulated journal of events were not new to American political deliberations. The Continental Congress had conducted several of its debates in secrecy, and there were state constitutions that owed their creation to sessions in which political figures felt free to speak their minds "without censure or remark."

The real question was not, was secrecy essential?—but, would it be possible? Could delegates resist the impulse to rehash the day's debate each evening as they gathered in Philadelphia's public taverns? Could a delegate be counted on to censor his comments in a letter home to a wife, son, or brother? Could men who saw their proposals voted down or their objections ignored keep their tongue in conversations with sympathetic friends and acquaintances? Surprisingly, self-preservation, if not true discretion, worked its magic on the delegates. Rumors might fly, speculations might multiply, but the proceedings of the convention remained confidential throughout the summer.

No sooner had George Wythe's report been approved, then another member of the Virginia delegation, Governor Edmund Randolph, rose from his seat. Randolph struck a perfect note of humility and sincerity as he made clear to the convention that he was not the author of the proposals he was about to present; he was only their messenger. The author himself sat at his table at the front of the room, no doubt aware that all eyes were upon him.

Slowly, Randolph began. He recited a familiar litany of the Confederation's many flaws and failures: the inadequacies of the requisitions system; the threat of social anarchy; the embarrassment of unpaid foreign debts; the violations of treaties, by foreign nations and even by some of the states; and the havoc produced by paper money. Perhaps his gentlemanly upbringing prompted Randolph to add that the authors of the Articles of Confederation must not be held responsible for these failings. Perhaps the sight of the man who first drafted those articles, John Dickinson, sitting stoically at the Delaware table, prompted Randolph's effort at absolution. Perhaps both motives were at play. But if it was true that no one was to blame, he continued, it was also true that the nation was in crisis. As Randolph drew a gloomy picture of a federal government unable to secure its borders, compete for commercial footholds in world trade, check the quarrels between states, or quell domestic rebellions, the specter of ruin and humiliation menaced the East Room. It was this specter that Virginia's political leaders had faced, un-flinchingly, Randolph declared proudly, and it was this specter that the Virginia plan he now lay before the con-vention was designed to dispel.

With that, Randolph offered up the fifteen resolu-tions that amounted to a constitutional revolution. Al-though the first of these called only for the Articles of Confederation to be "corrected & enlarged," the fourteen that followed, if adopted, would correct and enlarge the Confederation into a completely different government. Virginia had thrown down the gauntlet to the supporters of the Confederation and issued the call to arms for the nationalists. They would learn who was whom on the fol-lowing day.

# CHAPTER FOUR

❧

# The Perils of Power

## "How far do you intend to go?"

THERE MUST HAVE BEEN many restless sleepers that muggy Monday night, as dreams or nightmares based on the day's events formed in their minds. Did they have the authority to make the kind of changes Randolph proposed? Were they, in fact, about to overthrow their government? And could they agree on what to put in its place? Deep divisions were certain to arise if the convention began to construct a new and more powerful central government. And deep-seated fears of the abuse of power were certain to surface no matter what aspect of that government the delegates discussed.

The pace of events was itself startling. The convention was only a few days old, and yet a constitutional revolution appeared to have begun in earnest. Having seized the initiative, the nationalists now seemed determined to press their advantage. On Wednesday, May 30, Edmund Randolph rose to declare that, at the urging of Gouverneur

Morris, he requested a postponement of debate on his "corrected & enlarged" resolution. Instead, he offered the convention a bolder, balder resolution: "that a national Government ought to be established consisting of a supreme Legislative, Executive & Judiciary."

Supporters of the proposal moved quickly to outmaneuver its opponents. Charles Pinckney, displaying political insight that might not have been suspected, stole the thunder of those who might fear that the abolition of state governments was intended. Asking Randolph, "How far do you intend to go in reducing the power of the states?" Pinckney gave the Virginian the opportunity to assuage the fears of the more anxious delegates. On cue, Randolph responded that his only object was to replace the Confederation. He then urged the convention to proceed to the particulars of reform.

Once again, a confirmed nationalist posed the question that must have been on the minds of the more hesitant delegates. General Charles Cotesworth Pinckney, older and far more respected than his young relative, asked: Do we dare? Do we dare conduct a discussion of a system of government founded on principles so different from the federal constitution that now exists? What authority, in short, did the convention actually enjoy to even consider replacing the legitimate government of the United States?

Gouverneur Morris replied with a bluntness that would be his hallmark during the convention. The clear choice facing the convention was this: Shall we have a confederation or a nation? A federal government such as the Articles of Confederation created, Morris declared, was a mere compact, "resting on the good faith of the parties." A national or supreme government, however, had "compleat and compulsive operation." What Randolph proposed was not for the faint-hearted, Morris conceded, but it was based on the simple truth that there can be but "one supreme power, and one only."

The issue, of course, was not cowardice or bravery; the issue as Roger Sherman now pointed out was the limits of this convention's legitimate authority. Sherman agreed that the Confederation lacked sufficient power to be an effective government. He agreed that the jurisdictions of the federal and the state governments must not overlap. But—and here his arrow aimed straight at the heart of Virginia's rebel leadership—he questioned the right of the convention to make "great inroads on the existing system." Sherman's hesitation was more strategic than ideological. If the convention's first act was to abolish the Confederation, would the states respond by voting down this and any other reforms they might constructively propose? Begin slowly, Sherman was advising the delegates; follow the path of reform rather than revolution.

But a certain recklessness had overtaken the convention. As John Adams was so fond of saying on so many other occasions, the delegates had "crossed the Rubicon" and would not turn back. They would, indeed, discuss plans for a new government. Although they were cautious enough to cast their votes as a committee of the whole so that no official entry would be made in the convention journal, the delegates seemed ready, even eager, to give America a new government. With little debate and surprisingly little opposition, Randolph's resolution passed. Only Sherman's Connecticut proved unwilling to vote "aye."

Why had the Articles of Confederation been abandoned so calmly and so soon? The answer lay in the self-selected group that had gathered in Philadelphia. Some of the delegates might have entered Independence Hall uncertain, as Washington once put it, if the Confederation should be "propped up" or "annihilated." But few men who opposed drastic change had bothered to come at all. True, the New York delegation included two men openly hostile to the convention's agenda, but they were neither effective nor particularly respected political figures. The champions of the Confederation had chosen to boycott the meeting rather than mount an opposition from within the convention. On the need for change, then, the delegates were like-minded men. But on what kind of change—there the temple of accord became the Tower of Babel.

There was consensus on only one thing: A new and more effective central government was essential. But there was no consensus on what powers that government should have, the form that government should take, or how representation in that government should be determined. These were no small matters.

The Virginia Plan proved maddeningly vague on all these issues. It offered no clear statement of what powers the new government would have. Resolution 6 gave the

legislature the same powers the Confederation Congress
had enjoyed. But it also gave the new Congress power to
"legislate in all cases to which the separate States are incompetent, or in which the harmony of the United States
might be interrupted by the exercise of individual Legislation." What exactly "incompetent" meant or what
constituted "harmony" no one in the Virginia delegation
seemed prepared to say. The one added power that was
crystal clear owed its clarity, no doubt, to the memory of
a train of humiliations suffered by the Confederation at
the hands of certain powerful states. If Virginia had its
way, the central government would be empowered to "call
forth the force of the Union against any member of the
Union failing to fulfill its duty under the articles thereof."

On the design of the proposed government, the Virginia Plan was more explicit, and in this, it most fully
bore the stamp of its chief author, James Madison. Madison's forte was creating structures, and the Virginia resolutions provided a governmental skeleton, a structural
blueprint for the new Constitution. Because Madison
was a republican like all his fellow delegates, he believed
that the greatest powers must reside in the representative
legislature. For an American generation who rallied to
the cry of "No taxation without representation," the heart
and soul of any republican society must be the representative body that enacted the laws and levied the taxes, not
the executive who administered those laws, not even the
courts who administered justice. It was this conviction
that the legislature was the core and all else was periphery

that separates them from modern Americans, who look to the president for leadership and policy making.

But no matter where power was concentrated in the new government, eighteenth-century republicans tended to fear that concentration. They knew that excessive power in the hand of any group of men was a temptation to tyranny. Madison, deeply suspicious of human nature, was perhaps too trusting of organizational design as a remedy to human failings. In the Virginia Plan, he relied on the diffusion of power among three branches—legislative, executive, and judicial—to thwart that temptation to tyranny.

There was genius in Madison's reliance on the separation of functions, as English political traditions would affirm. But the idea was potentially explosive in the American setting. There were certain to be disagreements over the mode of selecting the executive or judiciary and over the powers they would enjoy. But these would pale before the controversies over the legislature—especially the legislature as Madison envisioned it. He proposed a bicameral legislature, with one house popularly elected by eligible voters in every state and the other elected by the members of the first from slates nominated by the state legislatures. Most controversial of all, membership in both houses was to be based on proportional representation.

With a surgeon's skill, Madison had cut the most important branch in half, creating a bicameral congress. But with a surgeon's hubris, he ignored the impact his call for proportional representation in both houses would have on

smaller states. The delegates would not allow him to ignore it for long. As weeks dragged into months, the convention debated, argued, and came dangerously close to
dissolving over the fundamental question: What was the
basis of representation in the legislature to be? It was easy
to predict that states with modest populations would rise
in opposition to proportional representation. For some
delegates, this was a matter of obligation as much as
choice. George Read, for example, was honor bound by
his instructions from Delaware to leave the convention if
the "one state, one vote" rule of the Confederation was
transgressed. From Delaware's perspective, that rule was
the only barrier protecting the small states against the
tyranny of the more populous states.

Proportional representation stirred up other hornet's
nests as well. If some states would gain and others would
suffer when heads were counted, then much would depend on whose head was to be counted. In North and
South Carolina, Maryland, and Georgia—and in Virginia itself—there were many people who, by law, were
not people at all but property. How, or if, slaves would be
included in determining congressional seats was, for the
Pinckneys and their slave-holding neighbors, a matter of
no small concern.

These issues were more than enough to shatter the
serenity of the convention. But the composition of the
congress also reawakened anxiety over an erosion of state
sovereignty. Edmund Randolph would comment after his
defection from the nationalist camp that the government

envisioned in the Virginia Plan was "a strong *consolidated* union in which the idea of states should be nearly annihilated." Randolph exaggerated in recollection. Yet if the state of Virginia had no intention of committing political suicide, its resolutions would indeed diminish state autonomy. The Confederation had reaffirmed the independence and sovereignty of the states by making the states the basic unit of representation within its congress. Indeed, it did not matter how many delegates a state sent to the Confederation Congress since only thirteen votes could be cast on any question. "One state, one vote" was not simply an equalizer for tiny Delaware and imposing New York; it was a confirmation that the basic political unit remained the state even if the political forum changed. The Virginia Plan weakened this political premise. It created a forum in which state identity was so transfigured that a state's interests were no longer expressed in one voice but in many. The implications of this were not yet clear. But to many delegates they were worrisome indeed.

Unless the delegates could agree on the form the legislature would take, its powers in relationship to the state legislatures, who that legislature would represent, and how its members would be chosen to serve—unless all this could be resolved, the nation would be in more danger than it was under the Articles of Confederation. Unless compromises could be reached, America would be in a political limbo more frightening than any state of nature or any tyranny its politicians, philosophers, or citizens had ever imagined.

Few delegates underestimated the difficulties that lay ahead. The burden facing them weighed heavily upon Virginia's George Mason, who wrote to his son: "The eyes of the United States are turned upon this Assembly and their Expectations raised to a vary [*sic*] anxious Degree. May God Grant that we may be able to gratify them, by establishing a wise and just Government." In the end, Mason would conclude that they had not. Here, at the beginning of the debates, Mason was somber but optimistic. Outside the tightly shuttered windows of the statehouse, men differed on the likelihood of the convention producing any positive results at all. George Washington's friend David Humphreys predicted that nothing would come of the convention. With Rhode Island boycotting and New York hoping to sabotage the proceedings, he asked, "What chance is there, then, that entire unanimity will prevail?" William Grayson, representing Virginia in the Confederation Congress, was equally cynical. "The people of America," he wrote his young friend James Monroe, "don't appear to me to be ripe for any great innovations." And an anonymous writer thought a medical analogy best suited the task facing the convention. In his diagnosis America was "a distempered Patient, whose recovery depends upon the skill of the Physician: Her situation is not desperate; but the nicest applications will be necessary to effect her cure." His prognosis? "The remedy is certainly in the power of the present Convention; and it is sanguinely expected that their united Wisdom will find out the healing balm and restore her to health and happiness."

On June 1 the delegates gathered once again as a committee of the whole to test the strength of that united wisdom. Their blueprint was the Virginia Plan, which they had accepted in principle but not in its specifics. Throughout the summer the plan remained their starting point, a mooring from which they could venture to the left or the right in their discussions. Yet it often proved difficult to decide what constituted a radical notion and what constituted a conservative one. Was it radical to advocate an independent executive branch, or did this reflect a reactionary nostalgia for monarchy? Was a demand for equal representation for the states in the national legislature a stubborn resistance to majority rule or a courageous effort to protect the weak against the strong? On occasion, delegates would take such surprising stances that their past behavior did not seem to guide their current opinions. Men known for their socially conservative views rose to advocate the popular election of the chief executive, and men with true affinities for the common citizen rose to demand his appointment by the Senate. In the course of their deliberations, the delegates were forced to confront their own as well as their colleagues' inconsistencies. They spoke as defenders of popular will on one issue and as guardians of elite judgment on the next. They voted to enhance the powers of the central government on a Monday and to protect the sovereignty of the states on a Tuesday. They reaffirmed their nationalism and then doggedly defended the interests of their region.

Veterans of the Continental Congress's wrangling over the Articles of Confederation and the men who had spent long hours arguing over every point in their state constitutions might have been more prepared than others for the arduous task before the convention. Still, even these seasoned politicians must have marveled at the manner in which debate on every issue, large or small, seemed to circle back upon itself, as arguments were fashioned and refashioned, sometimes into incoherence. Issues that seemed resolved were constantly reprised. In part, the structure of the proceedings made this cycle of "never done" inescapable. As long as the delegates sat as a committee of the whole, no vote was final, no topic ever closed. And as the committee had to forward its decisions to themselves as a convention, a disgruntled delegate or group of delegates had the opportunity, once again, to reopen debate on any issue.

Often the entire process seemed chaotic. Too many problems; too many proffered solutions. Too many issues; too many points of view. Yet a psychological bedrock could be discerned beneath that seemingly chaotic process. Madison's convention notes, like the less detailed notes taken by Massachusetts delegate Rufus King, are testaments to the convention's collective fear of power, or rather, its fear of its abuse, its anxiety about conspiracies and cabals, and its near obsession with setting trip wires and booby traps to ensnare the abusers and the conspirators. Few of the delegates held a view of human nature any rosier than Madison's, but most took pride in anticipating human frailties and taking steps to protect the nation against them. And their lawyerly obsession with anticipating every pitfall, protecting against every contingency, making airtight every clause seemed to them a great asset in assuring that protection. Yet many doubted that any design they came up with could preserve a republic that extended over such a large area and contained such a variety of people and interests. At best, they felt, they might be able to forestall the inevitable decline into tyranny. "I am apprehensive," wrote the normally optimistic Ben Franklin, "that the Government of these States, may in future times, end in a Monarchy. But this Catastrophe I think may be long delayed...."

When the delegates assembled that Friday, June 1, the work of delaying catastrophe began. The day began as usual with President George Washington calling the convention to order at around 10 A.M. While the delegates took their seats, the doors were locked, the windows closed, and the guards took up their posts around the statehouse. New arrivals then presented their credentials to Washington, who passed them along to the convention secretary, Major William Jackson. When these housekeeping chores were completed, the delegates once again assembled as a committee of the whole. Their agenda for the day was a discussion of Resolution 7 of the Virginia Plan, the resolution dealing with the executive branch.

Was it only serendipity that the debates began with Resolution 7? Surely not. Every delegate in the room, from ardent advocates of a strong central government to those hoping to preserve a balance between state sovereignty and national powers, knew that the most divisive arguments would come when Resolutions 2–6 were put on the table, for these dealt with the form and powers of the legislature. If the convention split apart, if delegations abandoned their tables and returned home, if the Confederation continued to oversee the demise of the nation, the death of the nationalists' hopes would undoubtedly come from the debate over the legislature. Thus, by plan or instinct, the delegates began with an issue that would not turn small states against large, region against region, protectors of state sovereignty against extreme nationalists. The coalition that Madison, Hamilton, and others had forged before the convention would not be challenged by a debate over the executive branch.

Resolution 7 provided little guidance to the delegates as they began their discussions. Even more than other parts of the Virginia Plan, the description of this branch was brief and missing several crucial details. Still, the delegates were not entirely at sea. Like many questions raised during the summer deliberations in 1787, the structure and duties of the executive had already been rehearsed on a state and national level. As members of their state legislatures and local constitutional conventions, delegates like George Mason, John Dickinson, and Elbridge Gerry had thrashed out questions of the executive and its functions as they transformed colonies into independent states. In writing state constitutions, they had debated the pros and cons of continuing the familiar colonial practice of a separate executive branch. Their decisions varied. Pennsylvania took the most radical course, abolishing both the governorship and the upper house of the legislature and entrusting all authority to enact and execute laws to a popularly elected assembly. Maryland, on the other hand, had shied away from what their political leaders considered democratic excesses. Its constitution created an executive branch and a bicameral legislature, setting high property qualifications for all of its officeholders in the process.

After the war several states appeared to reconsider the relative advantages of a separation of powers or a system based on complete legislative authority. In Massachusetts that reconsideration was spearheaded by John Adams, who outlined—much as Madison would before the Philadelphia convention—a new government for his state, based on the separation and balance of powers. The result was a new Massachusetts government, a government with a separate executive and a bicameral legislature. The sole, but significant, reminder of Massachusetts radicalism was that the governor was to be popularly elected. The Continental Congress, like Pennsylvania's constitution writers, had assumed that a government could function well without any executive at all. The nationalist attack on the Confederation put the wisdom of this decision, like others, in doubt. At the Philadelphia convention, the principles put forward by John Adams and embodied in the new Massachusetts Constitution held sway.

Few delegates disagreed that an executive branch should be created, but none expected that branch to dominate in the new government. Indeed, the delegates' vision of the executive will seem disturbingly foreign to the modern American, accustomed to a president who sets the agenda for congressional deliberations, who runs for office on a carefully articulated platform, and who dominates domestic as well as foreign policy making. For these eighteenth-century men, such a reversal of the flow of power between legislature and executive was unimaginable. In the scheme most delegates envisioned, the executive was to have a decidedly supporting role, more analogous to an errand boy for Congress than a powerful leader who sets the nation's course of action.

No matter how limited the executive's powers and functions proved to be, the convention still faced a formidable task in spelling out the details of both. The Virginia Plan offered nothing on the composition of the executive, the mode of election, the specifics of its duties and obligations. The resolution read simply: "Resolved, that a National Executive be instituted; to be chosen by the National Legislature for the term of —— years, to receive punctually at stated times, a fixed compensation for the services rendered, in which no increase or dimunition shall be made so as to affect the Magistracy, existing at the time of increase or dimunition, and to be ineligible a second time; and that besides a general authority to execute the National laws, it ought to enjoy the Executive rights vested in Congress by the Confederation."

Modern Americans are likely to be perplexed by the excessive attention paid to the executive's salary. But the delegates were eighteenth-century Americans, with

eighteenth-century concerns about the abuse of power. In
their minds, the executive—or the presidency as it would
later be called—carried inherent possibilities for corruption. Even as a servant of the legislature, empowered only
to execute what that body had enacted, the executive
could do serious damage to the nation. An ambitious
man, for example, might ignore or undermine the will of
Congress, acting as a partisan for an influential faction or
a special interest group within that legislature. Or if he
was to be elected by the legislature as Madison's Resolution 7 proposed, a man eager to retain office might agree
to do the bidding of a powerful group within Congress in
exchange for reelection. Or, driven by avarice, he might
sell out his nation's welfare or security to a foreign power
or to a cabal of the states.

Seen in this light, the close attention to the executive's
salary stands as one effort to protect against a potential
abuse of power. And this particular protection made perfect sense to men with political experience that stretched
back to colonial days. The executives that they knew before independence were, after all, a tyrannical king and a
long parade of his royal governors. Most delegates still
carried the scars of struggles for control between king
and colonists and between governors and assemblymen.
Many a royal governor, either a novice bureaucrat or a
man in the twilight of his career, had brazenly demanded
bribes for concessions to local interests or rewards for
their compliance in ignoring the king's instructions. To
be fair, of course, many a colonial legislature had forced a

governor's cooperation with brazen threats of reducing his salary or withholding it altogether. The lessons learned from these decades of power struggle were deeply etched in the minds of the delegates. They fully expected that members of their own national legislature, no matter what its composition, would fall into the old habits of bribery and cajolery. And they fully expected that a national executive would succumb to greed and corruption. A fixed salary for the executive was one safeguard against one avenue of abuse. The challenge was to find all the other avenues and close them off as well.

No such pervasive suspicions had arisen when Massachusetts created a relatively independent governor. But it was one thing to trust a state executive and quite another to put faith in a national one. The problem was largely a matter of scale. A state governor was a local man whose welfare was intimately entwined with the welfare of his state. The strengths and weaknesses of his character and intellect were well-known to those who had served with him in the legislature, on the bench, or in the militia. Most importantly, his actions could be monitored; his ambitions could be measured by both the political leadership and the citizens themselves. But a national executive would, of necessity, be a stranger to many of his constituents, his character unknown, the depth of his ambition uncharted. He would bring with him a regional perspective and a regional bias, and his loyalty to the entire nation would not be as strong as his loyalty to that region. In short, the sheer size of the Republic posed a novel problem of trust that the delegates were uncertain how to overcome.

Each of these concerns was raised, in turn, during the opening debates. Charles Pinckney, a man whose own ambition was boundless and who would often fall victim to temptation in pursuit of personal glory, spoke for those who wanted the executive's powers carefully limited. In his mind, and theirs, the Virginia Plan had transferred too much power to the executive. To give the executive the power to make war and peace was, in Pinckney's view, to make him as powerful as the king of England and as likely to become a tyrant as George III.

The crusty and obstreperous Elbridge Gerry of Massachusetts was more concerned about the dangers of sectional favoritism in the executive. The executive must be responsive to the interests of the whole nation, Gerry insisted, not simply to the region from which he had come. To protect against sectional or regional bias, the New Englander proposed the creation of a triumvirate, a three-member executive, each man representing a distinct region of the country.

Connecticut's Roger Sherman rejected both Pinckney's demand for limited powers and Gerry's call for a triumvirate. For Sherman, the issue was simple: The executive should have no independent powers at all. Speaking bluntly, his exaggerated New England accent grating on the ears of southern gentlemen like William Pierce, the Connecticut shoemaker turned judge declared that the executive was "nothing more than an institution for carrying the will of the Legislature into effect." As the executive must be accountable to the legislature, which, Sherman asserted, was "the depository of the supreme will of the Society," then the number of men composing that branch should be left up to the discretion of the legislature.

Thus, the question of the size of the executive seemed intimately joined to the question of how much power the executive would enjoy. Other related issues arose during the rambling discussions, whose sudden shifts in topic made them resemble an exercise in free association rather than a coherent dialogue. What administrative style should the nation expect from its executive? James Wilson considered this a critical question. After enduring years of slow and bumbling executive action by the Confederation Congress, Wilson thought Americans deserved a national executive able to act with energy and dispatch. For him, this ruled out a triumvirate since the cumbersome and tedious process of squabbling and compromise among three strong-minded men would cripple the office.

Elbridge Gerry was quick to respond, offering the convention yet another possible executive configuration: an advisory council for the executive. It was difficult to tell what motivated Gerry to make this proposal—conviction or general contrariness. It was likely he was prompted by both. One delegate declared that Gerry objected to everything he did not personally propose. For the moment he was intent on proposing that the convention adopt a device commonly used in most colonies. A council, Gerry reasoned, would add weight to and inspire confidence in the executive branch. It was likely, however, that Gerry wanted the council members to be watchdogs against tyranny as much as inspirational advisers. At the heart of his proposal was the question that nagged at every delegate, except perhaps Mr. Hamilton: How much power should be entrusted to a stranger?

Gerry's suspicion about the executive branch in general struck a chord in other, less irascible delegates. Virginia's own Edmund Randolph spoke for these men when he renounced the idea of "a unity in the Executive magistracy." To establish a single person in the executive office was to imitate the British government. Speaking more dramatically than usual, Randolph declared that a single executive was nothing less that "the foetus of monarchy." To this the soft-spoken Wilson could only reply, You are mistaken. A solitary magistrate was not a fetus of monarchy; it was "the best safeguard against tyranny."

Fetus of monarchy or safeguard against tyranny? Would a single executive be more likely to abuse his power than a triumvirate? Was the real threat to liberty likely to come from another source such as the legislature, as Wilson was suggesting? The delegates were far from certain, but they were in no mood to continue what suddenly seemed likely to become a heated debate. By common consent, Wilson's motion for a single executive was postponed, and the committee of the whole contented itself with approving the first fragment of the controversial clause, agreeing "that a National Executive be instituted."

The question could not be avoided long, however. It reemerged almost immediately when the method of appointing the executive came under discussion. James Wilson and Roger Sherman quickly locked horns once again. Wilson proposed the popular election of the executive, an idea he would doggedly return to during the convention, for he envisioned the executive as the champion of the people against all abuses by the legislature. Sherman opposed this idea vehemently, arguing that the executive must be absolutely dependent upon the legislature, even for his appointment. An independent executive, Sherman warned, recasting Edmund Randolph's fears, was the "very essence of tyranny." The two men agreed that power could and would be abused by all who wielded it; but whose abuse would be most dangerous for the nation?

Was there anything the delegates could easily agree upon? It seemed not. When the question of the length of the executive's term of office arose, the convention proved strongly divided. James Wilson proposed a three-year term, with the right to seek reelection. But the proposal immediately stirred fears in Virginia's George Mason. Would a short term coupled with the right to run for reelection lead a man to use bribery and trickery to regain the office? Would dangerous alliances between an executive bent on reelection and influential legislators eager to be kingmakers produce corruption and abuses? Mason preferred that the executive serve a term of at least seven years, without the option of reappointment by the legislature. By eliminating all hope of a second term, he ar-

gued, we will eliminate all temptation for intrigue between an overly ambitious executive and leading members of the legislature. Gunning Bedford, whose huge body
was usually more imposing than his arguments, challenged Mason's reasoning. Consider, he asked the delegates, how disastrous it would be to saddle the country for
seven years with a man who proved to be incompetent.

Was incompetence less dangerous than intrigue? By
the narrowest majority, the convention answered "yes."
When the committee of the whole took its last vote
of the day, New York, New Jersey, Bedford's own Delaware, Pennsylvania, and Virginia voted in favor of a seven-
year term for the executive. With that, the convention
adjourned for the day. The men made their way to boardinghouses and taverns, where they frustrated curious pa-
trons by discussing nothing more significant than the
oppressive weather.

On Monday the delegates reassembled. After greeting the newest arrivals—Connecticut's William Samuel
Johnson, Maryland's Daniel of St. Thomas Jenifer, and
New York's John Lansing Jr.—the convention chose to
tackle again the question of how the executive was to be
elected. The Virginia Plan called for election by the legislature, but this hardly satisfied the delegates. Other proposals were immediately laid on the table. As expected,
James Wilson called once more for the popular election
of the executive. In its first, rough form, his proposal was
noticeably cumbersome. The states were to be divided into
an unspecified number of districts. Any man in a district

qualified to vote for the popular branch of the legislature would be eligible to vote for electors, who, in turn, would choose the executive. The only restriction was that electors themselves were ineligible for the executive office. Wilson stressed the benefit of his scheme as he saw it, declaring that this form of election would insure the people's confidence in the "first magistrate."

But Wilson's proposal would insure more: it would establish the principle that this branch of the national government, at least, represented the citizens rather than the states. This same principle was, after all, what lay at the heart of Madison's fervent pursuit of proportional representation and his equally fervent desire to see the national government enjoy a veto over all state laws. What Hamilton, Wilson, Gouverneur Morris, and Madison— the core of the nationalist coalition—wanted was a government whose authority rested on "We the people," not because they were democrats or populists, but because this would establish a direct connection to Americans, unmediated by the state governments.

The wily Elbridge Gerry understood the implications of Wilson's proposal—and rejected them. Every mode of selection, Gerry conceded, contained its own dangers of intrigue and abuse of power. Election by the legislature opened up the door to conspiracies between candidates and lawmakers. The former had only to promise patronage and other rewards in exchange for support from the latter. But the dangers in popular election were far greater. It was, Gerry insisted, patently foolish to place so much responsibility in the hands of the people since the people were "too little informed of personal characters in large districts." Far worse, they were "liable to deceptions." Gerry's cynicism and contempt could be dismissed as reflections of his horror at Shays's Rebellion. But his next objection struck a chord less easily ignored. Popular election of the executive, Gerry charged, was simply another effort to insult and erode the authority of the state legislatures. It was these legislatures who ought, who must, choose the electors or choose the executive directly.

When the vote came, only Wilson's home state of Pennsylvania and neighboring Delaware supported popular election. No vote was taken on Gerry's counterproposal that the state legislatures control the election. At this point the committee of the whole preferred to trust the national legislature with the choice of the executive. The matter was far from settled, of course; like others, it would be reraised, reargued, and resubmitted in the months ahead.

If the relative power of the state and national governments was a sporadically emerging theme, the fear of excess power in any hands remained the major leitmotiv of these debates. The two bled into each other, however, no matter how the discussion began. That afternoon Benjamin Franklin asked to be recognized, and, begging the indulgence of the convention for his age and feeble health, he asked James Wilson to read some prepared remarks on the dangers of providing any executive salary at all. Both Franklin's topic and his style of presentation were a departure for the delegates; for the most part, the discussions had been conducted with few flights of oratory and few extended discourses on political philosophy. Indeed, Madison's notes preserved the awkward phrasing and backtracking typical of spontaneous comments rather than prepared speeches. Now Madison enjoyed the luxury of copying Franklin's prepared speech in a leisurely fashion rather than furiously scribbling down what he could as he listened.

Franklin's remarks were rich with political philosophy, almanaclike aphorisms, and historical references, but the proposal itself was straightforward: The executive should serve without pay. Behind his argument was the now-familiar fear of power and its abuses. "The love of power, and the love of money," the good doctor argued, wielded a powerful influence over the affairs of men. Separately, they drove men to action; united, they were potent and dangerous forces in any society. When a post of honor was also a place of profit, all men would "move heaven and earth to obtain it." The only remedy, Franklin concluded, was to sever the connection between ambition and avarice by eliminating the salary of the national executive.

As if by free association, Franklin's concern about overweaning ambition in a single man seemed to spur John Dickinson to return to the issue of overweaning power in a single government. It was not the executive's avarice or lust for power that troubled the Delaware delegate so much; it was the suggestion that the state governments ought to have no hand in monitoring the executive's behavior. "The happiness of this Country," Dickinson declared, "required considerable power to be left in the hands of the States." For that reason, he moved that the power to remove the executive officer be put in the hands of the state legislatures rather than the national legislature. Dickinson's goal was obvious. He hoped to preserve both a symbolic and a practical dependency of this branch upon the local governments.

Dickinson had read the intentions of the hardcore nationalists accurately. They did indeed hope to erode the sovereignty of the states, draining away their control over the lives of the citizens of the country and creating a bond between Americans and their national government. Both Madison and Morris spoke against Dickinson's motion, offering dire scenarios of endless intrigue among those state legislatures who disliked an executive and equally damaging counterintrigues among those who supported him. When Dickinson rose to offer dire scenarios of his own, he opened the real Pandora's box of sovereignty: Was the national legislature to represent the states or the citizens of the Republic? Dickinson, without a trace of fanaticism in his character, always ready to compromise, had digressed from the discussion of the executive to address the nature of the national legislature. Having ventured into this dangerous territory, he acted boldly, calling for a bicameral legislature, with one house representing the states, the other representing the will of the majority.

The delegates were far from ready to contend with the structure of the legislature. They summarily voted down Dickinson's motion regarding removal of the executive and carefully ignored his suggestions regarding the Congress. They spent the rest of the day in discussions tightly focused on the executive branch. They agreed to make the executive ineligible for a second term after seven years and then took up the question of whether the executive was to be a "he" or a "they." Unable to find common ground on this issue, they at last adjourned and went home.

When the convention reconvened the following Monday, the executive branch had vanished from their agenda. After four days of rambling, disjointed debate, the delegates seemed to shrug their collective shoulders and agree they must, after all, dive headlong into the question of the legislative branch. Although they had tried to avoid it, it was obvious that they would not resolve key issues about the executive branch until they answered key questions about the legislative one. And so, for the next six weeks or more, the battle over proportional representation or state representation, over how to elect members of the legislature and what their numbers would be, took central stage.

That the legislature became the central focus of debate does not mean that, sometimes unpredictably, issues about the executive did not arise. Throughout the convention the delegates would move back and forth, from one issue to another, from discussions of the judiciary to debates over the Congress, from arguments over terms of office for the executive to arguments over terms of office for the judges. And although it might seem to a casual reader of Madison's notes that this was some collective nervous tic, some inability to remain focused on the matter at hand, there was in fact a logic to the endless to-and-fro. Because the government the delegates envisioned was made up of interconnected parts, the smallest tinkering or adjustment to one required changes in another. The branches had to be able to cooperate, but they also had to be able to restrain one another. The tools of restraint given to one branch depended upon the dangers inherent in the powers given to another. Thus, the convention moved back and forth, making adjustments here in response to changes there, revising in the face of revisions, learning on a daily basis that they could not anticipate the consequences of every decision and so had to be ready to amend and alter what had once seemed permanently in place. In some, sheer stubbornness, a remarkable refusal to abandon a favorite notion or compromise a cherished belief, led them to reopen issues others considered resolved. But if a few seemed to pick away at constitutional scabs, most who reopened debate on an issue did so because they saw the need to realign a once-fixed element with a newly altered one. The process of fine-tuning was never ending, made always more difficult by the babel of voices and the discord even among men who carried the nationalist banner.

CHAPTER FIVE

Schisms, Threats, and
Compromises

"I do not, gentlemen, trust you"

IN JUNE 1787 JOHN DICKINSON wrote home to his wife,
Sally. "The Convention is very busy," he said, but, he
cheerfully added, the debates were "of excellent temper."
The old lawyer's optimism surely faded as the discussion
turned to the legislature. On June 9 the convoluted and
inconclusive discussion on the executive had petered out,
and the delegates moved to the heart of the matter: Who
would be represented in the lawmaking branch, and how?
Until that day it had seemed that nationalism coursed
through the veins of everyone present—except perhaps
Robert Yates and John Lansing of New York. But very
quickly the delegates discovered that there were many
strains of nationalism—and some were deadly to others.

The tone of the debates was immediately and noticeably different now. True, the discussion about the presidency had sometimes grown heated, but, on the whole, it
had reinforced the notion that the men cloistered in the

statehouse were generally in accord. Disagreements had seemed to arise from personal preferences, individual passions, or a man's vivid recollection of past experiences rather than from fundamental fault lines dividing region from region, state from state, political philosophy from political philosophy. It had been easy enough to imagine—or to hope—that men would speak their minds independently and that their peers would judge their suggestions with equal independence of mind. But self-interest did not seem to spur a man to his opinion, and votes on the executive's number, election, and powers did not reveal a steady pattern of cooperation among certain states.

It was not so innocent, of course. Virginia's delegates had caucused steadily in the days before a quorum was reached. Slowly but surely, Madison, Hamilton, Gouverneur Morris, and James Wilson—the central figures in the do-or-die nationalist circle—had drawn the Pinckneys and Rufus King into their embrace, and by the time the committee of the whole began its confused efforts to sort out the executive branch, a solid bloc of Virginia Plan advocates had been created from Massachusetts, Pennsylvania, Virginia, the Carolinas, Georgia—and Hamilton. But with no organized opposition—and no issue deemed critical enough for one to form—delegates could continue to believe, or claim, that this alignment was a natural confluence of opinion rather than a political bloc.

The delegates were not naive, but many did not seem fully prepared for what they faced. Certainly, few of them had arrived with well-defined plans for a new or even a revised government. Unlike Charles C. Pinckney or James Madison, who had both mulled over the flaws of the Confederation, consulted republics of the past and philosophers of the present, and sketched out detailed blueprints for a new government, most delegates had taken their seats in the East Room with a general sense that they were there to fix what was wrong—and go home to persuade their constituents that what they had done was right. The only caveats they all acknowledged were that they must do it in a manner that did not insult the republican inclinations of Americans and did not do damage to the welfare of their own state.

But now it appeared that divining what was best for the people or for one's state was no easy task. In the end, this assemblage John Adams praised for its "Ability, Weight, and Experience" relied far more on familiar political skills—caucusing, deal making, issuing ultimatums, and arranging compromises—than on full-blown plans or political philosophies. Fortunately for the nation, the framers were accomplished politicians.

For the extreme nationalists of the Hamilton/Madison stripe, two victories regarding the composition and powers of the legislature were essential. First, representation in the legislature had to be based on population rather than on the principle of equality among the states, large and small. They demanded proportional representation, or simply put, the more citizens a state had, the more voices it was entitled to in the legislature. The principle underlying *that* principle was even more important to these nationalists: The Union was a government of the people not of the states. It was to make this point even clearer that they pressed for their second goal: the right of the national legislature to veto any state law. Madison and Hamilton were adamant on both these issues. Even before the convention began, Madison had declared his unshakable commitment to both points to Washington, Jefferson, and anyone else who would listen. In 1798 James Madison would author the Kentucky Resolves, one of the most compelling defenses of states' rights before the Civil War, but in 1787 he stood at the head of a faction that seemed determined to crush the autonomy of the states.

In the first flush days of the convention, Madison believed his group of nationalists would be victorious on both counts. By the end of July, he knew how wrong he had been. For Madison's dream was a nightmare to nationalists like John Dickinson. Dickinson had no desire to preserve the Confederation, but he had no desire to see the equality of the states sent to oblivion with it. Aware that Madison's brand of nationalism was a potential threat to small states like his own, Dickinson, along with George Read, had made certain that their instructions prohibited their endorsement of any plan that denied the states an equal voice in the legislature. Dickinson's definition of nationalism was a far cry, it appeared, from Madison's; for him, it meant establishing a central government powerful enough to end the bullying of some states by others.

Having suffered long enough in the frying pan of large neighbors like New York and Pennsylvania, Dickinson's Delaware and William Paterson's New Jersey knew better than to jump into the fires of proportional representation.

Madison's vision also disturbed those delegates from large states who had no wish to preside over the death of the states. Among them were certainly men who "thought locally" rather than continentally, men whose loyalty radiated out from their county or parish to their state government, weakening as it stretched to the national scene. But their ranks also included men who believed that the best representative of the people's interests was their state government and the best role for the national government was as a forum in which the states could gather. They readily conceded the failures of the Confederation. They readily endorsed the decision to increase the scope and number of the national government's powers. But they were not ready to see the national government usurp the role of the states in representing the interests of the people.

Sparks began to fly from the first moment on June 9 when the champion of states' rights, William Paterson of New Jersey, asked the convention to take the question of suffrage head on. Everything about the five feet two inch Paterson, from his neatly placed wig to his spotless attire to his mild manner, seemed to signal his hatred of controversy, his love of order, and his devotion to a life of rules and regulations. He was, to put it bluntly, a prig. As state attorney general, he had expended an inordinate amount of time prosecuting fornicators and adulterers and advocating a decrease in the number of taverns in his home state. But he was also a nationalist, eager to see a staunch executive branch that could impose law and order on what he saw as an increasingly anarchical nation. Perhaps the same sense of moral outrage that sent him in pursuit of lascivious lawbreakers spurred him to overcome his natural inclination to avoid political conflict. For, like a states' rights David, he rose up to challenge the proportional representation's Goliath.

Despite the impassioned arguments of William Paterson, the committee of the whole voted on June 11 in favor of proportional representation in the Senate as well as the House. That would hardly be the end of it, however. Four days later Paterson presented his New Jersey Plan to the convention. The plan retained the basic structure of the Confederation with its unicameral congress and its one vote for each state. But the plan set out a compromise between the Confederation's executive committee system and the Virginia Plan's independent executive branch through the creation of an executive board, elected by the legislature but removable by a majority of state governors.

Paterson's plan also contained provisions that revealed its bias toward small-state economic interests. Under the New Jersey Plan, the national legislature would enjoy the right to lay duties on imports—thus providing protection for states like New Jersey against exploitation by states like New York. And it would be empowered to tax the state governments on the basis of population and to collect those taxes by force if necessary. The large states would thus be saddled with more taxes but deprived of any extra power.

Although it was the work of one man, the New Jersey Plan expressed the sentiments of a group of delegates, drawn from the small northern states, who would soon constitute an opposition bloc to Hamilton and Madison's already firmly established coalition. Rallying behind Paterson were men like Luther Martin, the brilliant but eccentric lawyer from Maryland. Martin and Paterson were the convention's odd couple, separated by temperament and habits but joined by a devotion to states' rights. It may not have been coincidental that Paterson raised the issue of representation in the Senate on the very day that Martin finally took his seat at the convention.

James Wilson led the assault on the New Jersey Plan. Veiled threats—soon to be made explicit—circulated that if the large states were thwarted in their desires for proportional representation in the Senate, they would withdraw from the Union and form their own nation. It seemed a wild notion, especially since New York would have none of it and the southern component of the extreme nationalist coalition would be left twisting in the wind. Still, the fear that the convention would break up seemed increasingly realistic over the next few weeks.

By the end of the day, Paterson realized that he had not mustered enough support for his plan to risk a vote. Resigned, he called for a postponement of the question.

Madison and his coalition did not delude themselves, however, that the threat was over. The New Jersey Plan might be defeated when the delegates reconvened on Monday, but at what cost? Before the day's adjournment, John Dickinson had laid the blame for the impending crisis squarely on Madison's shoulders. Drawing the Virginian aside, he said: "You see the consequences of pushing things too far.... Some of the members from the small States... are friends to a good National government; but we would sooner submit to a foreign power, than submit to be deprived of an equality of suffrage, in both branches of the legislature." Soon afterward the delegates left the statehouse, leaving nothing resolved and no one satisfied.

The following day, Sunday, small-state delegates gathered to caucus just as Virginia and Pennsylvania had so often done. Together Roger Sherman, Paterson, and their colleagues from Delaware and the large-state renegade, New York, hammered out a compromise proposal: a bicameral congress, one house based on proportional representation, the other ensuring equal representation for the states. There was nothing new in this Connecticut Compromise. In fact, Roger Sherman had proposed something remarkably similar to the Continental Congress in 1776. He had actually proposed it to this convention on June 11, but the large states, still confident, had ignored him. This time they ignored the proposal at their peril.

Inevitably, the Connecticut Compromise set the delegates off on a series of tangents. The discussion thus became both more heated and yet more diffuse. How the Senate would be composed turned out to be only one issue. What purpose the Senate served proved to be another. Was it simply a mechanism to diffuse power, another example of checks-and-balances designed to prevent the rise of an oligarchy or a tyrant? Or should the men who sat in the Senate represent some particular minority interest within the society—the propertied classes? With his typical combination of populism and elitism, Gouverneur Morris argued for a senate composed entirely of the nation's crème de la crème. The upper house, he argued, should be restricted to men of "great personal property," who served for life in a branch of government that openly boasted an "aristocratical spirit." The Senate, in short, should be a bastardized House of Lords, made up of men with fat pocketbooks rather than blue blood. If such a legislative branch existed, Morris continued, they would surely do wrong. And this, he added, relishing as always his own ironic insights, would be right for the nation. "The rich will strive to establish their dominion and enslave the rest. They always did," Morris declared. "They always will. The proper security against them is to form them into a separate interest. The two forces"—and by this he meant the more democratic House and the aristocratic Senate—"will then control each other." A realist after all, the hedonistic Morris preferred to isolate the enemy rather than attempt to convert him.

Morris's bald assertion that America did indeed have an economic and social elite and that its intentions were, if natural, still predatory sat badly with the delegates. Even Madison, who would defend the rights of this elite minority against the envy and passions of the less prosperous majority in his *Federalist* #10, cringed at so naked a description of his own social circle. Most delegates preferred to cast the issue in a different light: the Senate should be composed of "wise men," the best and the brightest of the nation. Serving longer terms than the elected representatives in the lower house, senators would be freed of immediate accountability to a fickle electorate. They could mull over issues without pressure from impassioned constituents. Their experience and education, combined with their unchallenged patriotism, would guide them as they advised, chastised, or reined in the lower house. They would be, as these eighteenth-century men liked to put it, disinterested participants in the governing of the nation.

A senate of sages—even if the majority of delegates preferred such a model, how would wise men be detected or selected? Would wise men be forbidden to serve in the House? In most delegates' experience, the men serving in their own state assemblies and councils were drawn from the same elite pool. Could a man sit in the house of the wise one year and sit in the representative assembly the next?

Paterson and Sherman considered this line of debate frivolous. They reiterated their demand that the legislature be unicameral, with equal representation for the states. If the convention could not be persuaded of this, then the central issue for the upper house was not the relative wisdom or wealth of the senators but whether the states were the basic unit represented in that house. The committee of the whole remained unbending, however. On June 19 the committee again endorsed the Virginia Plan's stipulation of proportional representation in both houses. Then they reported out their decision to themselves as the convention. With that, the debate began all over again.

Whatever hopes the small states held out for the New Jersey Plan were dashed on June 27. On that unbearably humid and uncomfortable day, Luther Martin rose from his seat and began a two-day marathon speech in support of states' rights. Perhaps he acted on his own; perhaps the small-state caucus had designated him their champion. Either way, it was a disaster. For three excruciating hours, the not-altogether-sober Martin managed to bore the delegates silly, droning on and on in a monotone that made it impossible for his audience to care what he said. Sadly, there was much merit—and considerable truth—buried in Martin's often incoherent monologue. In essence, he argued that the states were sovereign and that they, not the people, were the legitimate building blocks in any national political system. The problem with the Confederation, he believed, was not that it had made bad decisions, but only that it was too weak to enforce its good ones.

When Martin finally sat down, after holding the floor for three more hours on June 28, the small-state delegates could do little but lick their wounds. In quick succession, Wilson, Hamilton, and Madison rose to reassert the virtues of proportional representation in both houses. With the critical vote on proportional representation in the lower house approaching, and the danger that the convention would dissolve soon afterward, a desperate Benjamin Franklin moved that a chaplain be invited to open the next day's deliberation with a prayer. When the country's oldest Deist issued an appeal for religious intervention, it was obvious the convention had entered its darkest hour.

On June 29 Connecticut, New Jersey, New York, and Delaware cast their votes in the convention against proportional representation in the House. Maryland's delegates were divided. Six states reaffirmed the recommendation of the committee of the whole. And with that, proportional representation in the House of Representatives carried the day. As soon as the vote was taken, Oliver Ellsworth rose from his place at Connecticut's table to appeal for a compromise on representation in the Senate. The small states' olive branch, the Connecticut Compromise, was about to be extended once again.

For the moment, however, the leaders of the large-state bloc were in no mood to compromise. Although Hamilton had left the convention for an extended visit to New York, Madison and James Wilson remained behind, stubbornly committed to an all-or-nothing policy. When the small states suggested that Washington send an official letter to New Hampshire, requesting that their delegation please finally make its way to Philadelphia, the large states defeated the motion. The message was clear: We are not going to help you add another small state to your voting bloc.

Now it was the small states' turn to dig in their heels. They turned the large states' threat of bolting the convention back on their enemies, making it known that it was their delegates who would soon be packing their belongings and heading home. At last, Madison realized the seriousness of the situation. It was time to make some concessions before all was lost.

In the midst of this crisis, the irony of the situation was probably lost on the delegates. They were, after all, playing out a version of what they most feared: there, in the convention itself, cabals had formed and they were conspiring to advance self-interests. It did not matter that Alexander Hamilton had tried to dismiss the fears of domination among the small-state delegates by insisting that the large states would never find any issue that would unite them in the new government. Given "all the peculiarities which distinguish the interests of one State from the other," Hamilton said on June 18, there was no reason to fear cabals or conspiracies from the likes of Massachusetts, Virginia, and Pennsylvania. And yet, of course, the very issue-based coalition that men like Paterson feared was a reality in the East Room. Gunning Bedford, the lumbering giant from Delaware, was the first to bluntly accuse his enemies of conspiracy. "I do not, gentlemen, trust you," he told the large-state delegates. "If you possess the power, the abuse of it could not be checked...."

Looking into the future, the usually sanguine and jovial Bedford predicted that the issue of representation and sovereignty could only be settled by war.

It must have been with great relief that the delegates adjourned on the last day of June and prepared for a Sabbath respite on Sunday. But not everyone planned to return on Monday. By Sunday evening news had spread of a strange exodus from Philadelphia, with William Few and William Pierce of Georgia and William Blount of North Carolina on their way to New York City, where the Confederation Congress continued to meet. Many of the delegates to the convention, including the three Williams, still held seats in Congress, and their attendance in Philadelphia had brought the work of the already-floundering Congress to a virtual standstill. For several months certain southern interests had been hoping to pass partisan legislation when enough northern congressional seats were empty. When word reached the Williams that the moment was ripe, they hurried northward.

That the sudden departure of the Williams weakened the large-state coalition became obvious when the convention reconvened on Monday, July 2. Even more disturbing to Madison's group, the seat beside Luther Martin was noticeably empty. Daniel of St. Thomas Jenifer, the elderly, aristocratic planter who was both a confirmed bachelor and a confirmed nationalist, was nowhere to be found. With Dr. James McHenry away at the bedside of his dying brother and John Mercer and Daniel Carroll not due to arrive until mid-July, Luther Martin *was* the

Maryland delegation. When the voting came on equal suffrage in the Senate, Connecticut, New York, New Jersey, Delaware, and Luther Martin said "aye." The small states were one vote short of a majority.

When the vote stood at five to five, all eyes turned to Georgia. Here yet another William—the young and handsome, though not overly bright nationalist William Houstoun—sat beside the ablest Georgian at the convention, Abraham Baldwin. No doubt a smile flickered on the usually dour lips of Roger Sherman, for he knew, if others in the room did not, that Baldwin was born and educated in Connecticut. He was a Yale man who could analyze a problem in all its complexity.

As Baldwin saw it, Georgia's interests were tied to three major considerations. The first was how to thwart any attempt by northerners to end slavery. It was this concern that had brought Georgia into the Madison camp. Southern states like Georgia believed that the larger states would repay their support for the Virginia Plan with a guarantee of protection for slavery. The second consideration was how to protect Georgia's western lands from confiscation by other states or by the central government. But the most pressing threat to Georgia's well-being was its vulnerability in the face of southwestern Indians and their Spanish allies. Georgia needed the military and diplomatic protection of a strong central government, and Baldwin intended to do nothing that endangered the success of a convention certain to produce that government. He knew Roger Sherman—and thus he knew that the small states were not bluffing.

They would bolt the convention if proportional representation was established in both houses of Congress. Weighing all this, Baldwin cast his vote with the small states. Houstoun, on the other hand, cast his with the large states. Georgia had canceled itself out.

The small states had not won a victory—but they had not suffered a defeat. Subtly, power had shifted, and for the first time, James Madison found himself on the defensive. When Oliver Ellsworth, who had put the Connecticut Compromise idea on the table several times, moved that a committee of one man from each state be appointed to hammer out a compromise, not even the combined efforts of Madison and Wilson could prevent it. The composition of the committee gave a good indication of how anxious the delegates were to find a workable solution and how exhausted they were from the wrangling and threats. Luther Martin would serve; so, too, would William Paterson. Ellsworth was also selected but came down with a sudden, convenient illness and asked Roger Sherman to take his place. Thus, the powerhouses of the small states had been chosen while the leadership of the opposing bloc was nowhere to be found. Virginia's committee member was not Madison but George Mason, who by July was openly voicing his doubts about the extreme nationalists' attack on state sovereignty. Elbridge Gerry would represent Massachusetts and Benjamin Franklin, Pennsylvania.

Having appointed this committee, the delegates rewarded themselves with a few days' vacation. The Fourth of July was upon them, and they were relieved to take time off from creating a new government to celebrate the birth of their new nation. They joined enthusiastically in Philadelphia's festivities, marching in the parade and attending church services, where sermons focused on America's special destiny and God's special affection for the citizens of the Republic. Sometime during this much-needed recess, the committee fleshed out the compromise they would present on July 5. It was, of course, the Connecticut Compromise, with an added sop to the large states—all bills of appropriation would originate in the lower house, where they would dominate—and a considerable gesture of goodwill to the southern states—with the population base including slaves, at a ratio of three to five.

On Monday, July 16, the long ordeal ended. When the vote came, five states said yes to the compromise; four said no. Massachusetts was divided, and New York?— New York was gone. Hamilton, who had left before the July 4 break, had not returned. On July 5 Yates and Lansing had declared their firm opposition to the entire proceedings of the convention and gone home to the welcoming bosom of Governor Clinton's antinational party.

Madison had lost the battle for one of his two major reforms, a national government that represented the people directly rather than the states. On July 17 he lost the battle for the other. That day the convention voted down Congress's power to veto state laws. The constitution that would come out of the Philadelphia convention would be only a faint reflection of James Madison's grandest vision.

On July 23 a relatively satisfied William Paterson left Philadelphia, not to return until the delegates put their signatures on the completed Constitution. He missed, therefore, the final heated debate over slavery. It was not a debate over the continuation of slavery or over the three-fifths formula for including slaves in the population base for the House, for neither of these issues was especially controversial. The Confederation had operated on the three-fifths formula, and, arbitrary though it was, it was familiar enough to the delegates to be acceptable. Although southern delegates could not resist testing the waters on counting their slaves as full persons, they had already abandoned this by mid-June. Any attempt to raise the moral issue of slavery was just as quickly rejected, despite Gouverneur Morris's eloquent condemnation of this "nefarious institution" that called down the "curse of Heaven on the states where it prevailed" and the impassioned speeches of Virginia's George Mason and Massachusetts's Rufus King against the continuation of such an institution in a republic. The convention preferred to heed Oliver Ellsworth's advice. "Let us not intermeddle," he said, dismissing the problem with the optimistic prediction that "slavery in time will not be a speck in our country."

If neither slavery as a moral problem nor the absurdly arbitrary fractionalization of each enslaved man, woman, and child bothered the convention, what then was the issue? The southern delegates, especially those from South Carolina, wanted the convention's assurances that the slave trade could continue, at least for a time, and that the

Africans or Caribbean blacks brought to America would not be considered taxable imports. The southern demands opened the door for a second round of coalition building. The result was an unpredicted shift in alignments, temporary though it may have been. Throughout June Connecticut's Sherman had been searching for a way to drive a wedge between the southern states and the large-state axis. He now offered South Carolina and her sister states Connecticut's support on both issues. Sherman saw other no-less-important possibilities in this alliance with states whose economies were not only based on slave labor but on the exportation of staple crops. The mutual benefits to be gained were not lost on a man like South Carolina's John Rutledge. The fact was that Connecticut's economy, like that of South Carolina and Georgia, depended heavily on exports. If they presented a united front, the southern exporters and their northern ally could insist that no export taxes would be imposed and no imported slaves would be taxable. Before the convention ended, they had secured both of their goals.

The Great Compromise, as the vote on July 16 came to be called, ushered in a new spirit at the convention. It became clear that men were tired and missed their families and their own beds. "I believe the older men grow more uneasy [the longer] they are away from their wives," Oliver Ellsworth told his own wife on July 21. Delegates began to slip away for visits home. Even Roger Sherman overcame his rigid sense of duty and excused himself for a few days. Increasingly, the convention preferred to send thorny problems and even potentially troublesome ones to committees where compromises could be worked out. And increasingly they relied on committees to fill in the details of their grand design. It was in this mellower mood that the convention reopened the debate on the executive on July 17.

❧

# CHAPTER SIX

# Debating the Presidency Once Again

## "[Like] a trial of colours to a blind man"

ON JULY 31 THOMAS JEFFERSON wrote from Paris to John Adams, his fellow ambassador in London. The convention, he said, had at last settled on the "leading Principles or great Outlines" of a new constitution. Jefferson referred, of course, to the compromises on the national legislature. But if Jefferson and Adams could take a moment to rejoice, the delegates enjoyed no such luxury. By the time Adams received the news, the convention was hard at work once more, trying to fit the last major piece of the great puzzle of government in its place: the executive branch. As the weary delegates soon realized, they faced a double dilemma: Who could they trust to choose the president, and what could they trust that president to do?

This second discussion of the executive branch took place among dispirited, restless men. The delegates had been cooped up in a locked room for over a month and a half, listening to one another argue, bicker, and drone on about matters large and small, and everyone's patience was wearing thin. After weeks of carefully defining and illustrating what they meant by "tyranny," or "separation of powers," or "conspiracy and intrigue," a shorthand of mistrust had evolved. A delegate had only to mention "cabal" or "intrigue" and he could assume everyone present would fill in the details and respond with the proper emotions. The exchanges over the rest of July and the dog days of August suggest a certain mental exhaustion, for after carefully fitting together so many interlocking pieces of the constitutional puzzle, many delegates seemed unable or unwilling to assess how decisions on the executive would alter the picture. They had, after all, gone round and round on this issue already, and their irritation found its way into Madison's notes.

There were, of course, moments of sustained debate and brilliant argument. And there were interesting new alignments, for the earlier coalitions of interest had all but dissolved and men formed connections on an individual basis during this final major debate. Strange alliances emerged: Elbridge Gerry and George Mason, Luther Martin and Gouverneur Morris. The Virginia delegation, already strained by the debate on the legislature, began to air its differences openly, with Mason and Randolph edging closer every day to their final refusal to sign the Constitution.

The debates were also shaped by the arrival of newcomers with strong opinions and the departure of influential veterans of the debates. John Mercer, the young, opinionated delegate from Maryland, arrived in late July,

entered aggressively into the discussions on the presidency, accused the nationalists of being monarchists—and
left. Nicholas Gilman and John Langdon, New Hampshire's missing delegation, finally took their seats on July
23, the same day that William Paterson, author of the
New Jersey Plan, departed for home. Paterson would not
return until September 17, the day the delegates put their
signatures to the new Constitution. By July 6 the table at
which the New York delegates had sat was vacant. Lansing and Yates, the banes of Hamilton's existence, left
Philadelphia that day, after making their views about the
legitimacy of the convention clear once again. "Little
Mars" himself had returned to New York on June 29, and
although he may have come back briefly to Philadelphia
in mid-July, he did not take his seat at the convention.
The first time he appears again in Madison's notes is August 13. Hamilton's absence weighed heavily on some, especially the convention president George Washington,
who sent his former protégé a wistful note on July 10 saying, "I am sorry you went away—I wish you were back."

Hamilton's absence was less deeply felt by other nationalists at the convention. In truth, he had ceased to be
a major force at the convention on June 18 when he had
presented his own plan for a new government. No doubt
he knew that he would be swimming against a republican
tide and offending those who were sensitive to the usurp-
ation of state sovereignty even before he rose to speak.
Perhaps he thought his plan would put the more reasonable and measured Virginia Plan in a better light. He was

certainly capable of such a tactic. One thing was certain: he would not have left the convention simply because the "great Outlines" of the Constitution were not those he had sketched. More likely the frustrating composition of the New York delegation had driven him away from Philadelphia. It was humiliating for a man accustomed to dominate to be reduced to impotence by the likes of Yates and Lansing. Because of them, he had no power base at the convention and could not influence the voting by promising to cast New York's "aye" or "nay" when key issues were at stake. Yet Hamilton's departure also reflected a deeply ingrained preference for policy making rather than for the construction of a government. Madison was the Constitution's architect; Hamilton meant to breathe life into its structure. Where Madison saw completion, Hamilton saw potential: it was in the direction the new government chose for the nation, the laws it initially enacted, the programs it put in place, and the supporting institutions it spun off that Hamilton believed the promise of America would be realized. Thus, once the convention committed itself to the creation of a new government, a stronger government, Hamilton was less interested in its particulars than his Virginia counterpart. Whatever Hamilton's complex motives were, when the convention turned to the particulars of the executive on July 17, New York's table was empty.

If the old coalitions no longer applied, the old issues still plagued the convention. How should the executive be chosen and by whom? How long should he serve? How should he be removed from office if this was necessary? Yet a new issue would soon eclipse these older ones. As the debates unfolded, the central question proved to be whether the president should be empowered to police the legislature. For having created a bicameral congress and endowed it with broad-ranging powers, including the right to levy taxes and to regulate foreign trade, the delegates now wondered if the legislature needed some check upon its authority.

Some delegates might have willingly shored up the powers of the state governments in order to balance the broad powers of the national legislature. But the compromise that gave the states their Senate stronghold was as far as this convention of nationalist-oriented delegates was willing to go. If some counterweight to the legislature must be found, the executive branch seemed the most likely source. Slowly over the course of the next few weeks, the convention began to reconceptualize the executive branch. Before the month was over, delegates had begun to talk of the president as the representative of the people and as the people's guardian against legislative hubris. This new vision was never embraced by the entire convention, for the fear of executive tyranny remained strong.

The new concern about unchecked legislative power reopened the debate over the mode of electing the president. Should this power, too, be in the legislature's hands? Gouverneur Morris raised old fears—and added what for these overwhelmingly Protestant delegates was a chilling comparison to the practices of Roman Catholicism. "If the Legislature elect," Morris declared, "it will be the work of intrigue, of cabal, and of faction; it will be like the election of a pope by a conclave of cardinals; real merit will rarely be the title to the appointment." But it was James Wilson who put into words the uneasiness that was growing among the delegates. In some matters, Wilson declared, the legislature is entitled to our thorough confidence and to indefinite power; on other issues it should not be trusted.

If the legislature did not chose the president, there remained only one alternative: election by the people, either directly or through electors. An unlikely combination of naysayers spoke against this solution. Although he had risen from humble beginnings, Roger Sherman sounded the elitist trumpet. The people, he said, "will never be sufficiently informed of characters" to select wisely. Charles C. Pinckney, fed with the proverbial silver spoon, agreed. "They will be led," he warned, "by a few active & designing men." George Mason, master of the elegant Gunston Hall plantation yet author of the Virginia Declaration of Rights and defender of the people's liberties, also denied that ordinary citizens could be relied upon to select the nation's executive officer. "It would be as unnatural to refer the choice of a proper character for chief Magistrate to the people, as it would, to refer a trial of colours to a blind man."

The inadequacies of the people's judgment was not the issue for Elbridge Gerry. Gerry, always more drear in his outlook, more apocalyptic in his predictions, added a final caveat against popular election that proved remarkably prescient in light of the rapid rise of political parties during Washington's second administration. If the people elect the executive, Gerry said, any organized group that draws together men from across the nation will be able to control the outcome. He had an example ready at hand, one that many in the room would have refrained from citing out of delicacy and respect for the man who sat in the presiding seat at the convention. Gerry did not suffer from a surfeit of delicacy, however. With the benefit of an existing organization, ties of loyalty, and steady communication, he continued, the Society of the Cincinnati was most likely to choose the nation's president.

The people had their defenders, of course. For a brief and memorable moment, Luther Martin and Gouverneur Morris, the misfit and the bon vivant, became allies in the cause of popular election. An aristocrat through and through, Morris seemed nevertheless to be one of the few men with confidence in the people's judgment. "If the people should elect," he assured the convention, "they will never fail to prefer some man of distinguished character, or services; some man, if he might so speak, of continental reputation." Yet, on this opening day of the debate, the delegates were not willing to turn over the task of selection to their ordinary neighbors. When Luther Martin moved for a compromise version of popular election—selection via electors—the convention voted "no."

If the legislature retained the power to select the executive, the length of his term again became an issue.

That, in turn, depended upon his eligibility for reelection. Strong advocates of legislative selection were also strong advocates of allowing only one seven-year term. This seemed the best hedge against excessive legislative influence on the office, since the executive would not be tempted to ingratiate himself in order to retain his office. The objection to this lay in the waste of experience and talent that would result. No sooner had a man become familiar with and expert in the executive role, Morris observed, then he would be out of office, his talents lost to the nation. If the goal was to limit legislative influence, one logical solution was for the executive to serve for "good behavior." Morris approved the idea; George Mason was appalled by it. He saw a term of good behavior as the first step toward hereditary monarchy. And so, the convention seemed at a standstill. When Madison, once as cautious about individual power as Mason, ended the day by warning against throwing "all power into the Legislative vortex," it was clear that the delegates had indeed found new monsters under their beds.

No matter how the executive reached office, the question remained: What powers would he enjoy? On Saturday the delegates moved warily to this issue. When it was proposed that the judiciary should share veto power over legislation with the executive, it became immediately clear that the need to preserve the balance of powers vied with the need to preserve the separation of powers. Supporters of the proposal such as Oliver Ellsworth argued that adding the judiciary to the veto process would shore up the prestige of the executive and give him "more wisdom

& firmness" in dealing with the legislature. Elbridge
Gerry thought the plan was both foolish and dangerous,
solving one potential problem by generating another. The
executive could defend himself without any assistance,
Gerry said, and the convention should not make statesmen of judges.

No delegate with a political memory that stretched
back to the British constitution, the colonial governments, or their own state political organizations lacked a
commitment to the principle of separation of powers
evoked by Gerry. But they were equally aware of the importance of a balance among those powers. Even George
Mason worried that the transitory and weak position they
had created for the executive would leave the legislature
unchecked. Not every law passed by a legislature was just
or wise, Mason noted, and only the veto defended the nation against the pernicious work of demagogues. In the
end, it was Massachusetts's Nathaniel Gorham, one-time
sailor and the son of an artisan, a man without benefit of
formal education or natural brilliance, who pointed out
the delegates' true dilemma: If the judiciary was added to
the veto process in order to check the power of the legislature, what would prevent the judges from dominating
the process and further weakening the executive? No one
had an answer. The convention voted down the proposal
to give the judges a role in the veto process.

Surprisingly, James Madison now embraced the idea
of the executive as the people's last line of defense against
the wickedness or shortsightedness of the Senate. For

Madison, this may have been an inevitable shift in his thinking now that the Senate was a stronghold of the states. But there were other strategies for protecting against legislative hubris, and as the debate continued, new and often novel ideas were put forward. Elbridge Gerry suggested that the state legislatures choose the executive, a reinforcement of state power that surely sent a shiver up the nationalists' spines. James Wilson proposed an executive elected for six years by a small number of legislators chosen by lottery for the task. This pseudo-biblical scheme, one that surely offended devotees of Enlightenment rationality such as Benjamin Franklin, hinged on the acceptance of random chance as the best protection against intrigue. Outlandish as it was, the struggling convention grasped at it, willing to seriously consider any scheme that broke the deadlock between advocates of popular and legislative selection. But as hypothetical concerns mounted—What if unworthy men drew the winning lots? What if all the winning lots were drawn by men from the same state?—the delegates consigned the plan to the dust heap.

James Madison decided it was time to review the available options and provide a candid evaluation of the problems inherent in every proposal for the election of the executive. By now the litany was familiar to them all: To let the legislature select was to give it too much power; to let the state legislatures select was to put the decision in the hands of the very institutions that the convention had been called to restrain; to let electors chosen by the people select was to risk that the will of the uninformed would be expressed by the poorly informed; and to let the people select was, as Mason had so cruelly put it, to ask a blind man to make a color choice. Yet some mode of selecting the executive must be settled upon. Madison, with little past history of populism or love of direct democracy, made the leap of faith to direct election by the people. There were, he conceded, drawbacks—the large states would have an advantage over the small, the northern states, where more of the population were eligible to vote, would have an advantage over the slave-holding south— but these advantages were temporary, certain to pass as the country grew and slavery slowly vanished.

No one quibbled with Madison's summary of the weaknesses in every proposal. But popular election of the executive? George Mason continued to think it the utmost foolishness to burden "those who knew least" with a task best performed by those "who know most of the Eminent characters, & qualifications." Delegates who agreed with Mason—and there were many—were not necessarily contemptuous of the ordinary citizen. The fatal flaw in a popular election—the lack of familiarity with men outside the voter's native state—was a matter of practical circumstance rather than an intellectual or moral defect. The difficulty of acquiring a national reputation was nothing more than a reflection of the deficiencies of eighteenth-century American communication and transportation. The delays suffered as the delegates tried to reach Philadelphia that May was proof, if proof were needed, that the primitive roadways discouraged the easy movement of people from state to state. It took a cataclysmic event like the Revolution to wrench young men from their neighborhoods and carry them out of their hometowns and cities. The long marches—through mud, across rivers, on roads that were often little more than Indian paths—were journeys from place to place prompted by compulsion and necessity rather than wanderlust. "Thinking continentally" had been dearly paid for by the soles of the soldiers' feet.

Information traveled at an even slower, more erratic pace than horses, wagons, or carts. Modern Americans— accustomed to round-the-clock television and radio news, Internet access, overnight mail delivery, and a morning newspaper delivered to (or near) their door—would find the flow of eighteenth-century information excruciatingly slow. If eighteenth-century men and women knew no alternative, still they realized the limitations of their condition. Sources for information were sparse: the nation's few weekly newspapers were located in urban areas, mail delivery was erratic and expensive, and the cost of books was prohibitive for most farmers and artisans. Elite planters and wealthy merchants might correspond on what in the eighteenth century passed for a regular basis, Ben Franklin might create a public library in his hometown metropolis of Philadelphia, and diplomats, legislators, judges, and governors might find it possible to keep abreast of events in far-flung places, but cataclysmic events in New England might pass unnoticed by farmers in western Virginia or central Pennsylvania. News traveled best, if it traveled at all, from port city to port city, carried by ship captains and crew. Merchants in Charleston might be kept current on Boston political problems by visiting New England merchants, and planters' sons, returning from Princeton to their family homes in the Hudson Valley or Maryland, might arrive with the latest word on struggles between New Jersey and New York as well as on London fashions. Yet even at its best, information was imperfect, and often shockingly erroneous.

Neither wealth nor an active role in local politics and business guaranteed a man a broad, national circle of acquaintances. If many of the men in the East Room greeted one another familiarly on the first day of the convention sessions, it was because they had served together in the Continental Congresses, in the Confederation Congress, or in the officer corps of the Continental line. Not everyone at the convention could claim such cosmopolitanism, however. Young delegates, new to politics, had not forged friendships in these national forums spawned by the Revolution. William Pierce's sketches suggest that some of his subjects were only vaguely known to him by reputations and others were not known to him at all.

A delegate did not have to be elitist, therefore, to assume that ordinary voters would have little firsthand, or even secondhand, knowledge of the character or accomplishments of men who lived a thousand, or even two hundred, miles away. And no delegate would imagine that a candidate, even one burning with ambition, would undertake an exhausting, even perilous, months-long campaign from New Hampshire to Georgia to introduce himself to voters. It had taken a seven-year war to make General George Washington a household name; it was unlikely that any event in peacetime America would catapult another man to national fame. Thus, it was reasonable to assume, as several delegates suggested, that in a popular election, Virginians would vote for a Virginian, New Yorkers for a New Yorker, and Georgians for their favorite son. Thirteen, perhaps thirty candidates, would result—and who would decide among them?

July was ending, but the discussion dragged on, going nowhere. The only decisive movement occurred within the Virginia delegation, where the chasm was widening between Mason, Randolph, and the personally fastidious John Blair on one side and Madison, Washington, and the political novice Dr. James McClurg on the other. Before July was out, the Madisonian ranks had grown thin since Dr. McClurg had fled, returning to his home with a sigh of relief. No amount of urging could bring him back. "If I thought my return could contribute in the smallest degree to [the situation's] improvement," McClurg wrote Madison, "nothing should keep me away." In justifying his absence, the doctor was happy to acknowledge his inexperience and his lack of political reputation. But it was clear that the tensions within the delegation had distressed him. If he returned, they would continue, and perhaps increase. "My vote," he explained apologetically, "could only operate to produce a division, & so destroy the vote of the State, I think that my attendance now would certainly be useless, perhaps injurious." With Washington presiding and thus unwilling to enter into the discussions, Madison found himself disturbingly alone, the sole committed nationalist and the only advocate of a "president of the people" in his delegation.

The general outlines of the executive branch remained much the same at the end of July as they had been at the end of June. The executive would consist of a single person rather than a triumverate, elected by both houses of the national legislature to a term of seven years, without eligibility for reelection. Although no delegate seemed fully satisfied with these specifics, the convention clung to them out of boredom, exhaustion, confusion, and lack of a clearly superior alternative. On July 26, with almost palpable relief, the delegates turned over their entire handiwork to a newly created Committee of Detail made up of Nathaniel Gorham, John Rutledge, Edmund Randolph, James Wilson, and Oliver Ellsworth. They then declared the convention in recess for ten days.

While the Committee of Detail labored long hours to organize everything the convention had agreed upon thus far, luckier delegates fled the city. George Washington and his friend Bob Morris saddled horses and rode out of Philadelphia, following the path of a creek that marked where the Valley Forge encampment had been. Morris, a civilian throughout the war, passed the time trout fishing. Washington, once the commander in chief of the Revolutionary army, wrestled with his memories of barefoot and hungry enlisted men and the transformation of his ragtag army into professional soldiers by their eccentric drillmaster, the Baron von Steuben.

On August 6 the delegates gathered once more in the now-too-familiar East Room to hear the chair of the Committee of Detail, John Rutledge, report its draft of the new Constitution. The committee had made few if any changes to the outline of the presidency, his selection, his term, or his powers. The executive remained a single person, elected by both houses of the legislature for a seven-year term, without possibility of reelection. He had exclusive veto power over legislation, reversible by a two-thirds vote of the legislature, and could be removed from office if impeached by the House and tried and convicted by the Supreme Court. He could appoint all government officials whose selection had not been specifically granted to other branches. The committee had added a few flourishes to the description, however: the executive was to be called the president of the United States of America, and he was to be addressed as "Your Excellency."

For the next five weeks, the convention picked apart and revised virtually every clause of the committee's handiwork on virtually every aspect of the new national government. A certain hardness had set in by this time, the mark of men whose patience had worn thin. Heated debates over the regulation of commerce, thoughtful debates over determining suffrage qualifications, and cynical debates over slavery filled the sessions. But the delegates seemed determined to settle each disagreement before moving to the next. At the mere suggestion that an issue be returned to the committee, a wave of protest arose. Nathaniel Gorham, who had remained hunched over the convention secretary's minutes while Bob Morris reeled in his trout, shrank in horror from yet another committee session. Genuine despair marked Gorham's comments, as he declared that as "some could not agree to the form of Government before the powers were defined [and] others could not agree to the powers till it was seen how the Government was to be formed," he feared there would be no end to the delays and postponements. John Rutledge, also deprived of any bucolic interlude in his work, announced he was fed up with the "tediousness of the proceedings." And yet another committee member, Oliver Ellsworth, objected to any further committee service. "We grow more & more skeptical as we proceed," he said, speaking through the cloud of white snuff dust that perpetually surrounded his balding head. "If we do not decide soon, we shall be unable to come to any decision."

What had prompted this outpouring of frustration and anger from the members of the committee was the return to the mire of the presidential debate. On Saturday, August 14, with a day of rest beckoning the weary delegates, the recently arrived John Mercer turned the convention's attention back to the question of shoring up the executive's independence from the legislature. Mercer's comments were a measure of how far many delegates had come from their earlier, unconditional faith in the lawmakers. He reintroduced the idea of a council to assist the president, warning that the executive must have support in his battle against what he called "the aristocracy of the congress." In the same vein, another delegate urged that the president have an absolute, irreversible veto over legislation. Roger Sherman expressed amazement at these proposals. "Can one man be trusted better than all the others if they agree?" But the old, perfect faith in Congress was clearly fading. Although they were not willing to deprive Congress of its power to select the president, the delegates did vote to reduce its power to overturn a veto. The reversal process now required the support of three-quarters rather than two-thirds of the legislators.

On August 18 John Rutledge earnestly called for the delegates to conclude their constitution making. The sessions have gone on too long, he said, and both the public and the delegates wished the business of this convention to come to an end. It was perhaps fortunate that Rutledge could not see into the future, for the convention would continue its deliberation for another month. For the moment the delegates had to dispose of the question of a presidential council of advisers. The day was filled with arguments pro and con, and with the sensible suggestion that the president could and should consult with his own cabinet—including the secretary of war, of the treasury, and of the marine—rather than with a council of advisers drawn from the legislature. Before adjourning, the delegates acknowledged that they had reached an impasse and agreed to send the matter back to the Committee of Detail.

Four days later the committee presented this addition to section 2 of Article 10: The president was to have a privy council composed of the president of the Senate, the Speaker of the House, the chief justice of the Supreme Court, and the principal officers of the executive departments including foreign affairs, domestic affairs, war, marine, and finance. A modern reader would be quick to note that the president of the Senate was not the vice president, for the office did not yet exist in the minds of the delegates.

On August 24 Daniel Carroll of Maryland proposed, once again, the popular election of the president, and, once again, it was voted down. And yet the nagging doubts about the unbridled power of the legislature continued to gnaw at the delegates. Gouverneur Morris fed the fire of these doubts, warning now of "legislative tyranny" and of a president who would pander to Congress into which he would surely move once his single term of office ended. Still, the convention did not change its mind. Another vote on the popular election of the president was taken; another defeat was recorded.

On August 29, with the presidency still unsettled in many of its details, the final break between Mason and Randolph and the Virginia nationalist, James Madison, came. "There were features so odious in the constitution as it now stands," Madison recorded Randolph saying, "that [he] doubted whether he should be able to agree to it." The possibility that the man who presented the Virginia Plan and set in motion the creation of a new government might, in the end, refuse to endorse their hand-iwork must have stunned the delegates. That Friday the convention abandoned its collective responsibility and created a new committee of eleven men, designated the Committee on Postponed Matters. All unresolved issues henceforth rested in the hands of Nicholas Gilman of New Hampshire, Rufus King of Massachusetts, Roger Sherman of Connecticut, David Brearly of New Jersey, Gouverneur Morris of Pennsylvania, John Dickinson of Delaware, Daniel Carroll of Maryland, James Madison of Virginia, Hugh Williamson of North Carolina, Pierce Butler of South Carolina, and Abraham Baldwin of Georgia.

The Committee on Postponed Matters, like many of the committees that preceded it, was composed of one representative, chosen by ballot from each state except the absent New York. It was, in effect, a convention in miniature. In June and early July, the delegates would have been reluctant to cede decision-making powers to such committees, jealously guarding their right to debate every issue as members of a committee of the whole. But the debates over representation in the legislature had shown them the wisdom of sending controversial issues to small committees, sparing the majority of the delegates the debilitating effects of yet another protracted struggle. No matter how intense the debate, the number of advo-cates and the number of positions they might advocate were certain to be fewer when a smaller group of men gathered in a room together. Long-winded speeches were out of place in this more intimate setting, and compromise and resolution were likely to be reached much sooner. Over the course of August, most of the delegates in attendance had seen some committee service. The indefatigable Gouverneur Morris and Roger Sherman did more than yeoman's duty, representing their delegations on several Committees of Eleven or on the Committee of Detail that reported back to the convention with amendments and rewordings and additions to sections and articles of the still-protean Constitution.

The Committee on Postponed Matters boasted a stellar array of delegates. Madison, Morris, Sherman, and Dickinson were there, representing large states and small, extreme and more moderate nationalism, populist and elitist views. The remaining members, if less notable, were able representatives of their delegations. With William Paterson gone, New Jersey's chief justice, David Brearly, was the convention's logical choice. Abraham Baldwin, Georgia's committeeman, was the acknowledged leader of his delegation, and Hugh Williamson, although not the senior member at North Carolina's table, was the state's best debater and most active participant in the convention discussions. Irascible figures had been avoided, and thus the amiable Rufus King represented Massachusetts rather than Elbridge Gerry. Men of unpredictable or antisocial behavior had been avoided, too, which explained why Luther Martin was noticeably absent, passed over in favor of the rising newcomer to Maryland politics, Daniel Carroll. The only surprising choice was Pierce

Butler of South Carolina, for that delegation included, after all, Colonel Pinckney, the brazen Charles Pinckney, and the respected John Rutledge. Rutledge's absence was most easily accounted for; having served a grueling stint on the Committee of Detail, he had made clear his eagerness to see the convention adjourn, sine die. The convention hardly dared to tax his patience further.

Rutledge was not alone, of course, in wishing to see the convention adjourn sine die. Outside the locked doors of the convention, patience was clearly growing thin. On September 6 William Gordon wrote to his friend George Washington, acknowledging the "very arduous business" that occupied the general, but expressing his hopes that that business would soon come to an end. Neither Washington nor his fellow delegates needed any reminder that time was running out. On that same September day, James Madison had confessed to Thomas Jefferson, "Nothing can exceed the universal anxiety for the event of the Meeting here." Despite the virtually unbroken code of silence the delegates had maintained, newspapers and private letters were rife with rumor and conjecture. The Confederation Congress, reduced to skeletal size and unable to enact any business at all, also seemed to radiate a restlessness that could be felt miles away in Philadelphia.

The Committee on Postponed Matters, well aware of the pressures upon them, met for almost a week. When David Brearly delivered their report on September 4, it did little to calm the frayed nerves of the delegates. To the outrage of several, the delight of a few, and the surprise of the entire convention, the committee had decided to endorse the popular election of the president through state electors. Their proposal read like a patchwork of several suggestions that had surfaced over the summer. Each state would appoint a number of electors equal to the whole number of its senators and members of the House of Representatives. The state legislatures were free to determine how the electors were chosen, leaving room for popular balloting or legislative appointment. The electors would meet in their own state, rather than as a collective body, and vote by ballot for two persons, one of whom could not be an inhabitant of an elector's own state. A list of all persons voted for and a tally of the votes each received would be signed, certified, and transmitted to the president of the Senate. He, in turn, would open these certified lists and oversee the counting of the votes. The person receiving the greatest number of votes, as long as it was a majority, would be the nation's president. If more than one person received a majority, and both had the same number of total votes, the Senate would immediately choose between them. If no one had a majority, however, the Senate would select from among the five highest on the list. The person among the remaining candidates who had the greatest number of votes would become vice president, an office that was an innovation in itself. In the case of a tie among two second-place candidates, the Senate would select one of the eligible candidates by ballot. The state legislatures were entitled to decide when their electors would assemble and how their votes were to be certified and transmitted.

The committee's report covered several other presidential issues, including the impeachment process and the president's treaty-making powers, but it was his mode of election that brought both Edmund Randolph and Charles Pinckney to their feet. Both men demanded to know how this dramatic change in the mode of electing the president had come about. How indeed? Several years after the convention, John Dickinson claimed full credit for the creation of the electoral college. He arrived late for one of the committee meetings, he explained in a long letter to a relative, delayed as he often was by the illness that had dogged him all summer. He found the members of the Committee on Postponed Matters on their feet, ready to adjourn for the day. They had agreed on the election of the president by the legislature, they said, and would move on to other business tomorrow. But Dickinson begged his colleagues to reconsider. He believed that the acceptance of the new government hinged on the people's reaction to the presidency and its powers. And he was certain that the people would not accept a president endowed with such far-reaching powers as the right to make treaties, command the armed forces, and appoint ambassadors, unless they had a role in selecting him. "The only true and safe principle on which these powers could be committed to an individual," he declared, "[was] [t]hat he should be in a strict sense of th[e] expression, *The Man of the People...*" rather than the tool of the legislature. Instantly persuaded of the wisdom of Dickinson's views, Gouverneur Morris gestured to the men standing around him and said, "Come Gentlemen, let us sit down again, and converse further on this subject." Madison took out a pen and paper, and promptly sketched out the election procedure that Brearly presented to the convention on September 4.

It was a dramatic account, though a questionable one, and it was a cavalier one at that. Dickinson may have proposed the electoral college on that September afternoon, but the idea itself belonged to James Wilson, who had patiently, persistently argued for some form of popular participation in the choice of the national executive since early June. If the Committee on Postponed Matters readily acceded to Dickinson's plea, it was because Wilson had made them comfortable with the idea long before Dickinson advocated it.

On September 4, however, what the indignant delegates from Virginia and South Carolina really wanted to know was not "how" the electoral college came about but "why." Gouverneur Morris took on the task of explaining the committee's decision, carefully ticking off reasons the delegates had heard many times before. Despite Dickinson's later claim that a concern for the people's confidence had motivated the committee, Morris made no mention of this. Instead, he focused on the convention's bedrock fear of abuse of power, conspiracy, and corruption. The election of the president by the national legislature had been rejected, Morris said, because of the inherent danger of intrigue and faction it had always involved. The only way to avoid that danger was to limit a president to a single term, and this came at too high a cost. It deprived the country of a leader's valuable experience and talents. These dangers evaporated once a system of electors was put into place. The electors would cast their ballots at such a distance from one another that it would be impossible for a cabal to form among them or for an outside cabal to corrupt them. A president chosen in this fashion could serve a shorter four-year term and could be eligible for reelection.

A system of electors eliminated other problems, Morris continued. Putting the election of the president in the legislature's hands had complicated the search for a viable impeachment process, since it was inappropriate for the body that selected the president to impeach or try him. Under the committee's plan, the Senate could impeach and the Supreme Court could try a president accused of treason or bribery.

Then, with his typical aplomb, Morris switched gears, sliding smoothly out of the realm of practicalities and into the realm of interpretation. It was the committee's perception, he said, that no one in the convention was really fully satisfied with the election of the president by the legislature—even though they had voted, repeatedly, for this method. "Many" delegates, however, seemed eager to see a popularly elected president since this would insure his independence from the legislature.

The committee may have been presumptuous in claiming to read the minds of the delegates, but this does not mean they were inaccurate. George Mason, no longer a friend to the new Constitution, admitted as much. Yet delegates quickly pointed out the major flaw in the committee's reasoning: Most presidential elections would wind up in the Senate, for no candidate was likely to receive a majority of the electors' votes. Even if the electors had served in their state legislatures, or in one of the national congresses, they were unlikely to be able to identify the most viable out-of-state candidate, the man most likely to be favored by other electors as far-flung as Georgia and New Hampshire. Only George Washington had such a national reputation. After he stepped down from the presidency, who else could capture the votes of a majority of the electors?

The always thoughtful James Wilson had a solution. If the election were sent to the House rather than the Senate, perhaps the problems that sprang from the scarcity of national figures could be avoided. Since the membership of the House changed more frequently than the Senate, then a permanent faction committed to a particular candidate was less likely to develop. And, in case of impeachment, there would be no infringement of the separation of powers.

The issue was not destined to be resolved that day. The proposal of the Committee on Postponed Matters was postponed, and the convention moved on to the next committee report. The following morning, however, debate on the presidency began again. By this time the opposing camps had coalesced. Charles Pinckney, John Rutledge, and George Mason led the attack on the committee's plan; Morris, Madison, and Wilson led the de-

fense. No new ideas surfaced in their heated debate.
Pinckney continued to stress the impossibility of voters or
electors knowing "the fittest men." He and Rutledge continued to insist that the election would, in the end, fall to
the Senate, making the actions of the electors nothing
more than a waste of time and energy. There was, they
concluded, no way around it: the president would be the
creature of the Senate, and he would conspire with them
against the House in order to gain reelection. If, as the
committee proposed, the president was made eligible for
additional terms, he could secure the office for life as long
as he bowed to the wishes of the senators. Months of debate had clearly not weakened the fear of power or the
certainty of its abuse. These powerful men gathered in
Independence Hall, the most likely candidates for the
Senate and the presidency, continued to fear themselves.

Although the convention voted down James Wilson's
suggestion to move the election to the House in case no
candidate won a majority of the electors' votes, the idea
was not entirely forgotten. The problem, as Roger Sherman soon pointed out, was that a House election raised
the specter once again of a government dominated by the
larger states. The larger states already had an advantage,
Sherman noted, in the number of electors they had. If the
House won the right to choose among the presidential fi-
nalists, that advantage would come into play a second
time. Fortunately, Sherman's skill at devising workable
compromises did not fail him. He proposed that the election fall to the House, but that the states each cast only

one vote apiece in selecting the president. This would eliminate the large states' double advantage, remove the threat of a senatorial-presidential unholy alliance, and allow the impeachment process to be initiated in the Senate without any infringement of the separation of powers doctrine.

James Wilson wholeheartedly approved of Sherman's idea. And by the end of the day, so did the convention. Sherman's motion carried by a vote of 10–1, with only Dickinson's state of Delaware dissenting. In approving Sherman's proposal, the convention had, in effect, approved the proposal establishing state electors. The amended report of the Committee on Postponed Matters on the method of electing the president now read:

> He shall hold his office during the term of four years, and together with the vice-President, chosen for the same term, be elected in the following manner.
>
> Each state shall appoint in such manner as its Legislature may direct, a number of electors equal to the whole number of Senators and members of the House of Representatives, to which the State may be entitled in the Legislature:
>
> But no person shall be appointed an Elector who is a member of the Legislature of the U.S. or who holds any office of profit or trust under the U.S.
>
> The Electors shall meet in their respective States and vote by ballot for two persons, of whom one at least shall not be an inhabitant of the same

State with themselves; and they shall make a list of all the persons voted for, and of the number of votes for each, which list they shall sign and certify, and transmit sealed to the Seat of the General Government, directed to the President of the Senate.

The President of the Senate shall in the presence of the Senate and House of Representatives open all the certificates & the votes shall then be counted.

The person having the greatest number of votes shall be the President (if such number be a majority of the whole number of electors appointed) and if there be more than one who have such majority, and have an equal number of votes, then the House of Representatives shall immediately choose by ballot one of them for President, the Representation from each State having one vote. But if no person have a majority, then from the five highest on the list, the House of Representatives shall in like manner choose by ballot the President. In the choice of a President by the House of Representatives, a Quorum shall consist of a member or members from two thirds of the States and the concurrence of a majority of all the States shall be necessary to such choice. And in every case after the choice of the President, the person having the greatest number of votes of the Electors shall be the vicepresident: But if there should remain two or more who have equal votes, the Senate shall choose from them the vice-President.

> The Legislature may determine the time of
> choosing the Electors, and of their giving their
> votes; and the manner of certifying and transmit-
> ting their votes—But the election shall be on the
> same day throughout the U. States.

With the agreement over the method of electing the
president, the convention moved closer to completing the
"great Outlines" of the Constitution. Over the next two
days, the delegates made minor changes to the committee's report on the executive branch. They approved the
requirement that the president be a natural-born citizen
or a citizen of the United States at the time of the adoption of the Constitution. They agreed that no one under
the age of thirty-five and no one who had not been a resident of the United States for at least fourteen years
would be eligible for the office. At George Mason's suggestion, they added "high crimes and misdemeanors" to
"treason and bribery" as grounds for impeachment. And
they confirmed that the president had the power to make
treaties, with the advice and consent of two-thirds of the
Senate, and to appoint, with the advice and consent of
the Senate, all ambassadors and other public ministers,
the judges of the Supreme Court, and all other officers of
the nation whose appointments were not already allo-
cated to other branches of government.

For the first time in well over a month, a note of good
humor and playful sarcasm made its way into Madison's
record of the proceedings. When Elbridge Gerry raised
an objection to the vice president sitting as ex officio

of the Senate, Roger Sherman quipped: "If the vice-President were not to be President of the Senate, he would be without employment...." In the end, they approved the Committee on Postponed Matters' outline of the duties of this Johnny-come-lately addition to the executive department, the vice president. He was to be ex officio president of the Senate, but, except in cases of a tie vote, he would not be allowed to cast a vote in Senate deliberations. In case of impeachment of the president, the vice president would step down and the chief justice would preside. Should the vice president take over the powers and duties of the president, the Senate was to choose a temporary presiding officer. Finally, the committee report and the convention as a whole rejected the earlier decision to create an advisory council for the president drawn from the Supreme Court or from Congress itself. Instead, it was agreed that the president could require the opinions of his principal officers within the executive departments on subjects related to their duties and responsibilities.

The president's powers were situational, potential, and dependent upon historical developments that the convention delegates could not be expected to predict or even imagine. Many of those powers were crisis-driven: In case of war, he would command the military operations; to prevent war, he could send diplomats to negotiate treaties. Even in such emergencies, the delegates did not intend for these powers to be absolute because they gave the legislature a major role in approving all treaties, even commercial ones. Other of the president's powers were intended to be purely administrative, focused on staffing embassies and appointing special envoys or diplomats. As America's role in world affairs changed, the significance of those appointments would change as well. As the role of the Supreme Court grew, the significance of the president's power to appoint its bench would grow as well. In the end, there was a protean quality to this branch of government that would make "original intent" more a historical curiosity than a Rosetta stone of interpretation.

Before adjourning on Saturday, September 8, the convention appointed its last, and surely its most eagerly awaited, committee, the committee to "revise the stile [*sic*] and arrange the articles" of the Constitution. While the delegates hurried to leave the East Room, the Committee on Style—William Samuel Johnson, Alexander Hamilton, Gouverneur Morris, James Madison, and Rufus King—lingered a moment, to decide when and where they should meet.

❧

# CHAPTER SEVEN

# The Convention Ends

## "I consent, Sir, to this Constitution because I expect no better"

L IKE MOST PHILADELPHIA DAYS in the summer of 1787, September 12 dawned hot and muggy. Wigs had already begun to droop, collars to sag, and perspiration to form in small beads on the foreheads of the delegates as they made their way to Independence Hall that morning. But an observer might have noted a sprightliness in the steps of some and an air of anticipation, even wary optimism, on the faces of many that had not been seen since the opening days of the convention. For on this Wednesday in September, the Committee on Style was scheduled to report the final draft of what the delegates called "the plan." The only question of importance was whether the convention would endorse that plan.

Never burdened by false modesty, committee member Gouverneur Morris boasted that he had played the major role in preparing this final draft of the Constitution. Writing to a friend several years later, he declared

that the Constitution "was written by the Fingers which
wrote this letter." Decades later Madison would confirm
that "The *finish* given to the style and arrangement of the
Constitution fairly belongs to the pen of Mr Morris." But
even without Madison's supporting testimony, no one
who knew Morris's remarkable command of language
would challenge his claim. For the document the committee presented to the convention bore all the hallmarks
of Morris's literary style. Awkward phrasing and stilted
language had been transformed, and crisp sentences had
replaced overly wordy ones. "Having rejected redundant
and equivocal Terms," Morris explained, he had made
the text "as clear as our Language would permit." He had
taken the twenty-three articles and combined them into
seven, gathering together all the decisions on the legislature, the executive, and the judiciary in such a way as to
finally make the form of the new government clear. He
had reworked the preamble, giving it an emotional force
that had been sorely lacking in earlier drafts. In his revision Morris captured perfectly the nationalist vision of
a supreme central government capable of knitting together a sprawling country and of overcoming the petty
divisions among its competitive states. Where once the
preamble spoke for "We the people of the States of
New Hampshire, Massachusetts, Rhode-Island and Providence Plantations, Connecticut, New-York, New-Jersey,
Pennsylvania, Maryland, Virginia, North-Carolina, South-
Carolina, and Georgia," it now spoke simply but power-
fully for "We, the people of the United States." And

where once the preamble did no more than declare that the Constitution that followed was ordained, declared, and established by the people of these thirteen states, now Morris gave a full accounting of the new government's purpose. The people of the United States had ordained and established this government, he wrote, "in order to form a more perfect union, to establish justice, insure domestic tranquility, provide for the common defence, promote the general welfare, and secure the blessings of liberty to ourselves and our posterity...." Embedded in this list of national goals were the corrections to the many flaws in the Articles of Confederation that men like Alexander Hamilton, James Madison, and George Washington had feared would be fatal to the young and newly independent America.

The newly reordered and renumbered articles, sections, and subsections in the body of the Constitution reflected an explicit hierarchy among the branches of government. The legislature holds pride of place in Article 1. The first seven sections of Article 1 spell out the composition, qualifications, and election procedures of the two branches of the legislature. Section 8 sets down the very extensive powers of Congress, including the right to lay and collect taxes, a power once jealously guarded by the states and denied to the Confederation. Despite the plague of suspicion about Congress's excessive power that had swept through the convention in July and August, the Constitution confirms that the delegates' greatest faith lay in the nation's legislative branch. In addition to all the enumerated powers of that Congress, the Constitution gives the legislature permission to "make all Laws which shall be necessary and proper for carrying into Execution the foregoing Powers"—a leap of faith to accommodate the unforeseen by men rarely given to such trust.

Article 2 is devoted to the executive branch. Section 1 sets out the procedure for electing the president and vice president, a procedure unchanged since the debates following the report of the Committee on Postponed Matters. It also establishes a fixed salary for the chief executive and provides the oath of office each president would be required to take. Sections 2 and 3 deal with the president's powers. Compared with the broad and multiple powers of the legislature, the president's were few indeed. He was to be commander in chief of not only the nation's army and navy but of the state militias and he could appoint military and naval officers. He could grant reprieves and pardons for all offenses against the United States except in cases of impeachment. He could require the written opinions of the heads of the executive departments on any subject relating to the duties of their respective offices. He had the power to make treaties, providing two-thirds of the Senate gave their consent, and he had the right to appoint ambassadors, consuls, judges of the Supreme Court, and all other officers of the United States whose appointments did not fall to other branches of the government, again, with the advice and consent of the Senate. He also had the right to receive foreign ambassadors and other public officials. If a vacancy occurred during the Senate recess, the president was empowered to make a temporary appointment to that body. And on "extraordinary Occasions," he could convene both houses of the legislature or either of them, and adjourn them if there was no agreement on adjournment among them. From time to time, he was obliged to give Congress information on "the State of the Union." On these occasions he was free to recommend to Congress any measures he considered necessary or expedient. Finally, he was enjoined to see that the laws of the nation were faithfully executed—an obligation of office rather than a privilege.

The fourth and final section of Article 2 establishes the procedure for removing the president from office. Treason, bribery, and other "high Crimes and Misdemeanors" were set as impeachable offenses. This section is testimony to the abiding fear of tyranny. Despite all the efforts to bolster the independence of the executive branch and to protect it from the malicious control of the Senate, the delegates remained haunted by memories of a tyrannical king and abusive governors who held office at the pleasure of that king. Section 4 insures that the Republic would not have to resort to revolution to remedy executive abuse of power. Indictment, trial, and conviction put the president *within* rather than *above* the law.

The president's powers were not insignificant, but neither were they sweeping ones. His greatest power was his command over the nation's military forces and his right to appoint military officers, but his freedom to act in military matters remained limited. He was not given the right to declare war or even to make peace at his own discretion. He could, it was clear, influence U.S. foreign policy through the appointment of ambassadors who signaled particular support or opposition toward other nations. But these appointments were never his alone to make as the Constitution makes diplomacy a joint effort of the Senate and the executive officer. He could urge Congress to consider new laws and new policies based on his understanding of the state of the Union, but the lawmakers were under no obligation to follow his suggestions. Fundamentally, he was—as he was conceived to be from the beginning by all except perhaps Alexander Hamilton—an administrator, executing the laws Congress enacted and appointing the support personnel he needed to execute them efficiently. In the end, his greatest strength may have come from the nature of his selection: the popular election of the president, indirect though it was, made it possible to see him as the symbol of the nation itself.

Article 3 covers the judiciary, creating a supreme court and a system of inferior courts, and extending its authority over all cases arising under the Constitution, the laws of the United States, and national treaties, as well as in cases to which the United States was a party or the controversy involved a state and citizens of another state, or citizens of this nation and a foreign nation. All trials except impeachments were to be jury trials. Section 3 defines treason as levying war against the United States or giving the enemy "Aid and Comfort." Two witnesses to an overt act of treason or a confession in open court were required for a conviction. Although Congress could declare the punishment for a convicted traitor, that punishment could not extend to the heirs or the property of the traitor after his or her death.

Article 4 is an umbrella for rules governing the relationship between the national government and the states, including the guarantee that citizens in each state are entitled to all the privileges and immunities of citizens in other states and the insurance that a fugitive from justice in one state would not find refuge in another. Slavery, unnamed but identified by the phrase "held to Service or Labour, under the Laws thereof," was indirectly upheld in section 2, which guaranteed that any person so held who escaped to another state would, like a fugitive, be delivered up to "the Party to whom such Service or Labour may be due." Section 3 sets procedure for the admission of new states into the Union, and section 4 guarantees a republican form of government to every state in the Union and pledges the national government's protection against invasion. It also guarantees that the national government would assist in quelling domestic violence if a state requested aid. Thus, if an uprising such as Shays's Rebellion happened again, or if a slave rebellion began, no state would be left to handle it alone.

Article 5 establishes the procedure for amending the Constitution, and Article 6 insures that debts incurred by the Confederation would be honored by the new constitutional government. It also establishes U.S. laws and

treaties as "the supreme law of the land" and requires all
Congress members and state legislators to support the
Constitution. Finally, it explicitly forbids any religious
test for office holding in the United States.

The last article declares simply that "the Ratification
of the Conventions of nine States, shall be sufficient for
the Establishment of this Constitution...."

FOR THE DELEGATES, no rationale or justification for the
Constitution and its contents was necessary. Each man in
the room could conjure up, if he wished, the bitter battles,
the acrimonious debates, the hesitant, probing discussions,
the compromises, and the concessions that went into almost every section of the seven articles in this document.
They knew how perilously close to dissolution the convention had been during the struggle over proportional
representation in Congress, and they knew how convoluted their reasoning had often been on the election of
the president. They could admire the skill with which the
Committee on Style had erased all traces of disagreement
and confusion, but their greatest admiration, no doubt,
was reserved for the committee's ability to shroud all
signs of anxiety about the distribution of power, all fears
that loopholes remained to let tyranny come creeping or
rushing in, all foreboding that they could not, had not,
anticipated and averted every opportunity for corruption
and conspiracy.

The rest of the world, however, knew nothing of the
process by which the Constitution had come to be. The

veil of secrecy had not been pierced during the months of deliberation, and although newspaper editors might have spread unfounded rumors or made unsubstantiated charges and private citizens might have conjectured and offered unsolicited advice, everyone outside Independence Hall had remained in the dark about the convention's deliberations and their outcome. When the Constitution was made public, its definitive tone might prove to be both its strength and its weakness. The delegates might be glad that the document bore no traces of their own fallibilities and foibles, but the American public could easily mistake this for arrogance or a lack of sympathy for local problems, traditions, or interests. Perhaps more importantly, local citizens might suspect their own delegates of selling out their interests.

Fortunately, the veteran politicians of the Committee on Style anticipated the problem. They included a letter along with the Constitution, addressed to the Confederation Congress but intended to gain the sympathy, or at least the understanding, of constituents back home. At the heart of this letter, written in Gouverneur Morris's hand, was an analogy between the familiar Lockean social contract and the union of the states. Just as "all Individuals entering into society must give up a share of liberty to preserve the rest," so, too, each state had to give up some share of its sovereignty to enter the Union. Deciding what rights, and how much sovereignty, each state had to surrender was, of course, the most difficult and delicate of tasks, made even more difficult because of the widespread differences among the states as to "situation, extent, habits, and particular interests." The potential for conflict, though great, was held in check by the delegates' unswerving attention to their larger goal, "our prosperity, felicity, safety, perhaps our national existence." This focus on the good of the nation insured that state delegations were less rigid on small matters and more willing to make concessions as they participated in the give-and-take of the convention. The delegates did not expect any state to be fully satisfied with the results, but they were confident that "each will doubtless consider that had her interest alone been consulted, the consequences might have been particularly disagreeable or injurious to others. . . ." The letter was the committee's gift to their fellow delegates—a preemptive strike against the local critics they would have to face when they returned home.

After reading the letter to the convention, Dr. William Samuel Johnson declared the committee's report complete. It seemed a moment to relish, but the delegates, being who they were, immediately began to propose last-minute additions and changes. All that afternoon, and the following day, and the next, they bickered over wording, rehashed issues in a desultory fashion, and voted down most of the motions anyone proposed. When George Mason, daily more disillusioned by the convention's work, rose to protest the absence of a bill of rights in the Constitution, the delegates allowed him only the briefest discussion of the issue. Since every state constitution contained such a list of guaranteed rights, an overwhelming majority saw a national bill of rights as redundant. When the vote came, not a single state supported Mason's proposal for a committee to draft a bill of rights. Benjamin Franklin and James Madison fared no better. Franklin's proposal to add canal building to the list of congressional powers was defeated; immediately afterward Madison's proposal for a national university met the same fate. The following day a last-minute scramble to increase the representation of both North Carolina and the absent Rhode Island proved futile.

Some changes were made, of course. Among them, the number needed to override the presidential veto was reduced from three-quarters to two-thirds of Congress. The decision came after a curt exchange between George Mason and Gouverneur Morris, two men who were now barely civil to one another despite their genteel training. Franklin, still concerned about the dangerous mix of "avarice and ambition," persuaded the delegates to add a restriction, at the end of Article 2, section 1, paragraph 7, that the president could not receive "any other emolument" than his salary during his term of office.

In the final day of debate, Roger Sherman asked the convention to consider, once again, the vulnerability of the states in the face of the powerful national government they had created. Sherman, who with William Paterson was the most consistent guardian of states' rights, laid out a dark scenario of a majority of states mobilizing the powers of the national government to victimize other states.

To help prevent the majority from doing "things fatal to particular States," Sherman urged that the Constitution expressly forbid the passage of any amendment that deprived a state of its equality in the Senate. The convention voted down Sherman's proposal, but Gouverneur Morris recognized the anxiety that Sherman had revived in delegates from smaller states and proposed that Article 5 include the proviso "that no State, without its consent, shall be deprived of its equal suffrage in the Senate." Morris's motion passed without debate and without dissenting vote.

The desire to make corrections, additions, and deletions seemed spent. Yet the delegates sensed that a perfect accord had not been reached. Few delegates were surprised when Edmund Randolph rose to declare that he could not endorse the Constitution. The power the convention had given to Congress, Randolph said, was too indefinite, too dangerous. He appealed to the delegates to submit the Constitution to state conventions, so that they could suggest amendments and revisions, and then to hold a second "general Convention" that could be guided by these suggestions as they produced a final draft of a constitution. Unless these additional steps were taken, it pained him to say that he could not put his name on the document.

Randolph's decision saddened many, but it came as no surprise to those who had followed his slow, steady alienation over the summer. The man who had presented the Virginia Plan had never been the kind of committed nationalist that its author, James Madison, had been. He came to the convention convinced that the Confederation was too weak and that its deficiencies threatened the stability of the nation. But the alternative government the convention proposed did more than shore up the central government. It siphoned away many of the powers of the states and, in Randolph's mind, created a powerful congress as dangerous to the nation's stability as the weak one had been. Edmund Randolph could not sign the Constitution—but he did not close out the possibility of supporting its ratification by his home state of Virginia.

George Mason's defection, which quickly followed Randolph's, was also expected. Mason had made little effort to hide his dissatisfaction with the convention's refusal to condemn slavery and its rejection of a bill of rights. He denounced the Constitution in words far harsher than Randolph's, predicting that the government the delegates proposed was certain to end either in monarchy or in a tyrannical aristocracy. "This Constitution," he said, "has been formed without the knowledge or idea of the people." Only a second convention would allow the people's voice to be heard. He would not sign this Constitution, he declared, and he would not support its ratification by Virginia.

The third and final open refusal came from Elbridge Gerry, who reeled off a long list of defects in the Constitution. He objected, among other things, to the length of the senators' term of office, to the power of the House of Representatives to conceal their journals, to Congress members' control over their own salaries, to underrepresentation of his home state in the House, and to the necessary-and-proper clause. Only the guarantee of a second convention would satisfy him.

A second convention? Impossible, said Charles Pinckney, and, more than that, useless. The state conventions would produce a thousand conflicting demands and suggestions, and the delegates to the national convention, bound to represent the will of their states, would have no grounds for agreement and no room for compromise. "Conventions," he said, "are serious things, and ought not to be repeated." A man with more humor than Pinckney might have added that conventions were too exhausting and time-consuming to be repeated.

When the vote on calling for a second convention came, Madison recorded that "all the States answered—no." When the vote to agree to the Constitution, as amended, followed, Madison recorded, "All the States, ay." And so it was done; the Constitution was ordered to be engrossed and the convention adjourned for the day.

On Monday, September 17, sixteen weeks after the convention began, the delegates gathered to hear the secretary, Major William Jackson, read the engrossed Constitution. When he was done, Benjamin Franklin rose, a speech in his hands. Once again the elderly doctor called upon James Wilson to read his words for him. "Mr President," Wilson began, as he read aloud the wry but judicious thoughts of a man who had—as he himself observed—lived long enough to have a different perspective on things than many of his younger colleagues in the room that day. "I confess there are several parts of this constitution which I do not at present approve, but I am not sure I shall never approve them.... [T]he older I grow, the more apt I am to doubt my own judgment, and to pay more respect to the judgment of others. Most men indeed as well as most sects in Religion, think themselves in possession of all truth, and that wherever others differ from them it is so far error." Despite the seriousness of the occasion and the gravity of his argument, Franklin could not resist illustrating his point with an account of a comic exchange between two French sisters. The tale, no doubt, lost something in the telling by the far-stodgier James Wilson.

Franklin continued, moving to the heart of the matter. "I agree to this Constitution with all its faults, if they are such," he said, "because I think a general Government necessary for us, and there is no form of Government but what may be a blessing to the people if well administered." Unlike Gerry and Mason, Franklin believed that the government would be well administered for many years. Unlike most of the delegates who spoke of the innate corruption of officeholders, Franklin believed that despotism, when it came, would be the result of the innate corruption of the people themselves. The character of the government, in short, mirrored the character of the people. This did not mean that Franklin had unquestioning faith in the political elite. There was little point in calling a second convention, he argued, for these men would be no less burdened by their prejudices, passions, errors of opinion, local interests, and selfish views as the delegates to this convention had been. "From such an assembly can a perfect production be expected?"

Perfection could not be achieved, in Franklin's view, no matter how many conventions were called. And this was why the work of the delegates gathered in Philadelphia was so admirable. They had produced a near-perfect system of government that Franklin was confident would "astonish our enemies, who are waiting with confidence to hear that our councils are confounded like those of the Builders of Babel," and that "our States are on the point of separation, only to meet hereafter for the purpose of cutting one another's throats." Franklin urged unanimous support of this astonishingly near-perfect constitution, not only here in Independence Hall but when delegates returned home to report to their constituents. "I hope," he continued, "for our own sakes as a part of the people, and for the sake of posterity, we shall act heartily and unanimously in recommending this Constitution (if approved by Congress & confirmed by the Conventions) wherever our influence may extend." Let any who, like me, still have objections to some part of the Constitution, he added, "doubt a little of his own infallibility" and put his name to the document.

Franklin ended his remarkable speech with a motion that the Constitution be signed by everyone present, although the endorsement would read "Done in Convention by the unanimous consent of the States present the 17th. Of Sepr. &c—In Witness whereof we have hereunto subscribed our names." The endorsement had been carefully worded not by the good doctor himself but by his friend, the crafty Gouverneur Morris. By calling for the consent of the states rather than the delegates, a few individual dissenters would not jeopardize the appearance of unanimity.

Franklin's motion should have climaxed the convention's deliberations, but, true to form, the logical flow of discussion was abruptly interrupted. Immediately after Wilson finished reading Franklin's speech, Nathaniel Gorham seized the opportunity to propose one last amendment to the Constitution. Gorham asked that the ratio of congressional representatives be changed from one for every forty thousand to one for every thirty thousand people in each state. The resulting increase, Gorham argued, would lessen popular objections to the Constitution. Remarkably, it was the presiding officer, George Washington, who rose to put the question to a vote. Washington felt it necessary to explain his sudden, active participation in the debates. Up until this moment, he had felt his position in the president's chair required his silence; but now he felt equally compelled to speak his mind. He favored this proposal that would expand membership in the House of Representatives and thus provide greater security for the rights and interests of the people. It would give, he concluded, "much satisfaction to see it adopted." Whatever the views of the delegates, no one wished to deny General Washington this satisfaction. The motion carried, unanimously.

Edmund Randolph brought the convention back to

the primary business at hand. He was sorry to disappoint
Dr. Franklin, but he could not add his name to the venerable names that would endorse the Constitution's "wisdom and its worth." He refused to sign, he now said,
because the Constitution was doomed to failure. It would
not be ratified by nine states, of that he was certain. Although Gouverneur Morris declared he was content to
see the majority of each state delegation sign the Constitution, Alexander Hamilton pressed the individual delegates to set aside their doubts and criticisms and make
the endorsement genuinely unanimous. He reminded the
convention—if it needed reminding—that no one's ideas
were more at odds with the particular plan of government
that appeared in the Constitution than his own, but in a
choice between anarchy and political convulsion on one
side and the "chance of good" on the other, what man
could refuse to support the convention's handiwork?

Despite Hamilton's appeal, Randolph and Gerry
stood firm. Randolph admitted that his refusal might be
the most awful step of his life, but because it was dictated
by conscience, he could not alter his course. Gerry, too,
confessed how painful his decision was. Yet he believed
the nation stood on the brink of civil war, a war that
in his home state of Massachusetts pitted followers of
democracy ("the worst...of all political evils") against
supporters of aristocracy. The Constitution would do
nothing to prevent this war; indeed, in its present form, it
would fan the fires of discord. He could not sign the
Constitution and thus pledge to abide by it. He must remain free to take any action he thought might alleviate

the conflict within his state. Gerry's genuine anguish did not diminish his egotism; he closed with an accusation that Dr. Franklin's comments were leveled directly at him and his fellow dissenters.

When the vote was taken on Franklin's suggestion that the states unanimously endorse the Constitution, ten states said "aye"; South Carolina's delegation was divided. There was only one piece of business remaining: whether to destroy the records of the convention's proceedings or preserve them? The choice hinged on what would best serve the interests of the delegates. No one wanted the records made public, but destroying them would leave the delegates without any means of defending their actions against false accusations. Better to place them in the custody of the president, they decided, hidden from the public eye but accessible if needed.

There was nothing left to do but sign the Constitution. The New Hampshire delegates, last to arrive at the convention, were first to put their names to the document. When Delaware's turn came, George Read signed for the ailing and absent John Dickinson. Luther Martin, who had said nothing of his intentions, left without signing, as did fellow delegate John Mercer, raising the number of delegates who refused to endorse the Constitution but not endangering the unanimity of the states. Alexander Hamilton was New York's sole delegate to sign; John Lansing and Robert Yates had departed for good in early July. Nine supporters had been called away, either on Confederation business or to manage personal affairs. Thus, the signatures of Oliver Ellsworth of Connecticut,

Caleb Strong of Massachusetts, William Few and William Houstoun of Georgia, William Houston of New
Jersey, and Dr. James McClurg and George Wythe of
Virginia were missing from the Constitution. As Georgia, the last delegation, rose to sign, Benjamin Franklin
could be heard to say that during the long months of debate, he had often wondered whether the sun painted on
the back of Washington's chair was rising or setting.
"Now at length," he said with obvious relief, "I have the
happiness to know that it is a rising and not a setting
Sun." With that, the convention dissolved itself by an adjournment sine die. . . .

That evening the delegates joined members of the
Pennsylvania assembly for a farewell dinner at the City
Tavern. While the determinedly uncouth Luther Martin
may not have been missed at the table, the delegates probably regretted the absence of John Dickinson, who had
gone home to Delaware, hoping to recover from the illness that had plagued him throughout the summer. Gentleman that he was, Dickinson had entrusted a bank bill to
George Read to help cover the expenses of the festivities
that evening. After a hearty meal and several rounds of
toasts, the men cordially parted company. Like George
Washington, many must have "retired to meditate on the
momentous work, which had been executed, after not
less than five, for a large part of the time six, and sometimes seven hours' sitting every day . . . for more than four
months." And like Washington, most delegates knew that
a second round of political battle was about to begin.

# CHAPTER EIGHT

## The Battle for Ratification

### "The Constitution is now before the Judgment Seat"

O N SEPTEMBER 19 THE delegates began their exodus
from boardinghouses and the homes of friends.
Most were headed home; some were bound for New York
City, to take their long-vacant seats in the Confederation
Congress. A few, like the irrepressible Gouverneur Morris, were already making plans to flee political life for
what they considered a much-deserved vacation. Most of
the delegates, however, were steeling themselves for the
next phase of the constitutional struggle: ratification of
"the plan" by their home states. Unless nine states approved the Constitution, the long months of debate, argument, negotiation, and compromise would prove futile,
and the crisis brought on by an incompetent government
would continue. Could they rally the support they needed?
No one knew.

At one o'clock that afternoon, General Washington,
Bob Morris, and Gouverneur Morris dined together for

the last time. Then the three men rode to Gray's Ferry on the Schuylkill River. Here, on the riverbanks, they parted—Washington turning south toward his beloved Mount Vernon, Robert Morris returning to his elegant home in Philadelphia, and the feisty Gouverneur Morris heading toward his lavish Morrisania estate. Their plans for the future were as different as their personalities: Washington hoped to retire from public life; Robert Morris hoped to save his precarious fortune; and the peg legged Gouverneur Morris hoped to travel abroad in search of cultural stimulation and, with luck, new amorous encounters.

That same day George Mason could also been seen making his way home to his Virginia plantation at Gunston Hall. Mason remained firm in his resolve to oppose the Constitution, although he knew he would pay a high price for his apostasy. His "Objections to the Constitution," first scribbled on the back of his copy of the plan, was already circulating in Philadelphia. By October he would send a more polished copy of this critique to Washington, an act that would strain their long-standing friendship to the breaking point. His once intimate friendship with James Madison already seemed beyond repair. Vicious gossip about Mason filled the Philadelphia papers, including unfounded rumors that he had been greeted as a traitor in his native state. The mayor of Alexandria and a delegation of leading citizens, it was said, had met Mason at the city borders and warned him to leave the city within an hour's time if he valued his life.

The story was untrue, but it suggested the bitter divisions between the supporters of the new plan of government and its opponents in the key state of Virginia.

The pugnacious Luther Martin and the irascible Elbridge Gerry were men better suited to the conflict that lay ahead than the mild-mannered Mason. Yet no delegate expected to avoid the battles over ratification soon to take shape. A copy of the Constitution and Gouverneur Morris's brilliantly politic letter were already on their way to the Confederation Congress. Once Congress accepted this report from the Constitutional Convention, state legislatures were expected to call for the election of delegates to special ratifying conventions. At these conventions the Constitution would be approved—or rejected. Once nine states had ratified, the Constitution went into effect and a new government was established for the United States. By October the machinery was set in motion in several states, and Pennsylvania's convention was already scheduled for mid-November.

"The Constitution," George Washington wrote somberly to his old friend Henry Knox, "is now before the Judgment Seat." For him, and for all the Federalists the question was: would nine states ratify? James Madison immediately began to count heads, just as he did in the excrutiating days of waiting before the Constitutional Convention began. Ironically, it was the small states that he could most confidently place in the "yes" column. Now that the Senate provided them a secure foothold in national affairs, they would see the advantages of a central government able to regulate trade—and thus relieve them of continuing exploitation by their larger neighbors. Madison felt confident that Delaware, New Jersey, and Connecticut would ratify. Early reports from Pennsylvania were also encouraging. There were signs an opposition was forming in Massachusetts, but Madison thought that state, too, would ratify. As for Rhode Island—few veterans of American postwar politics were surprised when the legislature of Rogue's Island voted not to hold a ratifying convention at all.

Ironically, the greatest danger lay in the home states of the two men most intimately associated with the new plan of government. In Madison's Virginia, a fierce contest was brewing, as powerful and influential men began to publicly denounce the Constitution. And in Alexander Hamilton's New York, the nation's only genuine party machine, the Clintonites, were already mounting an organized campaign of opposition. Without the support of these large and powerful states, any new government was doomed to failure.

Despite the opposition in New York, Alexander Hamilton was cautiously optimistic. The supporters of the Constitution had the distinct advantage, he argued, for they had "the very great weight of influence of the persons who framed it." Yet in many parts of the country, this was reason enough to vote "no." Antagonism between the elite and the poorer classes was as old as America itself, and in almost every state, long-standing divisions between the privileged class that the convention delegates represented and the struggling people of the backcountry reappeared in the battle over ratification. Whether the division was described as one between backcountry and coastal regions, debtor and creditor, paper-money advocates and hard-money men, or simply the rich and the poor, the line of demarcation had been drawn many years before the Philadelphia convention. In the western counties of Virginia, Pennsylvania, or Massachusetts, voters were certain to elect delegates who shared their deepseated distrust of merchants, tidewater planters, and lawyers, the very "influential men" Hamilton described.

The Constitution would find its supporters among the farmers and workingmen of the nation, of course. Urban artisans and small shopkeepers saw the advantages of a government powerful enough to increase commerce and trade. And backcountry subsistence farmers facing hostile Indians and their Spanish allies on state borders saw the virtue in a government strong enough to repel frontier enemies or negotiate favorable international treaties.

At the same time, not all the wealthy merchants or planters could be counted on to support the new plan of government. The opposition would boast a roster of notable political and economic leaders as well as Revolutionary heroes. Regional icons like Samuel Adams and Patrick Henry, activists like the Revolutionary propagandist Mercy Otis Warren, and powerful officeholders like Governor George Clinton would quickly emerge as articulate champions of the antiratification movement. In fact, the leaders of the opposition forces were more likely

to be men of wealth, education, and legal training than
common farmers, since the ratifying conventions, like most
eighteenth-century political arenas, were the provenance
of the orator and the lawyer, the well-educated and the
politically experienced. The backcountry men and women
would depend in great measure upon champions who
were from the same social class as the nationalist leadership. In many cases this proved their undoing.

From the beginning the supporters of the Constitution did have one advantage: a political savvy born of experience. They knew how to create a positive impression
and put, as modern Americans would say, the right "spin"
on events and decisions. They had found a way to claim
unanimous approval of the Constitution by the convention, even though some individual delegates had refused
to sign. They had taken ratification out of the hands of
the Confederation Congress—which could hardly be
expected to sign its own death warrant—and away from
the state legislatures, which were unlikely to endorse the
loss of their own power and prestige. They made full use
of the eighteenth century's available media, filling the
newspapers—which were largely urban and largely sympathetic to the nationalist perspective—with essays and
letters setting out the virtues of the Constitution. They
had at their disposal some of the most persuasive writers
of the day, including John Dickinson, "the Penman of the
Revolution," and some of the nation's most brilliant
minds, including John Jay, Alexander Hamilton, and
James Madison. Together these three men would defend
the Constitution article by article and section by section

under the pseudonym "Publius," in a collection of essays known to us as *The Federalist Papers*. In some areas of the country, the opposition found itself silenced, its power to communicate cut off by the newspapers' refusal to publish their views.

Perhaps the nationalists' most brilliant tactic in the battle of ideas ahead of them, however, was their decision to call themselves "Federalists" and their cause, "Federalism." The men behind the Constitution were not, of course, federalists at all. They were advocates of a strong national government whose authority diminished the independence of the states. Their opponents were the true federalists, men who continued to support a league of friendship and cooperation among independent sovereign states. But Hamilton and Madison did not need advanced degrees in linguistics or sophisticated treatises on "signifiers" to understand the power of words in the struggle ahead of them. By co-opting the name "Federalists," the pro-Constitution forces deprived their opponents of the ability to signal clearly and immediately what they stood for. To add insult to injury, the Federalists dubbed their opponents "Anti-Federalists"—marking them as men who stood against the very political ideas they embraced.

The Anti-Federalists suffered from more than the damaging misnomer. In most states they found themselves on the defensive, urging voters to be loyal to a government they conceded was in need of repair. Indeed, many confessed they wanted a new government; they just didn't want the government the convention was proposing.

Unfortunately for their cause, they had no effective alternative to offer. Over the next nine months, they could do little but criticize the Constitution, a strategy that validated their image as "Antis."

Even this strategy was hindered by circumstances. Unlike the Federalists—who had honed their arguments over four months of grueling debate, made their compromises, and reached a measure of consensus—the Anti-Federalists had no collective critique, no agreed-upon set of objections. Although they agreed that the proposed government was a national rather than a federal government, too powerful to be trusted, they differed widely on which elements of the new government were most dangerous to a republican nation.

What Anti-Federalists did share was a pervasive suspicion, a belief that the Constitution was the end product of a carefully laid conspiracy by a cabal of ambitious men. From the beginning some members of the Confederation Congress had warned that "plans have been artfully laid, and vigorously pursued" to change the nation's republican government into a "baleful aristocracy." Mercy Otis Warren, whose sharp wit and cutting satire had destroyed the reputation of many a Massachusetts Loyalist, characterized the Philadelphia convention as a breeding ground of "dark, secret and profound intrigues." If the Federalist leadership—who had labored so obsessively to prevent conspiracy and intrigue in the new government—recognized the irony in such accusations, they rarely acknowledged it. Instead, they met accusation with counteraccusation, describing their critics as disgruntled failures and misfits, ne'er-do-wells, or as ambitious, conniving, unscrupulous men, hoping to profit from the chaos and confusion rapidly overtaking the nation. The convention had not been called in 1787 to create an oligarchy or a monarchy, they argued, but to protect Americans from the "turbulence and follies of democracy" and to help it achieve an honorable place in the family of nations. Edward Carrington put the differences between the Anti-Federalist and the Federalist fears succinctly in a letter to Thomas Jefferson. "Some Gentlemen apprehend that this project is the foundation of Monarchy, or at least an oppressive Aristocracy," he wrote, "but my apprehensions are rather from the inroads of democracy." At their worst, both sides resorted to name-calling and labeling; "consider the source" was the central message of many of the pro and anti diatribes.

Substantive criticisms of the Constitution did emerge, of course, many of them echoing the concerns of the convention delegates themselves. Were there enough representatives in the House to truly express the needs and concerns of the people? Washington had been concerned enough about this issue to break his silence as the presiding officer of the convention and urge that the number be increased. Were the senators' terms too long and their eligibility for reelection too open-ended? The delegates had fretted over this throughout the final weeks of the convention. Fearing that the Senate might become an oligarchic threat to republicanism, the delegates had made last-minute efforts to bolster the power of the president as a check on the Senate. Anxiety over excessive Senate power had been a key factor in their acceptance of what would become known as the electoral college.

Over the ten months of argument and discussion that followed the completion of the Constitution, Anti-Federalists voiced few concerns about the presidency. Perhaps the strongest criticism came from Madison's own father, in a letter to his son in October. "A sole Executive, who may be for Life, with almost a Negative upon ye Legislature" was, Madison Sr. insisted, an insult to the principle of separation of powers. Yet in the public forums, neither the breach of this principle nor the method of electing the president, the length of his term, or the possibility of his reelection provoked much comment. In the ratifying conventions, the presidency was virtually ignored; none of the many amendments proposed in the New York, Virginia, or New Hampshire conventions, for example, focused on the office of the president.

The explanation for this lack of controversy is simple: George Washington. Like the Federalists, the Anti-Federalists were confident Washington would be the nation's first president if the Constitution was ratified. And like their opponents, they revered him. As Gouverneur Morris explained to Washington himself: "Truth is, that your great and decided Superiority leads Men willingly to put you in [the presidency]." Thus, it would be difficult to find anyone in the country who cared how the president was chosen or how long he served—as long as his name was George Washington.

In the end, the familiar suspicion that aristocracy was on the rise, the pervasive fear of conspiracy, and the certainty, burned into the American consciousness, that power given would be power abused came together over a single issue: the absence of a bill of rights. To many Anti-Federalists, the failure—or refusal—of the convention to include guarantees of fundamental rights such as freedom of speech or assembly was proof that the Constitution was not a solution to an existing American crisis but the source of a future one.

THE FIRST RATIFYING CONVENTION was set to meet in Philadelphia in late November. Weeks before this James Madison had already set up what modern Americans might call "command central," receiving from and forwarding to others the reports that poured in from all across the country. Although information traveled at a sometimes maddeningly slow pace, Madison reached out to contacts in distant New Hampshire and nearby Maryland, trying to gauge the potential support or opposition to the Constitution. Even before he returned home, Madison had sent his father his first predictions: Pennsylvania would ratify, New York faced an uphill battle, Massachusetts was too close to call, but Connecticut and New Jersey were certain to ratify.

Henry Knox, the obese Boston bookseller turned military strategist during the Revolution, did not share Madison's conservative predictions. On October 3 he wrote to George Washington that he was confident the Constitution would be approved, despite opposition in every state. Thinking no doubt of Elbridge Gerry, who was already campaigning hard for the new government's defeat, Knox added: "The germ of opposition originated in the convention itself. The gentlemen who refused signing it will most probable conceive themselves obliged to state their reasons publickly."

Knox was right. Gerry, Luther Martin, and George Mason had quickly made public the reasons for their refusal to endorse the Constitution. Mason, however, was eager to see Virginia call a ratifying convention. He vowed to fight any efforts by Anti-Federalists to prevent it. No doubt Mason believed that quick action would favor the Constitution's opponents since powerful Virginians, including Patrick Henry and Richard Henry Lee, were ready to campaign against ratification. Madison, who had traveled first to New York to attend the Confederation Congress, got word that only days after the convention adjourned, Virginia's opposing camps had begun to organize. A friend in Fredericksburg wrote that judgments "have already been deliver'd, and that work, which was the production of much labour & time, has been in a few hours either damn'd or applauded, according to the wish, sentiments, or interests of the politician...."

Still in New York in mid-October, Madison reassessed the mood in the northern and middle states in a letter to George Washington. It was hard, he explained, to get accurate information about the countryside, but "Boston is certainly friendly" and the Antis in Connecticut were small in number and weak in influence. New

Jersey was entirely in the Federalist camp. For his part, Washington had steeled himself for a long battle and an uncertain outcome. The Constitution, he wrote Henry Knox, has "its adversaries and supporters. Which will preponderate is yet to be decided—the former, more than probably, will be the most active, as the Major part of them will, it is to be feared, be governed by sinester [*sic*] and self important motives, to which every thing in their breasts must yield." The usually stoic Washington made no effort to disguise his hopes for ratification. "I never saw him so keen for any thing in my Life," a Virginian told Thomas Jefferson.

Jefferson was not "so keen" for the Constitution as the Federalists might have hoped. He was one of the few who singled out the presidency as a source of concern. John Adams, Jefferson's diplomatic counterpart in London, defended the executive's powers, especially in checking the Senate. Writing to Jefferson that December, he made their differences clear: "You are afraid of the one— I, of the few.... You are Apprehensive of Monarchy; I, of Aristocracy.... You are apprehensive of the President when once chosen, will be chosen again and again as long as he lives. So much the better as it appears to me ... as often as Elections happen, the danger of foreign Influence recurs." Jefferson was not persuaded. He repeated his concerns in letters to correspondents in England and America. He predicted that Virginia would reject the Constitution—and gave no indication that he would regret it. As Christmas 1787 neared, Jefferson confided to a friend: "As to the new Constitution I find myself nearly a Neutral...."

There were few other neutrals on the issue of ratification. Although Pennsylvania had rushed to convene its convention in November, it was Delaware who won the honor of ratifying the Constitution first. Delaware's delegates gathered on December 3 and within four short days had voted unanimously for the new government. Pennsylvania's convention, convened on November 21, did not cast its vote of 46–23 in favor of the Constitution until December 12. Nevertheless, some Pennsylvanians believed that the decision came with unseemly haste. "I cannot imagine," wrote one Philadelphian, "why the people in this city are so very anxious to have it adopted instantly before it can be digested or deliberately considered." He objected to the manner in which the state conservatives—or as he dubbed them, the "Tories"—hailed the Constitution as the nation's salvation and noted with a combination of amusement and distress that the "Quaquers" [Quakers] had run about "signing declarations and Petitions in favor of it...before they [had] time to examine it." The Federalists had wasted no time, he added, haranguing "the rabble"—language that suggests wealthy Anti-Federalists entertained as low an opinion of the people as their allegedly more elitist opponents. The rush was, of course, a calculated move. The two preexisting state parties—one representing urban and commercial interests, the other, western, rural interests—had quickly chosen sides on the issue of the new government. The urban, and now Federalist, forces controlled the Pennsylvania legislature, and they naturally hoped to take advantage of their position while they still held a majority. When opposition members refused to attend the legislative session, a mob dragged two of them back into the chamber so that a quorum was assured to issue a call for the convention. Federalists filled the newspapers with pro-Constitution essays, and it is doubtful if many voters realized there was any opposition to ratification at all.

By December 18 the New Jersey convention had endorsed the Constitution, 39–0. As 1788 began Georgia joined the ranks of the supporters, its convention voting 26–0 for ratification. George Washington was not surprised at the strong show of support from this state. "If a weak State with the Indians on its back and the Spaniards on its flank does not see the necessity of a General Government," he observed, "there must I think be wickedness or insanity in the way." And on January 9 the last of the small states, Connecticut, turned in a vote of 128–40 in favor of the new government. Thus, as the Massachusetts convention got under way, five of the nine necessary states were in the "yes" column.

Madison was keenly aware of the importance of the Massachusetts vote. Anti-Federalist forces were strong in North Carolina, New York, and Virginia, and were gaining surprising strength in New Hampshire. These states would be deeply influenced by the decision of the Massachusetts convention. When the delegates met on January 9, the spirit of Shays's rebels was evident. Western

hostility to Boston merchants translated into western opposition to the Constitution. Spurring the opposition on
was Elbridge Gerry, whose Anti-Federalist essays were
both excessive and effective. One Massachusetts Federalist minced no words in discussing the effect of Gerry's
propaganda: "*damn him—damn him*—every thing look'd
well and had the most favorable appearance in this State,
previous to this—and now I have my doubts.... I cannot
leave him without once more *damn'g him.*"

Rufus King conceded to Madison that "our prospects
are gloomy." In the face of strong opposition, Massachusetts Federalists fought fiercely but unsuccessfully to gain
control of the convention. Class-based attacks on the
supporters of the Constitution had proved highly effective in the elections. "The Opposition complain that the
Lawyers, Judges, Clergymen, Merchants and men of Education are all in Favor of the constitution," explained
Tench Cox to the increasingly anxious Madison, and, he
added, "for this reason they appear to be able to make the
worst appear the better cause...." When Massachusetts
Federalists realized that the Anti-Federalists held a small
majority, they worked hard to woo some of these delegates to their cause. The ethics of their tactics were often
questionable.They warned the poorer delegates, for example, that they would not be reimbursed for their expenses unless the Constitution was ratified.

But the Massachusetts Federalists succeeded, in the
long run, because they were superior debaters, more prestigious citizens, and had greater skill in political settings.

They courted all and any influential political figures, including the very popular John Hancock, whom they flattered by asking him to present the state's recommendations for constitutional amendments to the new Congress. They also hinted to the vain Governor Hancock that if Virginia failed to ratify, he rather than Washington would surely be the nation's first president. Visions of glory such as these were impossible for the ambitious and egotistical Hancock to resist, and he joined the pro-ratification camp. On February 6, in a close vote, the Massachusetts convention ratified the Constitution.

Madison did not receive word of the Federalist victory in Massachusetts for almost a week. Rufus King sent him the good news, adding that the Antis were "in good Temper" and "have the magnanimity to declare that they will devote their Lives & property to support the Government...." With six states in his "win" column, Madison now awaited news of the New Hampshire convention. He was uncharacteristically optimistic. "There seems to be no question," he wrote Washington, "that the issue there will add a *seventh* pillar, as the phrase now is, to the federal Temple."

New Hampshire proved him terribly wrong. Many delegates arrived at the convention bound by instructions from their communities—and those instructions were to vote "no." Although several delegates were privately supporters of the Constitution, they considered their hands to be tied. New Hampshire's Federalists showed their political skills by moving swiftly to avert disaster.

Nicholas Gilman and his allies managed to win an adjournment of the convention so that delegates could return home and win release from their constituents to vote as they saw fit. The result, however, was a long delay, and New Hampshire's decision would not come until spring.

With the adjournment in New Hampshire, the ratification drive seemed to stall. Although Maryland and South Carolina were preparing to convene and Virginia elections were set to begin in early March, the count remained at six states as April's promise of warmer weather began. In Virginia George Washington had greeted the news of the New Hampshire postponement with dismay. It lent encouragement to the Virginia Antis and to the New York opposition as well. The only bright spot seemed to be the public response to the series of essays by "Publius," now circulating throughout the states. These essays carefully and effectively addressed every aspect of the Constitution, anticipating objections and providing cogent rebuttals to them. Although the authorship was anonymous, most of Madison's correspondents knew that the essays were the work of John Jay, Alexander Hamilton, and Madison himself. Whether James Sr. knew of his son's role in this propaganda is uncertain, but he was ready with his praise of the anonymous essayist. "Whoever may be ye Author of them," the senior Madison wrote, "they are certainly well written, as far at least as I have seen them, & well calculated to promote ye great Object in View." The question was could Publius win the hearts and minds of the Virginia and New York convention delegates?

By the time the Virginia convention met, both Maryland and South Carolina had—as hoped—ratified the Constitution. In Maryland the Antis had counted several former state governors in their camp, not to mention Luther Martin, yet the opposition inexplicably failed to campaign for seats in the Maryland convention. According to Washington, the convention proved lively nevertheless. "Mr Chace [Chase], it is said, made a display of all his eloquence—Mr Mercer discharged his whole artillery of inflammable matter—and Mr. Marten I know not what—perhaps vehemence—but no converts were made—no, not one." When Daniel Carroll sent Washington the happy news of ratification, he added that there were "great illuminations . . . at Annapolis—The Members having given one Guinea for that purpose." In South Carolina Federalists proved more organized than their opponents and thus entered the convention with a comfortable majority. The city of Charleston, where the convention met, was unabashedly, even noisily pro-Constitution, and this may have dampened the opposition further. When the vote came, it was 149–73 in favor of ratification.

Eight states had accepted the new government. Although Virginia Federalists hoped that their state would be the ninth pillar of the federal temple, that honor went to New Hampshire. Reconvening in June, the New Hampshire convention voted 57–47 to support the Constitution. Virginia's convention, begun on June 2, did not end its deliberations until June 25. In the course of over three weeks, this state's delegation proved the exception to many rules. The wealthiest citizens were equally divided, with planters standing firmly on both sides of the controversy. In typical fashion, Madison could name the delegates likely to vote "aye" or "nay." The only man he placed in the "undecided" column was the young James Monroe, labeled an Anti-Federalist by many, but suspected by Madison of being a reluctant supporter. He was wrong. Monroe, who would be the nation's fifth president, voted against ratification. The backcountry was no more consistent than the tidewater, with West Virginia supporting the new government and the voters of Kentucky opposing it. George Washington commented to his old friend Lafayette on the peculiarities of his own planter class, saying: "It is a little strange that the men of large property in the South, should be more afraid that the Constitution will produce an Aristocracy or a Monarchy, than the genuine democratical people of the East." On June 2, Madison could at last breathe a sigh of relief, for by a vote of 89 to 79, his home state endorsed his handiwork.

All eyes now turned to New York. Although the new government was technically a reality, few people believed it could succeed without both Virginia and New York within its fold. If the struggle in Virginia had been fierce, the battle in New York was likely to be far bloodier. The unchallenged leader of the Federalist campaign in New York was Alexander Hamilton. The chief author of the "Publius" essays and the mastermind of the Federalist strategy at the state convention, Hamilton worked tirelessly to devise tactics that would snatch victory from the jaws of the Clintonites. Clinton, whose network of patronage and near monopoly of public offices outside New York City amounted to America's first party machine, took full advantage of his position. The Antis were confident enough to invade the Federalist stronghold, organizing a "Federal Republican Committee" in New York City to mobilize support for the opposition. Always the realist, John Jay wrote to Washington, "There is much Reason to believe that the Majority of the Convention of this State will be composed of anti federal Characters." Jay was right. Despite all their efforts, Hamilton and his Federalist forces had failed to win any delegates outside New York City and the surrounding ring of communities in Kings, Richmond, and Westchester Counties. Still, Jay held out some hope for his cause. "It is doubtful," he told Washington, "whether the leaders will be able to govern the Party. Many in the opposition are Friends to Union and mean well, but their principal Leaders are very far from being solicitous about the Fate of the Union."

Throughout June Hamilton's strategy was to stall proceedings in the convention until word came from Virginia. But his strongest weapon in the battle against Clinton was the threat that New York City and its neighboring counties would secede from the state and join the Union independently. Writing to James Madison in the midst of the convention, Hamilton conceded that the Antis had a clear two-thirds majority and were pushing for an adjournment until next spring or summer, claiming that this would give New York time to test the viability of the new government. Hamilton read this call for adjournment as the first clear sign of weakness in the Anti-Federalist camp. They do not want the Union, he said, yet they do not want to reject the Constitution either. If Virginia ratifies, would New York relish the thought of its isolation?

The answer proved to be no. Faced with news of Virginia's decision and fearing that Hamilton and his urban Federalists might make good on their secession threat, the Anti-Federalist majority bent to the will of the minority. By a vote of 30–27, New York joined the Union.

Federalist elation—and relief—was not diminished by the news, arriving from North Carolina that August, that the Carolina convention had voted against ratification. It would be November 1789 before this southern state would formally enter the Union. And it would not be until March 1790 that Rhode Island would set aside its roguishness and grudgingly ratify the Constitution. By that time the first president and Congress were already seeing to the business of the nation.

# CHAPTER NINE

# The Inauguration of President George Washington

## "This great and good man"

T HE NEW GOVERNMENT gathering in New York over-flowed with political celebrities. The House and Senate were filled with leading Federalists, and even the irascible Elbridge Gerry had set aside his doubts and his endless criticisms and decided to serve as a congressman. Yet the presence of so many distinguished political leaders could not hide the fact that the new government was just that, *new*, and this was its weakness. The loyalty of its citizens was untested, and thus its survival was uncertain. Its legitimacy rested, for the moment, solely upon the ratification process. If public support waned or protest against its policies and programs grew vocal, that legitimacy could easily be challenged. It could not fall back on a claim of divine endorsement, or evoke an attachment to long-standing traditions, or point to past achievements to soften the impact of criticisms.

For the moment what the new government needed was a charismatic figure who held the people's affection and loyalty by the force of personality and character alone—and who was willing to spread the protective blanket of that widespread devotion over the newly established government. Fortunately, it had such a man in George Washington. Thus, if the Constitution did not make the president the central figure of the new government, political necessity did.

On February 4, 1789, electors in eleven states had met to cast their votes for the first president of the United States. The votes were tabulated, and, as the Constitution instructed, they were forwarded to Congress, where the results would be read and recorded in a special joint session of the House and Senate. The process—straightforward and simple as it was—immediately hit a snag: Congress was having difficulty producing a quorum in either house. Winter snow and ice slowed travel on the roads leading to New York, causing senators and representatives to trickle into the nation's temporary capital throughout February and March. In truth, there was no functioning government until the April thaw. At last, on April 6, 1789, with New Hampshire's John Langdon presiding, Congress was able to "open all the certificates and count all the votes of the electors" and to announce what the whole nation already knew: "His Excellency George Washington, esq., was unanimously elected, agreeably to the Constitution, to the office of Prsident of the said United States of America."

The election was unique in American history, not simply because a unanimous vote had swept someone into office. No one had campaigned for election. There had been no speeches, no public endorsements, no election slogans, and no campaign promises. The leading candidate was well-known to be the most reluctant candidate; indeed, he had repeatedly expressed his desire to retire from public life and spend his remaining years as a farmer. There were no political polls to indicate who was ahead in the race for the presidency and little newspaper coverage of the event—and yet virtually everyone in the nation knew that "this great and good man," General George Washington, would be their first president.

Washington knew it as well. Weeks before official word of his election reached Mount Vernon, the general had begun to pack his bags and set his Virginia affairs in order. Quietly, he sent out an urgent request for a loan of at least a thousand pounds, for like most planters, he lived beyond his means and was in constant debt. He had little success raising the money. As a political figure, he was revered and honored; as a borrower, he was considered a credit risk. At the last minute a friend in Alexandria gave Washington five hundred pounds. It vanished quickly. By the time Charles Thompson, the secretary of the former Confederation Congress, brought the official word to the president-elect on April 14, Washington had been forced to borrow a hundred pounds more to cover the costs of the journey to the capital.

Debt was not the only thing troubling Washington that fateful spring. He was in poor health, suffering once again from debilitating bouts of rheumatism and the nagging pain produced by dentures made of everything from hippopotamus teeth to ivory and lead. At fifty-seven, he felt old, and his longing to spend his days riding the fields and enjoying the quiet comforts of his fireside was no guise to hide ambition. Yet who could resist a call to service that came, as Thompson put it, "not only by the unanimous vote of the electors, but by the voice of America."

Washington had spent a lifetime in pursuit of the respect of his countrymen. His formal reply to Thompson showed clearly that he recognized the relationship with those countrymen was reciprocal. "I have been accustomed to pay so much respect to the opinion of my fellow citizens that the knowledge of their having given their unanimous suffrages in my favor scarcely leaves me the alternative for an option. I can not, I believe, give a greater evidence of my sensibility to the honor which they have done me than by accepting the appointment." And, having accepted, Washington saw no reason to delay. He and Thompson left for New York two days later.

Washington's first stop was Alexandria, where he said his good-bye to his fellow Virginians. "Words, my fellow-citizens, fail me," he declared, *"Unutterable sensations must . . . be left to more expressive silence: while, from an aching heart, I bid you all, my affectionate friends and kind neighbours, farewell."* Here, as everywhere along the route to New York, crowds gathered to greet Washington. At every town welcoming speeches were made; in every city Washington was asked to lead a parade of dignitaries. Reaching Baltimore on the afternoon of April 17, he received and responded to a welcoming address by the citizens of the city. The following day Wilmington's council and the Delaware Society for Promoting Domestic Manufactures added their formal congratulations. Feted and toasted at every turn, met by cheers and hardy handshakes, the president-elect made his way slowly northward.

In anticipation of Washington's arrival, Congress appointed its own welcoming committee. Senators John Langdon, Charles Carroll, and William Samuel Johnson together with House members Elias Boudinot, Theodorick Bland, Thomas Tucker, Egbert Benson, and John Lawrence crossed the Hudson River to Elizabethtown, New Jersey, where they would meet the president-elect and escort him, by barge, to New York. Boudinot, who lived in Elizabethtown, extended an invitation to Washington to "alight at my house, where the committee will attend, and where it will give me . . . the utmost pleasure to receive you."

Meanwhile, Congress busied itself with finding appropriate housing for the president-elect and planning his inauguration. A letter went out to Washington, asking when and where he would like to take the oath. The congressmen added that it would take until Thursday, April 30, for preparations to be completed. Their first thought was that the ceremony be held in the House chamber, as it was larger than the Senate room. But by Monday, April 27, the preparations committee had changed their minds. Expecting huge crowds of citizens to fill the streets outside Federal Hall, they decided that the oath should be taken on the balcony, or "outer gallery," so that the public could view the historic event. As this balcony was off the Senate chamber, the two houses would have to squeeze into this tighter space. More details followed. A chair for the president was to be placed in the Senate chamber and, to the right of this seat, a second chair for the vice president, Massachusetts revolutionary John Adams, who had received the second largest number of votes in the electoral college. Additional seating was needed for the former president of the Confederation Congress, the governor of the Western Territory, the "five persons being the heads of the great Departments," the minister plenipotentiary of France, the consul of Spain, the chaplains of Congress, the president's personal entourage, as well as New York's governor, lieutenant governor, chancellor, state supreme court justices, and the city's mayor. Aware of possible status sensitivities, the joint committee handling the inauguration planning instructed their staff to assure all these dignitaries that "no precedence of seats is intended."

Members of both houses were asked to assemble in their chambers precisely at twelve noon. The representatives, led by their Speaker, were then to proceed to the Senate chamber to await the arrival of the president. After appropriate greetings, the vice president and the president would make their way to the balcony, joined by Chancellor Robert R. Livingston, who had been chosen to administer the oath. Congressmen and dignitaries would assemble around them, and, at last, the swearing in would begin.

Washington would not be among strangers on that crowded balcony, for many of the delegates to the Constitutional Convention had sought and won office in the new government. Abraham Baldwin of Georgia, Hugh Williamson of North Carolina, Daniel Carroll of Maryland, Thomas Fitzsimons and George Clymer of Pennsylvania, Roger Sherman of Connecticut, and Nicholas Gilman of New Hampshire had won seats in the House. Appropriately, James Madison was also there as a Virginia representative. And, of course, Elbridge Gerry. In the Senate Washington would recognize even more familiar faces: John Langdon of New Hampshire; Rufus King, now a New Yorker; Caleb Strong of Massachusetts; Oliver Ellsworth and William Samuel Johnson of Connecticut; Robert Morris of Pennsylvania; William Paterson of New Jersey; Richard Bassett and George Read of Delaware; Pierce Butler of South Carolina; and William Few of Georgia. Close friends and colleagues, missing from Congress, would appear in other capacities around Washington. His protégé, Alexander Hamilton, had eagerly accepted the reins of the treasury department. Fellow Virginian John Blair would be wearing the robes of a Supreme Court justice, along with the much-respected lawyer John Rutledge and the brilliant James Wilson. Even Washington's old friend Edmund Randolph, whose opposition to the Constitution had so recently strained their relationship, had agreed to serve as attorney general. Some men Washington might have hoped to see were missing. Gouverneur Morris was abroad, viewing firsthand the French Revolution. The still-ailing John Dickinson and the aging Charles Cotesworth Pinckney had both retired from public life. That so many of the men who framed the Constitution would be there to see it through its first years must have been heartening to the new president.

On April 30—inauguration day—the city was awakened to the sound of church bells and the roar of cannon from Bowling Green. In the early hours men and women began to fill the streets, dressed in their finest clothes. As the morning progressed the crowds grew thicker, as people poured into the city, clogging the roads, filling the ferries, and cramming into packet boats coming down the Hudson or sailing westward on the Long Island Sound. Scores of New Yorkers assembled in churches, where they heard their ministers "implore the blessings of Heaven on the nation." Coming out of church, they saw the clouds dissipate and the sun shine brightly, a sign to many that the heavens had responded to their request. On the winding streets of lower Manhattan, people were treated to the sight of military banners and to the sounds of martial music as several regiments prepared to join the inaugural parade. German grenadiers—elegant in their blue coats, yellow waistcoats and breeches, and their towering cone-shaped hats—vied for attention with Captain Harsin's New York grenadiers, composed of young men selected for their height and good looks, decked out in eye-catching blue coats with red facing and gold lace embroidery, their cocked hats adorned with white feathers. Nearby the Scotch infantry, in full Highland regalia, drew cheers from the crowd as they played their bagpipes.

At precisely twelve noon, the senators and representatives chosen to escort the president assembled at his home. They found Washington waiting. Always sensitive to the symbolic possibilities of dress, Washington had chosen to wear a dark brown coat, waistcoat, and breeches, and white silk stockings, all made from American cloth. The simplicity of his suit was offset only slightly by the brass buttons of his coat, decorated with eagles; the silver buckles of his shoes; and the dress sword worn at his side. Washington had also asked that the Bible on which he would swear his oath come from the nearby St. John's Masonic Lodge. The choice carried a more private symbolism, for Washington, like many of the Revolutionary leadership, had long been a member of the secret society know as the Freemasons. With little or no attachment to any church, Washington had two intense organizational commitments: Freemasonry and the Society of the Cincinnati.

Slowly, the procession to the newly refurbished and redesigned Federal Hall made its way through the narrow streets of Manhattan. Leading the way, the military escorts; behind them, the sheriff of New York; next, the Committee of the Senate and the Committee of the House, with George Washington between them; then John Jay, the secretary of foreign affairs, Henry Knox, the secretary of war, and Robert R. Livingston, the chancellor of the state of New York, who was accompanied by the secretary of the Senate, carrying the open Masonic Bible on a rich crimson cushion; and, finally, a train of "distinguished citizens." When the procession reached the corner of Broad and Wall Streets, where the capital building stood, the troops formed a line on each side of the street, remaining at attention until the president and his entourage passed into the building.

At the door to the Senate chamber, Vice President John Adams greeted the president. Unlike the president-elect, the short, chunky Adams had shown a preference for splendor over simplicity in selecting his inauguration-day suit. Washington acknowledged the elaborately dressed Adams politely but not warmly, for the two men were far from friends. Adams burned with a jealousy of Washington's fame and popularity that he was unable to hide. For his part, Washington found Adams too "Yan-kee" in his unpolished manners, blunt speech, and open ambition. Yet Washington had not opposed the move to encourage enough electoral votes for Adams in order to make him vice president. With a Virginian in the executive office, it was politic to have a New Englander by his side.

Adams saw the president to his chair. Then, he announced, with great formality, "Sir, the Senate and House of Representatives of the United States are ready to attend you to take the oath required by the Constitution, which will be administered by the Chancellor of the State of New York." To this, Washington replied simply: "I am ready to proceed." Together, Congress and the executive officer moved onto the balcony.

Robert R. Livingston raised his hand to silence the crowds below. Slowly and distinctly, Livingston recited the oath as it appeared in the Constitution itself. The Bible was raised and George Washington leaned low to kiss its open pages. As he did, he said, "I swear"—and then, visibly moved by the moment, he closed his eyes and added, "So help me God." With that, the chancellor murmured, "It is done," and turning toward the crowd below, he shouted, "Long live George Washington, President of the United States!"

"The scene," wrote one of those present at the inauguration, "was solemn and awful beyond description." Despite the cheers, the roar of cannon, and the strains of "The President's March," composed in honor of Washington by a captured Hessian soldier who remained in America after the Revolutionary War, the president's mood inside the Senate chamber was somber. "As the first of every thing, in our situation will serve to establish a Precedent," he later wrote to James Madison, "it is devoutly wished on my part, that these precedents may be fixed on true principles." Washington's concern for the task before him was evident in the short, but moving inaugural speech that followed his oath taking. His hands trembling and his voice unsteady, Washington described his election as a "vicissitude" rather than a delight and spoke frankly of his anxiety in the face of "the magnitude and difficulty of the trust to which the voice of my country called me." His talents, he had always argued, were modest, and now he spoke of his "incapacity" in the face of the challenge ahead. Having expressed his appreciation for the confidence the nation placed in him, and having asked that nation's forbearance of his limited abilities, he turned his audience's attention away from himself and toward God. With a Deist's sensibility and vocabulary, he spoke of America's dependence upon "the Great Author of every public and private good," whose "Invisible Hand" in the political affairs of men ought to be acknowledged by the American people. He invited Congress, and the citizens they represented, to join him in recognizing the influence of the Almighty Being in the "proceedings of a new and free government."

Acknowledging that one of his duties was to make recommendations to Congress, Washington nevertheless carefully avoided proposing any specific measures in his inaugural address. The Constitution itself should be the legislature's guide as they began their work. He would go no further, he said, than to offer a tribute to "the talents, the rectitude, and the patriotism" of the men sitting before him. Chief among their virtues, he continued, was the pledge that they would not succumb to "local prejudices or attachments...[nor] separate views nor party animosities." In this, Washington would be sorely disappointed, for by his second term in office, a growing division between the champions of agriculture and the champions of commerce, between Francophiles and Anglophiles, and between the followers of Jefferson and the advocates of Hamiltonian economics would create the very political parties Washington so abhorred. But on this last day of April in 1789, Washington could speak confidently of a politics of "virtue and happiness" rather than faction or party.

Having expressed his confidence in the patriotism and wisdom of Congress, Washington ended with a personal observation and request. He served, he said, because it was his duty and, therefore, he could not accept any payment for his services. Though his language was stilted, his meaning was clear: "I ... must accordingly pray that the pecuniary estimates for the station in which I am placed may during my continuance in it be limited to such actual expenditures as the public good may be thought to require." Deeply in debt, George Washington renounced his salary as president of the United States.

His inaugural speech ended, President Washington joined Congress at a prayer service at St. Paul's Chapel. Later he visited at the homes of Chancellor Livingston and General Henry Knox, where he had a perfect view of the fireworks exploding in the evening sky. Because his wife, Martha Custis Washington, had not yet arrived in New York, the inaugural ball scheduled for that evening had been postponed. Thus, by ten o'clock Washington was able to retire to the solitude of his new home. Had he wandered through the city streets that evening, he could have seen a large transparent painting mounted near Bowling Green, with a portrait of him in the center, surrounded by members of the House and Senate, all under the sheltering wings of Justice and Wisdom. Nearby, in the waters by the Battery fort, the ship *Carolina* was illuminated, and Federal Hall's windows shone with candles. Transparencies covered the front of the theater on John Street, the most striking of them portraying Washington crowned with immortality by an angel. Private homes were illuminated, and the French and Spanish ministers had vied with each other to produce the most lavish display. Paintings depicting the past, present, and future of the United States adorned the front of the French minister's mansion; transparencies of the Graces were interspersed with patriotic symbols in the windows of the Spanish consul's home. In their reports the following day, newspapers praised the "enchanting spectacle" provided by these foreign dignitaries. In the midst of all the celebration, only a few had been keen enough to observe that George Washington was no longer the dashing young military officer, the tall and proudly handsome gentleman of Virginia; instead, "time had made havoc" on the face of the first president of the United States.

❦

# CHAPTER TEN

# Epilogue

THE MEN WHO FRAMED the Constitution could not see into the future. They could not predict the rise of political factions in Congress, factions that would soon coalesce into the first national party system. Indeed, at the Philadelphia convention, they had done everything in their power to prevent this. Nor could they ever have imagined that James Madison and Alexander Hamilton, the two pillars upon which the new government had been based, would become bitter political enemies, leaders of two opposing political parties. In truth, had they been asked to peer into the future, they would have been far more likely to see a civil war, dividing slave states from free, than a fierce struggle over the meaning of a republic that would culminate in the election of Thomas Jefferson in 1800. In the same manner, the men who elevated George Washington to the presidency and declared him "the Father of His Country" would never have imagined that the executive office would become more than a symbol of national unity, but the center of policy making, directing congressional action rather than simply executing it.

Washington's ability to read the future was no greater than his fellow delegates to the convention. When he took office, he believed his role in the government was exemplary rather than directive. He understood what Madison had realized sometime in early September 1787: that the president must be a symbol of national unity, the people's champion, and the country's most distinguished citizen. He must be a model of patriotism, a living example of the virtues needed in every citizen if the Republic was to survive. In eighteenth-century parlance, the president was to be a *disinterested* leader, removed from the tarnishing effects of ambition, greed, and factional wrangling, a check upon the sectional or class interests of lawmakers in the House and Senate. This was no small task—and the burden of it accounted for much of the havoc that time worked upon Washington's countenance.

Things did not turn out as the founding fathers hoped—or expected. Even before Washington's first term had ended, men like Madison and Hamilton and Jefferson realized that the executive office would play a more active role in shaping the nation's future than anyone at the convention had ever imagined. Washington had understood, as he told Madison, that every step he took would set a precedent. Yet he had not dreamed this would be true not only in the symbolic realm—in his choice to be called

"Mr. President" rather than "Your Excellency"—but also in the very tangible realm of commercial expansion and the widening embrace of the market economy and in the rising role of America in world events.

In retrospect, it seems unavoidable. For as the executive branch moved to create institutions that would assist it, and as it took action to insure it could execute the law, the influence of the presidency increased and the power of the executive expanded. Consider, for example, the establishment of the Bank of the United States in 1792. The bank was Hamilton's brainchild, an institution that combined government funds with funds from private investors, creating a much-needed capital pool for the use of American entrepreneurs. The bank achieved what Hamilton devoutly desired: it helped set the nation's course as a commercial, industrializing country. But it also demonstrated the critical role the central government could play in plotting the trajectory of the national economy. Consider as well Washington's actions in 1794, when western Pennsylvania wheat farmers and whiskey distillers resisted the government's first excise tax. Taking seriously his obligation to enforce the law, Washington used his powers as commander in chief to raise an impressive army to march against the Whiskey Rebellion. This action, undeniably effective, opened a window to the potential power of a president in times of domestic resistance to federal authority.

More than anything else, diplomacy and foreign affairs forced Washington and his contemporaries to realize the real, rather than the symbolic, role of the president. The French Revolution and the war between England and France that followed on its heels forced Washington to assert his authority as president both in negotiations with foreign powers and in persuading Congress to support those diplomatic decisions. As he worked to see the Senate ratify the Jay Treaty, which averted war with England in 1794, he abandoned that deference to the wisdom of Congress he had shown in his first inaugural address. As president, Washington came to the Senate with a demand, calling upon them to endorse his decisions rather than to make their own.

Ironically, in every instance—the creation of the Bank of the United States, the suppression of the Whiskey rebels, the Jay Treaty—Washington helped moved the nation's political culture closer to a two-party system. The unity the Federalists demonstrated in their struggle to ratify the Constitution was quickly splintered as fundamental disagreements over the national economy, the limits of the central government's authority, the degree of democracy possible within a republic, and the shape of foreign alliances emerged. The presidency was not at the center of every issue that further defined the Federalists and their opposition, the Democratic-Republicans, but it was surely at the center of many of them. By the time Washington left office in 1796, both the followers of Hamilton and Adams and those of Jefferson and Madison understood that party loyalty could be the key factor in legislation, domestic policy, and foreign affairs. By the time Jefferson took office in 1801, the president had become an advocate for a party program and a defender of its priorities—and an active player in assuring the triumph of both. Although Jefferson insisted in his inaugural speech that "we are all Federalist, we are all Republicans," political leaders knew this to be rhetoric, not reality.

As we have seen in recent times, a national crisis can momentarily revive the notion of the president as a symbol of unity, a representative of the people, and an embodiment of the virtues the citizens value. This image has been reinforced by the great sea changes in transportation, communication, and the definitions of citizenship that have occurred since the Philadelphia convention. The nineteenth-century revolutions in transportation and communication allowed candidates to mount national campaigns and led to the reform of the system for choosing electors. In state after state, legislative selection gave way to popular choice in the voting booth, making the choice of the president a more direct reflection of popular will. And as voting restrictions based on social class, race, and gender vanished in the century following the Civil War, the conviction that a president is the people's choice rings more true.

Yet the president's symbolic role can no longer overshadow the president's role as the leader of a political party and the developer of policy, both foreign and domestic. We live, after all, in the era of what the distinguished historian Arthur Schlesinger Jr. has termed the "imperial presidency," in a time when the president goes before Congress to present his agenda for the coming year, to announce the legislation he wishes the House to propose, the foreign policy he wishes the Senate to endorse. We can only imagine what the delegates to the Constitutional Convention would make of these historic changes. Surely John Dickinson would protest; no doubt James Madison would fret. And even Alexander Hamilton would be shocked. In their surprise and dismay, they would reveal themselves to be the products of a very different era.

The founding fathers did not expect their constitution to endure for centuries. They could not predict the social, economic, or technological changes produced by the generations that followed them. Perhaps their ultimate wisdom, and their ultimate achievement, was their willingness to subject the Constitution they created to amendment. With this gesture—a true leap of faith—they freed future generations from the icy grip of the past.

# The Delegates to the Constitutional Convention

## NEW HAMPSHIRE

NICHOLAS GILMAN (1755–1814) Born in Exeter, New Hampshire, Gilman was the second son of a distinguished New Hampshire merchant. When the Revolutionary War broke out, he quickly enlisted in the Continental army and rose to the rank of captain. When the war ended, he began a career in politics, serving in the Continental Congress before becoming a delegate to the Philadelphia convention. The junior member of the two-man New Hampshire delegation, thirty-two-year-old Gilman was a person of ordinary abilities, a fact that he tacitly acknowledged by keeping a respectful silence during the convention debates. He proved his value to the nationalist cause, however, during the ratification battle in his home state. Gilman became a leading Federalist, supporting his party's policies in the House of Representatives from 1789 until 1797. He sat in the New Hampshire legislature in 1795, 1802, and

1804, and held the position of state treasurer during the War of 1812. Like John Langdon, Gilman slowly shifted his political allegiance to the Jeffersonian party and was elected to the U.S. Senate under its banner in 1804.

JOHN LANGDON (1741–1819) Born in 1741 near Portsmouth, New Hampshire, Langdon was forty-six when he attended the convention. A large, handsome man whose family had deep roots in New England, Langdon's natural talent for business earned him the nickname "the Robert Morris of New England" and more than compensated for his lack of formal education. He was an early and ardent supporter of the Revolution and risked his considerable fortune by financing American privateers during the war. Fortunately, the gamble proved profitable as well as patriotic. Langdon had extensive political experience before coming to the Philadelphia convention, serving in the Continental Congress, the New Hampshire State Senate, and as governor of his state. Always a generous patriot, Langdon covered the full expenses of the New Hampshire delegation to the Constitutional Convention. Although he and his fellow delegate, Nicholas Gilman, did not arrive in Philadelphia until mid-July, the confident Langdon joined the debates with gusto. A committed nationalist, Langdon consistently favored practical solutions to any problem that arose. John Langdon served in the U.S. Senate from 1789 to 1801. During these years Langdon gradually shifted his political loyalties, abandoning the Federalist Party for Thomas Jefferson's Democratic-Republicans. He ended his political career as governor of New Hampshire, holding that office from 1805 to 1809 and again from 1810 to 1812.

## MASSACHUSETTS

ELBRIDGE GERRY (1744–1814) Small, thin, with a hawklike nose and a squint in his eye, this Marblehead native was the third of twelve children of a wealthy merchant-shipper. When Gerry graduated from Harvard College, he joined his father and his brothers in the family export business. Despite a slight stutter, Gerry entered politics in 1772 and, as a protégé of Samuel Adams, became an outspoken advocate of independence. In 1776 Gerry became a member of the Continental Congress, where he focused his attention on military and financial matters. His steady call for better pay and equipment for the Continental troops earned him the name "Soldiers' Friend." Although he sat in the Confederation Congress from 1783 to 1785, Gerry found himself less suited to governing than to agitating for revolution. Dour, suspicious, and aggressive, Gerry made many enemies during his political career, but even his foes conceded that he was politically shrewd and clever. At the convention Gerry managed to antagonize almost everyone with his unpredictable stances on key issues. Although he began the convention as an advocate of a strong central government, he ultimately refused to sign the Constitution that it produced and worked against ratification in his home state. In 1789, however, he declared himself a supporter of the new government and was elected to the first Congress. Here he became a strong advocate of Federalist policies. By 1789 Gerry had shifted political loyalties once again. After several failures to win the governorship of his home state, Gerry at last took that office in 1810. When the Democratic-Republicans attempted to hold on to political power in Massachusetts by redistricting measures, Gerry's Federalist opponents coined the phrase "gerrymandering" to describe this political ploy. Nearly seventy years old, Gerry nevertheless agreed to serve as James Madison's vice president in 1813, the last political office of his long and stormy career.

NATHANIEL GORHAM (1738–1796) As affable as Gerry was cantankerous, Gorham was the son of an old Charlestown family of modest means. With little formal education, Gorham managed to establish a successful mercantile career. Although he was never fashionably dressed and was a poor speaker, Gorham's patriotism earned him political office. He served in the Massachusetts provincial congress in the years immediately before independence and was a member of the state's Board of War throughout much of the Revolution. He was a man of good sense though no particular genius, but he spoke often at the Constitutional Convention and served as chairman of the committee of the whole and on the influential Committee of Detail. A disastrous venture into land speculation kept Gorham out of political life for several years after the Constitution was adopted. He died in debt, a pariah to the Boston elite society in which he had once claimed membership.

RUFUS KING (1755–1827) Tall, handsome, with a disarmingly sweet speaking voice, King was born in a small frontier town in what later became the state of Maine. He was the eldest son of a prosperous farmer-merchant and thus received a good education, graduating from Harvard in 1777. He took up a career in law, but his impressive oratorical skills soon led him into politics. He served in the Massachusetts legislature from 1783 to 1785 and then in the Confederation Congress, where he gained a reputation as a brilliant speaker and an early opponent of slavery. King was only thirty-two when he joined the Massachusetts delegation to the Philadelphia convention, but his youthfulness did not deter him from taking an active role in the debates. He was a leading figure in the nationalist caucus and served on the Committee on Postponed Matters and the Committee on Style. Soon after the convention, King abandoned his legal practice and moved to New York. He was appointed one of that state's first U.S. senators and in Congress proved a strong supporter of Alexander Hamilton's fiscal policies. In 1796 King was appointed minister to Great Britain, a post he held until 1803. Despite the ascendancy of the Jeffersonian party, the Democratic-Republicans, Rufus King remained a staunch Federalist and was chosen as that party's presidential candidate in 1816. Throughout his long career in Congress, King remained a vocal critic of slavery, and in 1820 he denounced the Missouri Compromise. When he retired from the Senate in 1825, President John Quincy Adams persuaded him to serve once again as minister to Great Britain. However, illness forced him to return to New York and he died soon afterward.

CALEB STRONG (1745–1819) A self-made man of solid abilities, the tall, angular Strong was a Harvard-educated lawyer. He had established a thriving country law practice when he was called upon to serve as a delegate to the Philadelphia convention. He had been an active patriot during the war years, serving on the Northampton Committee of Safety and in the Massachusetts assembly. He was a strong nationalist who was responsible for the decision to give the House of Representatives the sole power to originate money bills. An illness in his family forced him to return home before the convention adjourned, and he thus was unable to sign the Constitution. He helped lead the fight for its ratification in Massachusetts, however. Strong was one of his state's first U.S. senators and a loyal Federalist throughout his term in office. In 1800 he defeated the unpopular Elbridge Gerry for governor and remained in that office for seven years, despite the growing strength of the Jeffersonians in his state. He was elected to that office once again in 1812 and remained governor until 1816 despite his open opposition to the War of 1812.

## CONNECTICUT

OLIVER ELLSWORTH (1745–1807) At forty-two, Connecticut delegate Oliver Ellsworth had a solid reputation as a shrewd, able, well-educated lawyer, a fine debater, and an eloquent speaker. His thick brows and broad forehead gave him a dramatic appearance, but his notorious stinginess gave him a reputation as a poor social companion. He was born in Windsor, Connecticut, and attended Yale College and the College of New Jersey (which became Princeton University). He built a prosperous law practice in his native Connecticut, earning him an appointment as state attorney for Hartford County in 1777. That same year he was chosen to serve in the Continental Congress. During the war years, he supervised his home state's military expenditures and took a seat on Connecticut's Council of Safety. At the Constitutional Convention, Ellsworth was a powerful voice during the debate on the Great Compromise. On his recommendation, the term "United States" replaced "national" as the title of the proposed new government. Like several other delegates, Ellsworth left the convention early and did not sign the final draft of the Constitution. Nevertheless, he played an active role in seeing the Constitution ratified in his home state, writing the influential *Letters of a Landholder* in support of the new government. Oliver Ellsworth served as one of Connecticut's first senators, holding that office from 1789 to 1796. In the spring of 1796, he was named chief justice of the Supreme Court. In 1799 and 1800, he served as a commissioner to France. When he returned to America, he retired from politics, settling in his hometown of Windsor.

WILLIAM SAMUEL JOHNSON (1727–1819) Sixty years old when he served as a delegate to the Philadelphia convention, Johnson had already amassed an impressive number of academic degrees. Dr. Johnson, as he was respectfully called, came from a scholarly family; his father was the first president of King's College (later Columbia University) and a well-known Anglican clergyman and philosopher. Johnson graduated from Yale in 1744 and then went on to earn his master's degree at Harvard. Later he would receive honorary degrees from Oxford University. He took up a career in law after leaving Harvard and was an immediate success. He moved quickly into politics, serving in Connecticut's colonial assembly and its council. When the Revolution came, however, Johnson's loyalties were divided. He believed most of Britain's policies in the 1760s and 1770s to be unwise, but he had strong personal ties to England and a strong association with the Anglican Church. As tensions increased, Johnson attempted to remain neutral and to work for a peaceful settlement of differences. He was briefly arrested in 1779 by the Revolutionaries, but when the war ended, he was welcomed back into the state's political arena. He served in the Confederation Congress and played a major role at the Philadelphia convention as an advocate of the Connecticut Compromise. With Ellsworth, he was appointed to the first Senate by Connecticut. He abandoned politics in 1791 to devote his considerable energies to the presidency of Columbia College.

ROGER SHERMAN (1721–1793) Tall and awkward, Sherman provided a striking contrast to the suave Dr. Johnson at the Connecticut delegates' table. The ungainly Sherman was an autodidact who devoured books in what spare time he could eke out while doing farm chores and learning the cobbler's trade from his father. Although he was born in Massachusetts, he moved to Connecticut as a young man following his father's death. There he purchased a store, learned surveying, and won appointment to a number of local offices. With no formal education, Sherman managed nevertheless to pass the bar in 1754 and establish a reputation as a distinguished jurist and political leader. His skills in political debate and his shrewdness in political negotiations were well-known by the time he came to the Philadelphia convention. Despite his constant political duties before the Revolution, Sherman was able to publish an essay on monetary theory and a series of almanacs containing his own astronomical observations and his own poetry. In 1761 Sherman gave up his legal practice and returned to shopkeeping. He did not give up politics, however. He served in the Continental Congress and was on the committees that drafted both the Declaration of Independence and the Articles of Confederation. Although his finances were failing, Sherman agreed to take time away from his business interests to serve at the Philadelphia convention. He was one of the prime spokesmen for the interests of the smaller states and played a critical role in creating the Connecticut Compromise. A solid supporter of the Constitution, Roger Sherman served in the first House of Representatives and later in the Senate. He remained a Federalist throughout his life.

## NEW YORK

ALEXANDER HAMILTON (1755–1804) A genuine American rags-to-riches story, Hamilton's life began on the tiny island of Nevis, where he was born the illegitimate son of a Scottish merchant and an English-French Huguenot mother, and it ended with the largest funeral honoring a distinguished New Yorker ever held in that state. Brilliant, ambitious, and fortunate in his ability to find powerful mentors, Hamilton came to America just as the Revolutionary crisis was beginning. He quickly emerged as a leader of the independence movement in New York, and when war broke out, his skill as an artillery captain caught the attention of General George Washington, who invited the young officer to join his "family" as an aide-de-camp. Marriage to the daughter of one of New York's leading landholders, combined with the devotion of Washington, secured Hamilton a place in the top echelons of society. But it was his genius and his legal talents as much as his charm and connections that made him welcome. A dedicated nationalist from the start, it was Hamilton who orchestrated the groundswell for a Constitutional Convention. Hampered by his state's antinationalist delegation, he took a backseat to Madison and Morris at the convention but was critical in securing New York's ratification afterward. He was an author, with James Madison and John Jay, of the influential *Federalist Papers* and was chosen to serve as the nation's first secretary of the treasury. It was his plans for fiscal responsibility—including funding the debt and the creation of the Bank of the United States—that set the country on the path of remarkable economic growth. Hamilton's support for a commercial and industrial economy clashed with Jefferson and Madison's vision of a primarily agrarian society, and as the Jeffersonian party gained power, Hamilton confined his influence to New York. In 1804, at the age of forty-nine, Hamilton was killed in a duel with longtime political enemy, Aaron Burr. At his funeral New York City's financial, political, and educational leaders as well as former Continental army officers joined scores of other mourners honoring a man they considered the driving force behind a strong new nation.

JOHN LANSING JR. (1754–1829) Born in Albany, New York, this wealthy landowner and lawyer served as military secretary to General Philip Schuyler during the Revolutionary War. When his military service ended, Lansing turned to politics and served six terms in the New York assembly, eventually becoming the speaker of that assembly. For two years he was a delegate to the Confederation Congress before leaving that body to serve as Albany's mayor from 1786 to 1790. A staunch supporter of Governor George Clinton, to whom he owed much of his political success, Lansing went to the Philadelphia convention suspicious that it might go beyond simply amending the Articles of Confederation and concerned that it might produce a challenge to New York's autonomy. After only six weeks, both Lansing and fellow Clinton supporter, Robert Yates, left the convention in protest against its obvious intention to consolidate the United States under one powerful central government. At the New York ratifying convention, Lansing was a vocal opponent of the Constitution. After ratification Lansing confined his political career to his home state, serving for eleven years on the supreme court of New York and from 1798 to 1801 as its chief justice. From 1801 to 1814 Lansing served as chancellor of the state, and in 1817 he became a regent of the University of the State of New York. He died mysteriously, disappearing without a trace during a visit to New York City.

ROBERT YATES (1738–1801) A native of Schenectady, New York, Yates was a well-educated lawyer considered by many to be a vain and pompous man. After admission to the bar, Yates moved to Albany, where he became immediately involved in local politics. A strong supporter of independence, he served on the Albany Committee of Safety and in the provincial congress. He played a key role in drafting the first constitution for New York State. By 1777 Yates was a member of the New York Supreme Court and presided over the court as chief justice throughout the 1790s. A determined opponent of the Constitution, Yates left the Philadelphia convention in protest. With his fellow delegate John Lansing Jr. he wrote a joint letter to Governor Clinton that detailed the dangers of a centralized government and the illegitimacy of the Constitutional Convention. He worked vigorously against ratification when the state convention met, writing a series of letters, signed "Brutus" and "Sydney," that criticized the Constitution. Like Madison and Hamilton, Yates took personal notes at the convention, and in 1821 these were published as the *Secret Proceedings and Debates of the Convention Assembled...for the Purpose of Forming the Constitution of the United States*.

## New Jersey

David Brearly (1745–1790) Born near Trenton, Brearly attended the College of New Jersey (later Princeton) and then took up a career as a lawyer. He was an avid patriot, arrested by the British for high treason but rescued by a band of Revolutionaries. He was a member of the New Jersey convention that drew up the first state constitution, and during the war he rose from the rank of captain to colonel in the New Jersey militia. He was an active member of the controversial Society of the Cincinnati, although his greatest organizational commitment appeared to be his Masonic Lodge and the Episcopal Church. When he came to the Philadelphia convention he was only forty-two but already the chief justice of his state's supreme court. Elegantly dressed, his wig carefully coiffed, Brearly seemed content to take a backseat to the delegation's acknowledged leader, William Paterson. He took a leadership role at the ratification convention, however, presiding over its deliberations. President Washington appointed him a federal judge in 1789, and he remained on the bench until his death.

Jonathan Dayton (1760–1824) Only twenty-seven when he took his seat, Dayton was one of the youngest delegates at the Philadelphia convention. He was born in Elizabethtown, where his father, a local storekeeper, was active in local and state politics. Dayton graduated from the College of New Jersey in 1776 and immediately enlisted in the Continental army. During his military career he saw considerable action and apparently acquitted himself well, rising to the rank of captain by the age of nineteen. He was briefly a prisoner of war. When peace came Dayton returned to New Jersey and took up the practice of law. He sat on the New Jersey assembly for one year, from 1786 to 1787. He arrived late to the Constitutional Convention and entered into several of the debates—revealing in the process a hasty temper and a noticeable lack of political experience. Although he objected to some of its provisions, he signed the Constitution. When the new national government was established, Dayton became a leading Federalist, serving in the House of Representatives from 1791 to 1799. He proved a strong supporter of Hamilton's fiscal policies as well as the controversial Jay Treaty with England. In 1806, however, Dayton narrowly escaped participation in Aaron Burr's illicit expedition to conquer Spanish territory in the Southwest and establish an independent empire. Although illness kept him at home while Burr's forces made their abortive conquest attempt, Dayton was indicted for treason. He was not prosecuted, but his national career was ruined. He remained in state politics, holding local offices and serving briefly in the assembly.

WILLIAM CHURCHILL HOUSTON (c. 1746–1788) A graduate of the College of New Jersey, Houston was one of the few professional educators at the Philadelphia convention. He served as master of his alma mater's college grammar school and in 1771 was appointed professor of mathematics and natural philosophy. In 1775 Houston became deputy secretary of the Continental Congress but joined the military once independence was declared. He was a captain in the Somerset County militia and saw combat at Princeton. He served in his state assembly during the war and on its Council of Safety. By 1779 he was back in the Continental Congress. Despite his political activities, Houston found time to study law and was admitted to the bar in 1781. His legal practice ultimately led him to resign from his academic position at the College of New Jersey. Houston was a New Jersey delegate at both the Annapolis and the Philadelphia conventions. His participation at the latter convention was brief since illness forced him to go home after only a week. The following year he died of tuberculosis.

WILLIAM LIVINGSTON (1723–1790) At sixty-four, Livingston was one of the oldest men at the convention. Tall and reedlike, the son of a distinguished landholding family from New York's Hudson Valley, Livingston was known to friends and enemies alike as the "Whipping Post." Livingston rejected his family's suggestion that he take up life as a fur trader or a New York City merchant, becoming a lawyer instead. Despite his aristocratic background, Livingston was a defender of popular causes in his native New York and an antiestablishment crusader during the 1750s. When the liberal faction he belonged to split over the Stamp Act in 1760, Livingston pulled up stakes and moved to New Jersey, where he built an elegant estate, Liberty Hall, and retired from public life to write poetry and live as a gentleman farmer. The Revolution ended Livingston's seclusion. He served in both the First and the Second Continental Congresses, and when war began he became a brigadier general in the New Jersey militia. In 1776 he was elected the first governor of the state of New Jersey, a post he held for fourteen consecutive years. His duties as governor prevented him from attending every session of the Philadelphia convention, and he missed several weeks of debate in July. He was a supporter of the New Jersey Plan but worked tirelessly for ratification of the Constitution in its final form. Despite his many political commitments, Livingston managed to conduct agricultural experiments and to work in the antislavery movement.

WILLIAM PATERSON (1745–1806) Paterson was born in Ireland, but his family immigrated to America when he was only two years old, settling first in Connecticut and later in Trenton, New Jersey. The family prospered and Paterson was able to attend the College of New Jersey. After receiving his master's degree, he took up the practice of law. During the war he served in the provincial congress, the state constitutional convention, and New Jersey's legislative council. From 1776 to 1783, he was the state attorney general. After the death of his wife in 1783, Paterson retired from politics and devoted his energies to his legal practice. His selection as a delegate to the Philadelphia convention revived his political career. The five feet two inch Paterson—fastidious in his dress, mild-mannered, and modest in his demeanor—played a central role in the Constitutional Convention as the author of the New Jersey Plan. Although he left the convention after the issue of representation in the Senate was resolved, he returned to sign the Constitution. Paterson was a member of the first U.S. Senate and later governor of his state. From 1793 to 1806, he served as an associate justice of the U.S. Supreme Court.

## PENNSYLVANIA

GEORGE CLYMER (1739–1813) Clymer became an orphan within a year of his birth but had the good fortune to be taken in by a wealthy uncle. He was made a partner in his uncle's mercantile firm and eventually became its sole proprietor. His wealth increased when he merged his business with another prosperous mercantile family. British economic restrictions on his business made Clymer an early advocate of independence.

He led the opposition to the Tea Act in Philadelphia, and when war came he personally underwrote the war by trading his specie for unstable continental currency. Quiet and unassuming, Clymer served in the Continental Congress without often entering into debate or discussion, but he willingly served on several key committees. When Congress fled Philadelphia in December 1776, he risked his life by remaining behind to carry on vital congressional business. British troops ransacked his home in Chester County, causing his wife and children to flee to the safety of nearby woods. After the war Clymer served in the Pennsylvania legislature, where he advocated replacing the unicameral legislature with a two-house system. At the Philadelphia convention, he behaved true to his character, speaking rarely but attending conscientiously. When the new national government was established, Clymer served in the House of Representatives. In addition to political activities, he became involved in scientific and cultural improvements, including the Philadelphia Society for Promoting Agriculture and the Pennsylvania Academy of Fine Arts.

THOMAS FITZSIMONS (1741–1811) Like William Paterson, Fitzsimons was born in Ireland, coming to America in his late teens or early twenties. He became a successful merchant in Philadelphia, marrying the daughter of a prominent businessman and going into partnership with one of her brothers. Fitzsimons was an enthusiastic supporter of independence, and during the war he commanded a militia company. His firm helped supply the military and made a sizable donation to the Continental army. Fitzsimons began his political career in the Continental Congress. Although he was a strong nationalist, he said little at the Philadelphia convention. He served three terms in the House of Representatives, beginning in 1789, and was a strong supporter of Hamilton's policies. After 1795 Fitzsimons returned to private life, concentrating his energies in his mercantile business. Yet he remained a staunch Federalist and opposed Jefferson's Embargo Act in 1807. Although he had been one of the founders of the Bank of North America and a director of the Insurance Company of North America, he was not immune to financial ruin, suffering a setback in 1805. Despite the fluctuations in his fortunes, Fitzsimons was a steady contributor to his local Roman Catholic Church, a supporter of public education, and a trustee of the University of Pennsylvania.

BENJAMIN FRANKLIN (1706–1790) The tenth son of a soap and candlemaker, Franklin, like Alexander Hamilton, stands as an example of the rags-to-riches story. Apprenticed first to his father and later to his half-brother, the printer James Franklin, he demonstrated his literary talents early by publishing anonymous essays in James's newspaper while he was still a teenaged boy. In 1723 Franklin moved to Philadelphia, where, after a two-year hiatus in London, he began a successful career as a printer. His *Poor Richard's Almanack* gained him fame at home and abroad. A man of Renaissance interests, Franklin was an educational reformer, a philanthropist, and a scientist. His political career was long and distinguished, beginning in the 1750s when he served as a member of the colonial legislature and deputy postmaster of the colonies. He lived in England for much of the period from 1757 to the outbreak of the Revolutionary War, acting as the colonial agent of his own Pennsylvania and several other colonies. He became well-known during the decade of increasing tensions leading to the Revolution, defending the American position on taxation before the House of Commons. Franklin served in the Continental Congress and was one of the members of the committee that drafted the Declaration of Independence. He was chosen to preside over the Pennsylvania constitutional convention as well. During the war Franklin's diplomatic career in France and at the Paris peace treaty negotiations made him the toast of Paris. Dr. Franklin, as he was known, returned to Pennsylvania in 1785 to serve as president of the Supreme Executive Council of his state. By the time of the Philadelphia convention, Franklin was plagued by ill health, but he attended faithfully, expressed his views on a number of key issues, provided expert advice to the nationalist leadership, and was a firm defender of the proposed Constitution. Despite his age and failing health, in 1787 Franklin accepted the position as first president of the Pennsylvania Society for Promoting the Abolition of Slavery. He died three years later, still active in civic affairs.

JARED INGERSOLL (1749–1822) Ingersoll was born in Connecticut, where his father was a British colonial official and a prominent Loyalist. He received an excellent education, graduating from Yale in 1766. After graduation he joined his father in Philadelphia to establish a legal practice. In the early years of the war, Ingersoll avoided any political commitments by studying law in London and touring Europe. When he returned to Philadelphia, his politics were decidedly more favorable toward American independence, and in 1780 he served in the Continental Congress. At the Philadelphia convention, Ingersoll was unusually silent despite his skills at debate and his long-standing conviction that the Articles of Confederation were inadequate. After the convention Ingersoll held a number of local positions, serving as attorney general of Pennsylvania and Philadelphia city solicitor and presiding judge of the Philadelphia District Court. He remained a loyal Federalist and in 1812 ran as his party's vice presidential candidate.

THOMAS MIFFLIN (1744–1800) The son of a wealthy Quaker merchant, Mifflin was educated in Quaker schools and later received a diploma from the College of Philadelphia (which became part of the University of Pennsylvania) at the age of sixteen. Mifflin became a highly successful Philadelphia merchant but turned his attention to politics by the early 1770s. He was a champion of the American cause in the Pennsylvania legislature and served as a delegate to the Continental Congress from 1774 to 1776. As war approached he helped raise troops and was appointed a major in the Continental army. His military service led to his expulsion by the Quaker Church. Mifflin served as one of the earliest aides-de-camp for General Washington and later held the post of quartermaster general. Mifflin's relationship with George Washington became strained, due in part to his preference for battle rather than his assigned quartermaster duties, but largely because of his participation in the cabal to replace Washington as commander in chief with General Horatio Gates. Mifflin left the military with the rank of major general, and by 1778 he was once again active in Pennsylvania politics. He served in the state assembly and then took a seat in the Continental Congress, where he became presiding officer in 1783. Mifflin, like Ingersoll, played no significant role at the Philadelphia convention. After the convention he returned to state government, chairing Pennsylvania's constitutional convention in 1789 and serving as state governor from 1790 to 1799. By the 1790s Thomas Mifflin had moved into the emerging Democratic-Republican political camp. Despite his financial successes, Mifflin's lavish lifestyle brought him to ruin. He died pursued by creditors and was buried at the state's expense.

GOUVERNEUR MORRIS (1752–1816) Born to wealth and privilege on his family's impressive Morrisania estate in New York, Morris was educated first by private tutors and then by the faculty of King's College (later Columbia University). As a young man, Morris lost his leg in a freak carriage accident, but this did not appear to diminish his very active engagement with women. He trained as a lawyer but entered politics as the movement for independence gained ground. A social conservative, he nevertheless joined the patriots' camp and served in New York's Revolutionary provincial congress. Despite his wooden leg, Morris served in the militia as well. Acknowledged as a brilliant stylist, he was appointed to the committee that drafted New York's first constitution. In the late 1770s, Morris served in the Continental Congress, where he was one of the youngest and most intellectually impressive of the delegates. When Governor George Clinton's party defeated him in his bid for reelection to Congress, Morris moved to Philadelphia and opened a legal practice. By 1781 he was once again involved in public service, working as an assistant to the superintendent of finance for the United States during the Revolution. Gouverneur Morris was one of the leading figures at the Philadelphia convention, speaking more often than any other delegate, his analytical powers leavened by his keen satiric sense. His nationalism was strengthened by his experiences working with Robert Morris and his conviction that a strong central government and a sound fiscal policy were essential to the survival of the country. It was Morris who produced the final draft of the Constitution. After the convention he returned to private life, took possession of the family estate at Morrisania, and settled once again in New York. A man of broad-ranging intellectual and cultural interests, Morris spent many of the years after the Philadelphia convention abroad. He was in France as that nation's revolution began, and in 1792 President Washington asked him to take over the duties of minister to that nation from Thomas Jefferson. An ardent Federalist until his death, Morris once again retired from politics when the Jeffersonian party began to dominate the national political scene. In his last years, he became a vocal critic of the Democratic-Republicans and of the War of 1812.

ROBERT MORRIS (1734–1806) Robert Morris (no relation to Gouverneur Morris) was born near Liverpool, England, but immigrated to Maryland with his father when he was thirteen years old. Moving to Philadelphia, Morris joined a shipping-banking firm and soon became a partner. His commitment to independence grew slowly after the Stamp Act crisis, but by 1775 he was a strong critic of British policies. He entered politics after his firm began to supply the Continental army with arms and ammunition, serving in the provincial assembly, the state legislature, and the Continental Congress during the early years of the war. When the vote for independence came, however, he voted against it, declaring it was premature. Despite his views, Morris continued to assist the Continental army procure what it required. His efforts earned him the suspicions of others that he was profiteering; though he was cleared of charges, his reputation was marred. In 1781 Morris made a complete commitment to independence by accepting the office of superintendent of finance for the Confederation government. He was generally credited with keeping the nation afloat fiscally during this era. Convinced that the nation needed a stronger central government and firm regulation of its interstate commerce, Morris attended the Annapolis convention and the following year served as a delegate to the Philadelphia convention. He spoke only twice during the entire convention and did not do service on any of the convention's many committees. He did serve in the first U.S. Senate, however. Morris's personal finances were faltering when the Philadelphia convention met, and his circumstances grew more precarious in the years that followed. He speculated wildly, overextending his credit to purchase western lands, and soon had to flee his Philadelphia creditors. He was arrested for debt in 1798, thrown into debtors' prison, and not released until 1801. His last years were spent in poverty and depression, supported by an annuity obtained for his wife by the generous Gouverneur Morris.

JAMES WILSON (1742–1798) Scottish by birth, Wilson received an excellent education at the universities of St. Andrews, Glasgow, and Edinburgh. He immigrated to America just as the Stamp Act protests were beginning in 1765. His first position was as a Latin tutor at the College of Philadelphia, but he soon gave up teaching for a career in law. He earned a reputation as one of the ablest lawyers in the country and became a leading advocate of American independence. He was a man who elicited respect rather than affection, appearing stern and forbidding to most who met him. Having set up a law practice in western Pennsylvania, Wilson became a political leader in his county. He served in the first provincial assembly, distinguishing himself by writing a tract on the issue of parliamentary authority in the colonies. By 1774 he was in the Continental Congress, and he signed the Declaration of Independence. In most regards, Wilson was a conservative and he opposed the liberal constitution first adopted by Pennsylvania. Popular opposition to his views only hardened them, and his ties with the state's leading aristocratic and conservative political figures increased. With Robert Morris, Wilson served as one of the directors of the Bank of North America. Wilson was an indisputable leader of the nationalist forces at the Philadelphia convention, second only to Madison in his role in crafting the new government. He led the battle for ratification in Pennsylvania and was the architect of the new, more conservative constitution drafted for Pennsylvania in 1789–90. He was disappointed when President Washington did not appoint him chief justice of the Supreme Court but accepted a position on that bench as an associate justice. A student of the law as well as a practitioner, Wilson welcomed an appointment in 1789 as the first law professor at the College of Philadelphia, and he soon began to compile an official digest of the laws of Pennsylvania. Despite his recognized brilliance and his erudition, Wilson did not distinguish himself on the Supreme Court, perhaps because he mixed business interests with his duties. He barely escaped impeachment when he tried to influence legislation in his home state that would favor land speculators like himself. Wilson suffered from the same compulsive speculative behavior as his friend Bob Morris, and, like Morris, he wound up fleeing creditors. Fearing imprisonment, he moved to New Jersey. Suffering from extreme anxiety over his circumstances, Wilson collapsed at the home of a friend in North Carolina and died there in 1798.

## DELAWARE

RICHARD BASSETT (1745–1815) Bassett was born in Maryland, the son of a tavern keeper who deserted his wife and family and left them destitute. Bassett was fortunate to be taken in by a wealthy relative from whom he inherited an estate. After passing the bar, Bassett moved to Delaware, where he succeeded both as a lawyer and a planter. Thus, despite his stormy childhood, Bassett rose to wealth and social status, the owner of not one but three elegant estates in Maryland and Delaware. During the Revolution he served in the military as a captain of a state cavalry unit. Entering politics, he served as a delegate to Delaware's constitutional convention and enjoyed terms in both houses of his state legislature. His nationalist leanings led him to attend the Annapolis convention in 1786. At the Philadelphia convention, he was virtually invisible, saying nothing and serving on no committees. Yet after the Constitution was adopted, Bassett's political career blossomed. He served in the U.S. Senate from 1789 to 1793, and from 1793 to 1799 he was chief justice of the court of common pleas. He was a loyal Federalist, despite his opposition to Hamilton's plan for the federal government to assume state debts, and a supporter of John Adams for the presidency. He became governor of Delaware in 1799 and only left this post in order to accept appointment as one of John Adams's last-minute appointees to the U.S. Circuit Court. When the Jeffersonians abolished his judgeship, he retired from public office.

GUNNING BEDFORD JR. (1747–1812) An imposing man in both heft and stature, Bedford came from a distinguished family with roots in Virginia and Delaware. An honors graduate of the College of New Jersey (later Princeton), Bedford was a classmate of another convention delegate, James Madison. After studying law Bedford moved first to Dover and then to Wilmington, where he rose quickly in local and state politics. He sat in the state legislature, on the state council, and in the Continental Congress. For much of the 1780s, he was Delaware's attorney general. At the Philadelphia convention, Bedford frequently took the floor during debate, usually to champion the interests of the smaller states. Sociable and good-natured, Bedford was well liked by most members of the convention. In 1789 President Washington appointed Bedford to the federal district court of Delaware, an office he held for the remainder of his life. After his appointment to the court, Bedford abandoned politics, preferring philanthropy, working for the abolition of slavery, and living the life of the gentleman farmer. Never self-conscious about his obesity, Bedford would probably not have minded his epitaph, which read "his form was goodly."

JACOB BROOM (1752–1810) The oldest son of a blacksmith turned farmer, Broom began as a farmer and a surveyor but soon developed a prosperous career as a shipper, importer, and real estate speculator. He played no active role in the Revolution, seemingly content to serve in local Wilmington government throughout the 1770s. He sat in the state legislature from 1784 to 1786 and again in 1788. Although he was chosen as a delegate to the Annapolis convention, he did not attend. At the Philadelphia convention, he was especially conscientious, never missing a session, but he played a minor role in the deliberations. When the convention ended, Broom returned to local Wilmington politics and to a position as chair of the board of directors of that city's Delaware Bank. He was a vocal supporter of internal improvements, endorsing the construction of more toll roads, canals, and bridges, but his primary enthusiasm seemed reserved for local philanthropic and religious activities.

JOHN DICKINSON (1732–1808) Dickinson was born in Maryland, the son of a prosperous farmer who moved his family to Delaware while Dickinson was still a boy. He was educated by private tutors and then studied law in Philadelphia and London. Brilliant and talented, he moved quickly into politics, serving in both the Delaware and the Pennsylvania colonial assemblies during the 1760s. A conservative, he was often pitted against Benjamin Franklin in political battles between Pennsylvania proprietor interests and the popular faction. When tensions began to develop between England and the colonies, Dickinson defended colonial interests in the pamphlet wars of the 1760s and 1770s. His *Letters from a Farmer in Pennsylvania*, critical of British policy but urging a peaceful resolution to the conflict, earned him the nickname "Penman of the Revolution." His support for the colonial cause was undercut by his resentment of the radicalism of New England's political leadership, and he continued to work for a peaceful solution to the political problems despite increasing support among others for independence. In the Continental Congress, Dickinson voted against the Declaration of Independence, but as soon as it passed, he enlisted in the military. He refused to serve in Congress as a representative of Delaware and resigned his seat in the Pennsylvania assembly, retiring from politics for several years. In 1779 he returned to the Continental Congress, where he signed the much-revised version of the Articles of Confederation he had drafted in 1776. He continued to move back and forth between the political worlds of Delaware and Pennsylvania, serving as president of Delaware's Supreme Executive Council in 1781 and president of Pennsylvania the following year. A nationalist, he chaired the Annapolis convention. Throughout the Constitutional Convention, Dickinson was plagued by illness; at fifty-four, he looked far older, an emaciated figure, usually dressed in black. Despite his failing health, Dickinson took an active and influential role in the Philadelphia convention, helping to put the Great Compromise in place. He was forced to leave the convention before its work was ended and was not present to sign the Constitution, which he had played a vital role in creating. After the convention Dickinson devoted his energies to writing about politics rather than participating in them.

GEORGE READ (1733–1798) Born in Maryland, Read grew up in Delaware, the son of a wealthy landholder. He received a good education and, like so many of the convention delegates, took up the practice of law. His successful practice included both a Delaware and Maryland clientele. By the 1760s Read had entered local politics, serving as the Crown's attorney general in Delaware, but following the Stamp Act, he abandoned royal appointment for a seat in the colonial legislature. Moderate by nature, he supported nonimportation and protests that he considered dignified rather than rowdy. He took a seat in the Continental Congress but attended only sporadically. Like his friend John Dickinson, Read voted against independence although he eventually signed the Declaration. Once the war began, he concentrated on state rather than national politics until poor health forced him to retire from politics altogether in 1779. He returned to public life in 1782 and in 1786 attended the Annapolis convention. At the Philadelphia convention, Read championed the interests of small states, but he proved less effective than other small-state champions because he was a poor speaker. He led the ratification movement in Delaware and was rewarded with a seat in the first U.S. Senate. He resigned from national office to accept the post of chief justice of Delaware and remained on that bench until his death.

## MARYLAND

DANIEL CARROLL (1730–1796) Carroll was born into a prominent Irish Catholic family of Maryland. He received an excellent parochial education, studying for six years under the Jesuits in Flanders. After touring Europe he returned to his home colony but took no active role in public life until 1781. In that year he was elected to the Continental Congress. Soon after he began a lifelong career in the Maryland Senate. Carroll did not take his seat at the Philadelphia convention until July 9, but he attended regularly after that, took the floor to speak on several occasions, and served on the influential Committee on Postponed Matters. Carroll won a seat in the first U.S. House of Representatives, where he voted for most Federalist measures. In 1791 his friend George Washington named him to the commission to survey and define the District of Columbia, an area in which Carroll held extensive land. Bad health forced him to resign from this post after four years, and he died soon afterward.

DANIEL OF ST. THOMAS JENIFER (1723–1790) A man of consistent good humor, Jenifer inherited a large estate near Annapolis, where he lived in comfortable bachelorhood for the rest of his life. As a young man, Jenifer held a variety of appointive offices for the proprietors of Maryland. During the early 1770s, he served in the royal governor's council. Despite his long association with the proprietors and the Crown, Jenifer supported the independence movement. He served as president of the first state senate of Maryland, and he sat in the Continental Congress from 1778 to 1782. A strong nationalist, he was an early supporter of granting the power to tax to the central government. He attended the Mount Vernon conference as well as the Philadelphia convention. Although he rarely spoke at the Constitutional Convention, he supported Madison on almost every occasion. After the convention Jenifer retired from public office.

LUTHER MARTIN (1748–1826) One of the most controversial figures at the Philadelphia convention, Martin was a complex and tragic figure. He graduated with honors from the College of New Jersey, taught school in Maryland for a few years, and then studied law in Virginia before making his home in Maryland. He was an early advocate of independence and served on several patriotic committees before the war began. He was highly successful as a lawyer and was named attorney general of Maryland before he was thirty. He was known for his generosity to poorer clients, but also for his rudeness toward men of his own social class. He became increasingly eccentric, however, sometimes appearing disheveled and often appearing drunk in public. At the Philadelphia convention, Martin was an immediate and consistent opponent of the Constitution, voting against the Virginia Plan and questioning the decision that the convention's meetings be held in secret. When he took the floor to speak, he often engaged in loud and long harangues, delivering a three-hour speech at a crucial moment in the debates over representation. He eventually walked out of the convention before it adjourned, joined by fellow delegate John Francis Mercer. During the ratification struggle, Martin campaigned vigorously against the adoption of the Constitution, opposing the increased power of the central government over the states, proportional representation in the House, the inclusion of slaves in determining state populations, and the absence of a jury in Supreme Court deliberations. His criticisms reflected the fundamental Anti-Federalist position. Yet by 1791 Martin had joined the Federalist camp, driven there by his hatred of Thomas Jefferson. Throughout the rest of his career, Martin did not flinch from taking on controversial legal cases. He successfully defended his friend Supreme Court Justice Samuel Chase when Chase was impeached, and he served as a defense lawyer for Aaron Burr when Burr was on trial for treason in 1807. A brilliant lawyer, Martin argued Maryland's position in the landmark Supreme Court case *McCulloch v. Maryland.* In his last years, however, heavy drinking and illness diminished Martin's fortune and his reputation. He suffered a paralysis in 1819 that forced him to retire as Maryland's attorney general, and he died a poor man in 1826.

JAMES McHENRY (1753–1816) McHenry was born in Ireland and received a classical education in Dublin. He arrived in America in 1771, and the following year the rest of his family immigrated here as well. While his father and brother established an importing business, McHenry studied medicine with the well-known Philadelphia physician Dr. Benjamin Rush. During the Revolution McHenry served as a military surgeon. He was captured by the British in late 1776 but was exchanged in March 1778. He was assigned to Valley Forge and became

General Washington's secretary. His work for Washington may have influenced McHenry's decision to give up the practice of medicine for the world of politics and administration. He remained on Washington's staff until 1780 and then went on to serve the marquis de Lafayette. He had a seat in the Continental Congress from 1783 to 1786. McHenry missed much of the Philadelphia convention because of his brother's illness and contributed little to the debate when he was there. He was a firm nationalist, however, and campaigned for ratification of the Constitution in his home state. In 1796 McHenry accepted President Washington's appointment as secretary of war, a position he continued to hold during John Adams's administration. McHenry's preference for Hamilton's political guidance rather than Adams's annoyed the president, and in 1800 Adams forced the Marylander to resign. McHenry's political career thus ended, but he remained a firm Federalist and thus opposed the War of 1812.

JOHN FRANCIS MERCER (1759–1821) Born in Virginia, Mercer attended the College of William and Mary. When the Revolution began, he joined the Third Virginia Regiment and became General Charles Lee's aide-de-camp in 1778. When Lee was court-martialed, Mercer resigned his commission and took up the study of law. In 1782 Mercer was elected to the Virginia House of Delegates and soon after to the Continental Congress. In 1785 he moved to Maryland and attended the Philadelphia convention as a Maryland delegate. At twenty-eight, he was among the youngest men there. Like Luther Martin, Mercer was a strong opponent of centralization of government, and he spoke out against the Constitution during the convention, ultimately leaving the convention before it was signed. In the 1790s Mercer aligned himself with the Democratic-Republican

Party of Jefferson and Madison. He served in the U.S. House
of Representatives from 1791 to 1794 and served two terms as
governor of Maryland in the early nineteenth century. When
Jefferson became president, Mercer renounced the Democratic-
Republicans and joined the Federalist camp.

### VIRGINIA

JOHN BLAIR (1732–1800) Gentle in manner and careful in
dress, John Blair was born into a prominent Virginia family.
He graduated from the College of William and Mary and
studied law in London, returning to Virginia to establish a
solid legal practice in the capital city of Williamsburg. He
served in his colony's assembly, known as the House of Burgesses, from 1766 to 1770, leaving to accept the position of
clerk of the colony's upper house. Blair was a patriot, supporting the nonimportation agreements passed by Virginia's radi-
cals and serving on the committee that drafted Virginia's
Declaration of Rights. In 1778 he was elected a judge of the
general court and soon became its chief justice. With fellow
delegate George Wythe, Blair served on the high chancery
court as well. At the Philadelphia convention, Blair attended
faithfully but never took the floor and never served on a committee. In 1789 the new president appointed Blair as an associate justice of the U.S. Supreme Court, a position Blair held
until 1796. In that year the unassuming jurist retired to
Williamsburg, living quietly but comfortably until his death.

JAMES MADISON (1751–1836) The oldest of ten children born to
a distinguished planter family, Madison received a good educa-

tion from tutors and the College of New Jersey. Despite a long and relatively healthy life, Madison was something of a hypochondriac, perhaps due to a sickly and frail childhood. Even before he chose a profession, Madison decided on a life in politics; he threw himself enthusiastically into the independence movement, serving on the local Committee of Safety and in the Virginia convention, where he demonstrated his abilities for constitution writing by framing his state constitution. During the war he served in the assembly and in the Council of State, kept from military service by poor health. In 1780 Madison became the youngest delegate to the Continental Congress. An early advocate of a strong central government, Madison attended both the Mount Vernon conference and the Annapolis convention before earning the title "Architect of the Constitution" for his work at the Philadelphia convention. He campaigned tirelessly for ratification in Virginia and reached out to influence New York as well by his contributions to the essays known as *The Federalist Papers.* Madison won a seat in the first House of Representatives, where he served until 1797. By this time he was a committed leader of the Democratic-Republicans, and he became secretary of state in 1801 when his friend and cofounder of that party, Thomas Jefferson, became president. Madison succeeded Jefferson in 1809, and it was during his administration that the long-standing tensions between Britain and the United States finally erupted into war. After his second term as president, Madison retired to his plantation, Montpelier, where he edited the journal he kept during the Constitutional Convention. He wrote newspaper articles supporting fellow Democratic-Republican and Virginian President James Monroe and acted as Monroe's informal adviser on foreign policy. In his last years, Madison became actively involved in the American Colonization Society, an organization that encouraged the emancipation of slaves and their resettlement in Africa.

GEORGE MASON (1725–1792) Perhaps the most effective opponent of Madison and the Federalists, Mason was raised by his uncle, John Mercer, following his father's death when Mason was a young boy. Mercer boasted one of the largest private libraries in the colonies, and Mason read widely in these fifteen hundred volumes. As the owner of Gunston Hall, one of Virginia's largest plantations, Mason was a wealthy and socially influential man. He became involved in western land speculation, buying an interest in the Ohio Company, and wrote a stinging defense of colonial entitlement to the Ohio Valley region when the Crown revoked the company's rights. Mason served as a justice of the peace before taking a seat in 1759 in the House of Burgesses. He took up his pen once again to defend the colonial position on the Stamp Act, and by 1774 he had emerged as a leader of the patriot movement in Virginia. Mason drafted the Virginia Declaration of Rights in 1776. By the early 1780s, Mason had grown disillusioned with public life and retired to Gunston Hall. He agreed to attend the Mount Vernon conference in 1785 but did not go to Annapolis despite his appointment as a delegate to that convention. Mason played a leading role at the Philadelphia convention, speaking frequently and exerting considerable influence over the deliberations. He became increasingly critical of the direction the convention was moving, however, and in the end, Mason refused to sign the Constitution. Among his primary objections was the absence of a bill of rights. Mason actively campaigned against ratification in Virginia, causing a breach in his friendships with both Washington and Madison.

JAMES McCLURG (1746–1823) McClurg was born in Virginia and attended the College of William and Mary. After graduating he went abroad to study medicine, receiving a degree from the University of Edinburgh in 1770. He continued his medical studies in Paris and London, publishing studies that earned him considerable notice from the English scientific community. McClurg returned to Virginia in 1773 and during the Revolution served as a surgeon to his state militia. He was appointed to the faculty of William and Mary in 1779. His reputation as a physician grew, and he was named president of the state medical society. But McClurg had an interest in politics as well as medicine, and when Richard Henry Lee and Patrick Henry refused to serve as delegates to the Philadelphia convention, McClurg gladly accepted a seat in the Virginia delegation. At the convention McClurg supported extensive executive power and independence from congressional control. He left the convention in early August and thus did not sign the Constitution. After ratification McClurg served on Virginia's executive council, but he never again attained a role in national politics.

EDMUND RANDOLPH (1753–1813) Born into a prosperous planter family, Randolph received his education at the College of William and Mary and then went on to study law with his father. When the Revolution began, Randolph's father chose to remain loyal to the Crown; the younger Randolph supported independence. He served as one of General Washington's aides-de-camp during the war. At twenty-three, Randolph was the youngest member of the state convention that adopted Virginia's first constitution in 1776. Soon afterward he became mayor of Williamsburg and then the state's attorney general. He entered national politics with his election to the Continental Congress in 1779. In 1786 Randolph became governor of

Virginia. It was Randolph who presented the Virginia Plan to the Philadelphia convention, but as the weeks went by, his support for a strong central government diminished. He reluctantly declared his unwillingness to sign the Constitution at the convention, but when the ratification battle began in Virginia, Randolph once again returned to the Federalist camp. He served as President Washington's first attorney general, and when Jefferson resigned from his cabinet post as secretary of state in 1794, Randolph stepped into that position. He attempted to remain neutral in the growing political division between Jefferson and Hamilton, and perhaps because of the strain this caused, he decided to retire from public life in 1795. He returned to the practice of law and devoted his free time to writing a history of Virginia.

GEORGE WASHINGTON (1732–1799) Washington was born into the Virginia gentry, the oldest of six children from his father's second marriage. His father's estates included a plantation that would later be known as Mount Vernon. Washington had a limited education, probably from tutors, but he did train as a surveyor. For several years he conducted surveys in Virginia and in what later became West Virginia. In 1753 the royal governor of Virginia appointed him a major in the militia, and by 1754 he had risen to the rank of colonel. When he was demoted because of the expected arrival of British regulars, Washington resigned his commission and leased Mount Vernon from his brother. By 1755, however, he was back in the military as an aide to General Edward Braddock. In 1759 he returned to civilian life, married, and focused much of his energy on farming. He found time, however, for political activity. Between 1759 and 1774, he sat in the House of Burgesses, where he was a strong supporter of colonial resistance to the new British policies. Washington served in the First and Second Continental Congresses, and in 1775 he accepted command of the Continental army. His military experience intensified his conviction that the nation needed a strong central government, and Washington was active in helping to orchestrate the call for the Philadelphia convention. He served as host to one of its predecessors, the Mount Vernon conference. After some hesitation, he agreed to join the Virginia delegation to the Philadelphia convention, where he was immediately elected presiding officer. In 1789 Washington became the first president of the United States by unanimous election. During two administrations Washington supported programs and policies consistent with his Federalist views, more often accepting Hamilton's position than Jefferson's on both foreign and domestic matters. Although many encouraged him to serve a third term as president, Washington declined. Rheumatism and other ailments prompted him to retire to his beloved Mount Vernon, where he died at the age of sixty-seven. Although he had not made the abolition of slavery one of his central causes, he did emancipate all his slaves when he died.

GEORGE WYTHE (1726–1806) Born into a planter family of Virginia, Wythe was orphaned as a child and grew up under the guardianship of his older brother. Despite the fact that he received little formal education, Wythe became a highly respected jurist and teacher. By 1754 he was the colony's attorney general. Although he inherited the family estate soon afterward, Wythe preferred to remain in Williamsburg, where he could pursue his study of the classics and of law. He served in the Virginia House of Burgesses for almost twenty years, from the mid-1750s until 1775. He also played an active role in the life of the College of William and Mary. During the Revolution Wythe was a delegate to the Continental Congress, signing the Declaration of Independence in 1776. In 1778 his appointment to the newly created Virginia High Court of Chancery began a twenty-eight-year career on the bench. Despite his legal skills and his impeccable reputation as a judge—he was known as "Wythe the Just"—Wythe's first love was education. In 1779, when the College of William and Mary created the nation's first chair in law, George Wythe was the first scholar to receive that honor. In the course of his long teaching career, he trained Thomas Jefferson, James Monroe, and John Marshall in the law. Although he attended the Philadelphia convention, the sixty-year-old Wythe was not an active participant in the debates and left early, without signing the Constitution. He did, however, work for its ratification. In 1791 Wythe retired from his college position, but he continued to train lawyers privately. One of his last pupils was Henry Clay. It is possible that Wythe was poisoned to death by his grandnephew, who was heir to Wythe's extensive estate.

## NORTH CAROLINA

WILLIAM BLOUNT (1749–1800) The son of a prosperous planter, Blount received a good private education. During the war he served in the North Carolina military as a paymaster. When he returned to civilian life, Blount began an uninterrupted career in politics. He sat in the lower house of the state legislature from 1780 to 1784 and in the upper house from 1788 to 1790. In between he served in the Continental Congress. At thirty-eight, he was a member of the North Carolina delegation to the Constitutional Convention but rarely participated in the debates. He signed the Constitution with considerable reluctance, although he supported its ratification in his home state. When he was passed over for the first U.S. Senate, Blount left North Carolina, settling in what became the state of Tennessee. Washington appointed Blount as governor for the Territory South of the River Ohio and superintendent of Indian Affairs for the Southern Department. In 1796 he chaired the constitutional convention that created the state of Tennessee. That same year Blount was chosen as one of Tennessee's first U.S. senators. His political victory was overshadowed by personal financial difficulties, however. He became involved in a wild scheme to conquer Spanish-held Florida and Louisiana, and this led to his expulsion from the Senate. Despite this humiliation, Blount remained popular in Tennessee and was elected to state office in 1798, two years before his death in 1800.

WILLIAM RICHARDSON DAVIE (1756–1820) Born in England, Davie was brought to South Carolina in 1763 by his father in order to place him in the care of the boy's maternal uncle. Davie's uncle adopted him and educated him, sending him to the Queen's Museum College in Charlotte, North Carolina, and later to the College of New Jersey. Davie studied law and began a practice in North Carolina. When the Revolution began, he helped raise a cavalry troop and rose to the rank of colonel. He was wounded in a battle at Stono in 1779. In January 1781 Davie was appointed commissary-general for the critical Carolina campaign. After the war Davie settled in Halifax, North Carolina, practicing law and earning praise for his courtroom presentations. He was well liked by his community as well as well respected. Halifax sent him to the North Carolina legislature for a dozen years, beginning in 1786. There he worked to encourage all efforts to strengthen the national government. At the Constitutional Convention, Davie swung his state's vote in favor of the Great Compromise. He left the convention on August 13 but continued to be a strong supporter of the Constitution and worked for its ratification in North Carolina. He was a founder of the University of North Carolina, playing an active role in the selection of its instructors and its curriculum. For his contribution to state education, the trustees of the university named him "Father of the University" and granted him an honorary degree of Doctor of Laws. Davie became governor of the state in 1799 and served as one of President Adams's peace commissioners to France in 1799. He retired from politics in 1805.

ALEXANDER MARTIN (1740–1807) Martin was born in New Jersey, but his family moved first to Virginia and then to Guilford County, North Carolina, where he grew up. He returned to his birth state to attend the College of New Jersey. After graduation Martin began a mercantile career in North Carolina but devoted most of his energies to a political career as justice of the peace, deputy king's attorney, and, by 1774, judge of the Salisbury district. When members of the backcountry movement known as the Regulators staged a violent protest in Martin's courtroom, he was severely beaten by the protesters. In the years before the war, Martin, who never married, served in the North Carolina House of Commons and in its provincial congresses. When war broke out, he was appointed a lieutenant colonel in the Second North Carolina Continental

Regiment. He saw military action in South Carolina, but when he joined Washington's army in 1777, he was arrested for cowardice after the Battle of Germantown. Although acquitted, Martin resigned his commission. The embarrassment of his military experience did not seem to impede Martin's political career. He was elected to the North Carolina Senate in 1778 and served there for eight years, often as that body's speaker. In 1781 he became acting governor and the following year was elected to that office in his own right. From 1785 to 1787, Martin was a delegate to the Confederation Congress. At the Philadelphia convention, Martin showed little commitment to the nationalist agenda. He took no active role in the debates, perhaps because he had limited skill in public speaking, and left before the Constitution was signed. From 1789 to 1792, Martin again sat in the governor's seat of North Carolina. By 1790 he had joined the ranks of supporters of the Jeffersonian party, and by 1792 the Democratic-Republicans had placed him in the U.S. Senate. His national career ended, however, when he voted with the Federalists for the Alien and Sedition Acts. By 1804 he was back in the state senate, where he again served as speaker.

RICHARD DOBBS SPAIGHT SR. (1758–1802) Spaight, born into a distinguished family of English and Irish descent, was orphaned at the age of eight and his guardians sent him to Ireland in order to insure he was well educated. He returned to North Carolina, perhaps with a degree from Glasgow University, in 1778. He was given a commission in the military and served as an aide to the state militia commander. In 1780 he saw combat at the Battle of Camden. In 1781 Spaight returned to civilian life in order to devote himself to politics. He served in the state legislature from 1780 to 1787, taking two years off in 1783 to serve in the Confederation Congress. Only twenty-nine when the Philadelphia convention began, Spaight spoke on several occasions during the debates. Back home in North Carolina, he campaigned actively for ratification. His political career did not fare well after this. He was defeated in a bid for governor in 1787 and lost an election for the U.S. Senate in 1789. Soon afterward illness forced him to retire from public life. In 1792 Spaight returned to politics, this time in a successful campaign for the governorship. In 1798 Spaight—now a Democratic-Republican—took a seat in the U.S. House of Representatives. While serving in Congress, he voted against the Alien and Sedition Acts and for Jefferson in the presidential election of 1800. At the age of forty-four, Spaight was killed in a duel with a Federalist politician.

HUGH WILLIAMSON (1735–1819) The versatile Williamson was born into a large family in Pennsylvania. His parents hoped for a career for him as a clergyman and, toward that end, gave him a fine education. He was a member of the first class at the College of Philadelphia (later part of the University of Pennsylvania) and went on to become a licensed Presbyterian minister, although he was never ordained. He took a teaching position in mathematics at the College of Philadelphia rather than a pulpit. In 1764 Williamson rather abruptly abandoned his academic career and took up the study of medicine at Edinburgh, London, and Utrecht. He received a medical degree from the University of Utrecht and came home to Philadelphia, where he opened a practice. Unfortunately, he found a career in medicine emotionally exhausting. His interests in science led him to publish *An Essay on Comets,* for which he was recognized with an LL.D. degree from the University of Leyden.

For his next career, Williamson decided to found an academy. On a fund-raising trip, he witnessed the Boston Tea Party, but when the British government called on him to testify about the event, he warned them that their unfair policies were provoking rebellion. Increasingly sympathetic to the American cause, Williamson wrote a pamphlet while in England, asking the English Whigs to support the colonists. Still abroad when the Declaration of Independence was signed, Williamson returned to America and settled in North Carolina. There he established a mercantile business and began to practice medicine again. During the war he served as surgeon general to the state troops. In 1782 Williamson opened up a new phase of his life by entering politics. He was elected to the lower house of the state legislature and then to the Continental Congress. He left Congress to return to state office and in 1787 was chosen to join the North Carolina delegation to the Constitutional Convention. There he proved himself an effective debater and was chosen to serve on a number of key committees, including the Committee on Postponed Matters. In 1789 he began the first of two terms in the U.S. House of Representatives. In 1793 Williamson moved to New York City in order to better pursue his literary and philanthropic interests. He published a number of political, educational, historical, and scientific works and became a leading member of the New-York Historical Society.

## South Carolina

PIERCE BUTLER (1744–1822) The younger son of a British baronet, Butler was born in Ireland. As he would not inherit his father's title or estate, Butler decided to pursue a military career. He became a major in a regiment that was sent to

Boston in 1768 in an effort to reduce the hostilities against the British government there. In 1771 Butler married a wealthy woman from South Carolina and resigned his military commission in order to take up the life of a southern planter. When the Revolution broke out, Butler was a staunch patriot. He served in the state assembly in 1778 and the following year again donned a uniform as an adjutant general in the South Carolina militia. Despite his aristocratic background, Butler became a spokesman for and champion of the backcountry farmers against his own planter class. He lost much of his property and wealth in the war but continued to serve his adopted state, sitting as a delegate to the Confederation Congress and to the Philadelphia convention. There he attracted attention in his powdered wig and his coat trimmed in gold lace—and his readiness to remind the gathering of his noble birth. The nationalists welcomed him, however, as he was a vocal supporter of strong government and a key figure in the nationalist caucus. At the same time, he defended the interests of southern slaveholders like himself. Butler served on the critical Committee on Postponed Matters. He served in the U.S. Senate from 1789 to 1796, but his voting record did not mark him as a loyal Federalist or a convert to the newer Jeffersonian party. For example, he supported Hamilton's fiscal program, but he opposed the Jay Treaty with Great Britain. He showed the same independent bent when he returned briefly to the Senate in 1803 to fill out an unexpired term. In his last years, Butler moved to Philadelphia presumably to be near a married daughter there.

CHARLES PINCKNEY (1757–1824) The cousin of fellow South Carolinian Charles Cotesworth Pinckney, Pinckney was the son of a wealthy lawyer and planter. Unlike many wealthy young men, Pinckney did not attend college but received all his education and his legal training in his home city of Charleston. Late in the war, Pinckney enlisted in the militia. He rose to the rank of lieutenant and served during the siege of Savannah. When Charleston fell, the young officer was captured and remained a British prisoner until the summer of 1781. Meanwhile, Pinckney had begun a political career, serving in the Continental Congress from 1777 to 1778 and later in the Confederation Congress. He also served several terms in his state legislature. A nationalist, he wanted the government to be strong enough to insure American rights to navigate the Mississippi. At the Philadelphia convention, Pinckney commanded notice. He was ambitious, bold, an excellent speaker, and a key member of the nationalist caucus, although his inflated claims that he had submitted a draft of a plan for the government that was the real basis for the Constitution are unfounded. After the convention he rose rapidly on the South Carolina political scene. He became governor in 1789, an office he held until 1792, and in 1790 he chaired the state constitutional convention. At first a Federalist, Pinckney slowly began to shift his allegiances. He opposed the Jay Treaty and began to align himself with the backcountry farmers who were the heart of the Democratic-Republican Party in his state. In 1796 Pinckney was again in the governor's seat, and in 1798 he went to the U.S. Senate with the backing of the Democratic-Republicans. In 1800 he served as Jefferson's campaign manager in South Carolina. As a reward, President Jefferson appointed Pinckney minister to Spain. When he returned from Europe, he took over the reins of the Democratic-Republican Party in his home state. He served a third term as governor from 1806 to 1808. In 1819 he reentered national politics as a member of Congress, but poor health forced him to retire from political life in 1821.

CHARLES COTESWORTH PINCKNEY (1746–1825) The eldest son and heir of a prominent planter, lawyer, and political figure and a remarkable mother, the agriculturalist Eliza Lucas Pinckney, Pinckney had every advantage educationally and financially. He was schooled in England and went to Christ Church College, Oxford. For his legal training, he attended London's famous Middle Temple. After he was accepted to the English bar in 1769, he spent almost a year touring Europe and studying with leading European scientists. After his travels Pinckney returned to South Carolina to set up his legal practice. He was immediately elected to the provincial assembly, where he supported the growing opposition movement against Great Britain. When war broke out, he joined the First South Carolina Regiment as a captain and rose rapidly to the rank of colonel. He saw combat in the defense of Charleston and in the Battles of Brandywine and Germantown. When Charleston fell in 1780, he, like Pierce Butler, was taken prisoner by the British. He was not released until 1782. Like his cousin, Pinckney was a leader at the Constitutional Convention and a strong advocate for a powerful national government. After the Constitution was ratified, he became a loyal Federalist, although he refused several national appointments, including secretary of war and a place on the Supreme Court bench. In 1796 Pinckney did agree to serve as minister to France, but the revolutionary leaders of that country refused to receive him. He was one of the American ministers who rejected French efforts to bribe them during what became known as the XYZ affair.

Pinckney returned to America in 1798 and was appointed a major general in command of U.S. forces in the South until the threat of war ended in 1800. He was the Federalist candidate for vice president that year and in 1804 and 1808 the party's presidential nominee. Following the 1808 defeat, Pinckney returned to South Carolina and his legal practice. He continued to serve in his state legislature and to participate in philanthropic activities. He was a charter member of the board of trustees of South Carolina College (later the University of South Carolina), head of the Charleston Library Society, and a prominent member of the Society of the Cincinnati.

JOHN RUTLEDGE (1739–1800) Born into a large family of Irish immigrants, Rutledge received his early education from his physician father. He was sent to London's prestigious Middle Temple for his legal training and was admitted to English practice in 1760. He returned soon afterward to his native Charleston, married, and began a successful legal career. He made his fortune, however, from his plantations and slaves. By 1761 Rutledge had won a seat in the provincial assembly and remained in this legislative body until independence was declared. There he earned a reputation as one of the greatest orators of his day. As tensions increased between the colonies and Great Britain, Rutledge defended American rights but worked for a peaceful resolution of differences. In 1774 he was a delegate to the Continental Congress, and there, too, he pursued a moderate course. Once independence was declared, however, he played an active role in helping to reorganize his state government and in writing South Carolina's state constitution. Although a patriot, Rutledge was a political conservative, resigning his position in the state legislature when democratic

revisions of the state constitution were passed. His views did
not prevent his election to the governorship in 1779. When
Charleston was taken by the British in 1780, Rutledge suffered
severe financial losses. His extensive property holdings were
confiscated, and Rutledge was forced to flee to North Carolina.
He never recovered his fortune. Rutledge served in the Continental Congress from 1782 to 1783 and then returned to state
offices. At the Philadelphia convention, he was a moderate nationalist, speaking frequently on issues and serving on several
important committees. His deepest concern at the convention
was the protection of southern interests. President Washington
appointed Rutledge as an associate justice of the U.S. Supreme
Court, but he left that bench in 1791 to become chief justice of
the South Carolina Supreme Court. Washington again called
upon him to serve on the U.S. Court in 1795, this time to replace John Jay as chief justice. His appointment was not confirmed by the Federalist-dominated Senate, however, due in
part to his vocal opposition to the Jay Treaty of 1794 and in
part to signs of mental illness brought on by the death of his
wife. The rejection led Rutledge to retire from public life.

## GEORGIA

ABRAHAM BALDWIN (1754–1807) Baldwin was a transplanted
northerner, born in Guilford, Connecticut, the second son of a
blacksmith. Baldwin's father had high hopes for his twelve
children and went into debt in order to provide them a good
education. Baldwin graduated from Yale College in 1772.
Soon afterward he became a minister and a tutor at his alma
mater. In 1779 he served as a chaplain in the Continental army.

After the war he gave up both the ministry and academic life to take up a career in law. By 1784 Baldwin had moved to Georgia, where he purchased land, established a law practice, and entered state politics. In 1785 he sat in the assembly and served as a delegate to the Confederation Congress. When his father died two years later, Baldwin took on the responsibility of paying off the family debts and covering the costs of educating his remaining siblings. At the Constitutional Convention, Baldwin did not play a prominent role, although he served on its key committee, the Committee on Postponed Matters. His most important contribution was to support the small states in their demand for equal representation in the Senate. Baldwin was one of several delegates to the Philadelphia convention who served in the first Washington administration, sitting in the House of Representatives for ten years and in the Senate for eight. A bitter opponent of Hamilton's policies, Baldwin allied himself with the emerging Democratic-Republican Party. Baldwin, a bachelor all his life like Maryland's Jenifer, focused much of his civic interest on education. He was a driving force in Georgia's efforts to create a state college, working from 1784 until 1798, when Franklin College was founded. Franklin was later expanded to become the University of Georgia.

WILLIAM FEW (1748–1828) Few was one of the convention's rare self-made men whose fortune came from his own enterprise rather than marriage. Born in Maryland into a poor family, Few received little education. When he was ten years old, his family moved to North Carolina, where his father hoped to improve their economic situation. In North Carolina Few, his father, and his brother became members of the Regulators, the backcountry farmers who sought more responsive and less corrupt government in their frontier area. Few's brother was hanged for his protest activities, the family farm was destroyed, and Few's father became a fugitive, moving the family to Georgia for their safety. Despite his lack of formal education or any legal training, Few successfully won admission to the Georgia bar. During the Revolution he served as a lieutenant colonel in the dragoons, demonstrating natural leadership abilities. He gravitated toward politics, serving in the Georgia provincial congress and after independence in the state assembly. He was appointed surveyor-general and Indian commissioner in the late 1770s. Few was one of six men chosen as delegates to the Philadelphia convention, although only four ultimately attended. Two of his state's delegates left before the convention adjourned, and Few was absent during July and much of August attending the Confederation Congress. Although he did not participate in the convention debates, Few proved his value to the nationalists in the end. He was influential in persuading the Confederation Congress to approve the Constitution. Few was one of Georgia's first U.S. senators, serving from 1789 to 1793. At the end of his term, he returned to the Georgia assembly. He became a federal judge for the Georgia circuit in 1796 but resigned three years later when he moved to New York City. The move to New York did not slow Few's political career. He served four years in the New York assembly and was appointed to a number of positions, including inspector of prisons and U.S. commissioner of loans. He became involved in the city's financial growth, as a director of the Manhattan Bank and president of City Bank. Until his death in 1828, Few was also an active philanthropist.

WILLIAM HOUSTOUN (1755–1813) A handsome man of ordinary intelligence, Houstoun was the son of a nobleman who served as a council member for the royal governor of Georgia. Houstoun received a fine education, including legal training at London's Inner Temple. When the Revolution began, Houstoun returned to Georgia to find his family divided on the issue of independence. Many of the Houstouns chose to remain loyal to a Crown that had been generous with its patronage over the years; William, however, championed the cause of revolution. He served as a delegate to the Confederation Congress from 1783 to 1786 and was chosen to attend the Philadelphia convention. He remained at the convention only briefly, leaving in mid-July, but he was there to cast a critical vote on the issue of equal representation in the Senate. He split the Georgia delegation's vote with his "nay" against Abraham Baldwin's "aye."

WILLIAM LEIGH PIERCE (c. 1740–1789) Little is known about Pierce's early years, although it is assumed he was born in Georgia and raised in Virginia. He served as an aide-de-camp to General Nathanael Greene and left the military with the rank of brevet major. His bravery at the Battle of Eutaw Springs won him a ceremonial sword, presented to Pierce by Congress. After the war Pierce settled in Savannah, organizing an import-export company in 1783. In 1786 he took a seat in the Georgia House of Representatives and was chosen as a delegate to the Confederation Congress. At the Philadelphia convention, Pierce took the floor during three debates but was not an influential member of the convention. He was concerned that the integrity of the states be preserved, but he acknowledged an urgent need to strengthen the central government. He left the convention early to attend to a business crisis. Soon afterward he was bankrupt and died deeply in debt. Pierce is best remembered for the notes and character sketches he produced at the convention, which were published in the *Savannah Georgian* in 1828.

# The Articles of Confederation

A GREED TO BY CONGRESS November 15, 1777; ratified and in force, March 1, 1781.

## Preamble

To all to whom these Presents shall come, we the undersigned Delegates of the States affixed to our Names send greeting. Articles of Confederation and perpetual Union between the States of New Hampshire, Massachusetts-bay, Rhode Island and Providence Plantations, Connecticut, New York, New Jersey, Pennsylvania, Delaware, Maryland, Virginia, North Carolina, South Carolina and Georgia.

## Article I.

The Stile of this Confederacy shall be "The United States of America."

## Article II.

Each state retains its sovereignty, freedom, and independence, and every power, jurisdiction, and right, which is not by this Confederation expressly delegated to the United States, in Congress assembled.

## *Article III.*

The said States hereby severally enter into a firm league of friendship with each other, for their common defense, the security of their liberties, and their mutual and general welfare, binding themselves to assist each other, against all force offered to, or attacks made upon them, or any of them, on account of religion, sovereignty, trade, or any other pretense whatever.

## *Article IV.*

The better to secure and perpetuate mutual friendship and intercourse among the people of the different States in this Union, the free inhabitants of each of these States, paupers, vagabonds, and fugitives from justice excepted, shall be entitled to all privileges and immunities of free citizens in the several States; and the people of each State shall free ingress and regress to and from any other State, and shall enjoy therein all the privileges of trade and commerce, subject to the same duties, impositions, and restrictions as the inhabitants thereof respectively, provided that such restrictions shall not extend so far as to prevent the removal of property imported into any State, to any other State, of which the owner is an inhabitant; provided also that no imposition, duties or restriction shall be laid by any State, on the property of the United States, or either of them.

If any person guilty of, or charged with, treason, felony, or other high misdemeanor in any State, shall flee from justice, and be found in any of the United States, he shall, upon demand of the Governor or executive power of the State from which he fled, be delivered up and removed to the State having jurisdiction of his offense.

Full faith and credit shall be given in each of these States to the records, acts, and judicial proceedings of the courts and magistrates of every other State.

## *Article V.*

For the most convenient management of the general interests of the United States, delegates shall be annually appointed in such manner as the legislatures of each State shall direct, to meet in Congress on the first Monday in November, in every year, with a power reserved to each State to recall its delegates, or any of them, at any time within the year, and to send others in their stead for the remainder of the year. No State shall be represented in Congress by less than two, nor more than seven members; and no person shall be capable of being a delegate for more than three years in any term of six years; nor shall any person, being a delegate, be capable of holding any office under the United States, for which he, or another for his benefit, receives any salary, fees or emolument of any kind.

Each State shall maintain its own delegates in a meeting of the States, and while they act as members of the committee of the States.

In determining questions in the United States in Congress assembled, each State shall have one vote.

Freedom of speech and debate in Congress shall not be impeached or questioned in any court or place out of Congress, and the members of Congress shall be protected in their persons from arrests or imprisonments, during the time of their going to and from, and attendance on Congress, except for treason, felony, or breach of the peace.

## *Article VI.*

No State, without the consent of the United States in Congress assembled, shall send any embassy to, or receive any embassy from, or enter into any conference, agreement, alliance or treaty with any King, Prince or State; nor shall any person holding any office of profit or trust under the United States, or any of them, accept any present, emolument, office or title of any kind whatever from any King, Prince or foreign State; nor shall the United States in Congress assembled, or any of them, grant any title of nobility.

No two or more States shall enter into any treaty, confederation or alliance whatever between them, without the consent of the United States in Congress assembled, specifying accurately the purposes for which the same is to be entered into, and how long it shall continue.

No State shall lay any imposts or duties, which may interfere with any stipulations in treaties, entered into by the United States in Congress assembled, with any King, Prince or State, in pursuance of any treaties already proposed by Congress, to the courts of France and Spain.

No vessel of war shall be kept up in time of peace by any State, except such number only, as shall be deemed necessary by the United States in Congress assembled, for the defense of such State, or its trade; nor shall any body of forces be kept up by any State in time of peace, except such number only, as in the judgement of the United States in Congress assembled, shall be deemed requisite to garrison the forts necessary for the defense of such State; but every State shall always keep up a well-regulated and disciplined militia, sufficiently armed and accoutered, and shall provide and constantly have ready for use, in public stores, a due number of filed pieces and tents, and a proper quantity of arms, ammunition and camp equipage.

No State shall engage in any war without the consent of the United States in Congress assembled, unless such State be actually invaded by enemies, or shall have received certain advice of a resolution being formed by some nation of Indians to invade such State, and the danger is so imminent as not to admit of a delay till the United States in Congress assembled can be consulted; nor shall any State grant commissions to any ships or vessels of war, nor letters of marque or reprisal, except it be after a declaration of war by the United States in Congress assembled, and then only against the Kingdom or State and the subjects thereof, against which war has been so declared, and under such regulations as shall be established by the United States in Congress assembled, unless such State be infested by pirates, in which case vessels of war may be fitted out for that occasion, and kept so long as the danger shall continue, or until the United States in Congress assembled shall determine otherwise.

## Article VII.

When land forces are raised by any State for the common defense, all officers of or under the rank of colonel, shall be appointed by the legislature of each State respectively, by whom such forces shall be raised, or in such manner as such State shall direct, and all vacancies shall be filled up by the State which first made the appointment.

## *Article VIII.*

All charges of war, and all other expenses that shall be incurred for the common defense or general welfare, and allowed by the United States in Congress assembled, shall be defrayed out of a common treasury, which shall be supplied by the several States in proportion to the value of all land within each State, granted or surveyed for any person, as such land and the buildings and improvements thereon shall be estimated according to such mode as the United States in Congress assembled, shall from time to time direct and appoint.

The taxes for paying that proportion shall be laid and levied by the authority and direction of the legislatures of the several States within the time agreed upon by the United States in Congress assembled.

## *Article IX.*

The United States in Congress assembled, shall have the sole and exclusive right and power of determining on peace and war, except in the cases mentioned in the sixth article—of sending and receiving ambassadors—entering into treaties and alliances, provided that no treaty of commerce shall be made whereby the legislative power of the respective States shall be restrained from imposing such imposts and duties on foreigners, as their own people are subjected to, or from prohibiting the exportation or importation of any species of goods or commodities whatsoever—of establishing rules for deciding in all cases, what captures on land or water shall be legal, and in what manner prizes taken by land or naval forces in the service of the United States shall be divided or appropriated—of granting letters of marque and reprisal in times of peace—appointing courts for the trial of piracies and felonies committed on the high seas and establishing courts for receiving and determining finally appeals in all cases of captures, provided that no member of Congress shall be appointed a judge of any of the said courts.

The United States in Congress assembled shall also be the last resort on appeal in all disputes and differences now subsisting or that hereafter may arise between two or more States concerning boundary, jurisdiction or any other causes whatever; which authority shall always be exercised in the manner following. Whenever the legislative or executive authority or lawful agent of any State in controversy with another shall present a petition to Congress stating the matter in question and praying for a hearing, notice thereof shall be given by order of Congress to the legislative or executive authority of the other State in controversy, and a day assigned for the appearance of the parties by their lawful agents, who shall then be directed to appoint by joint consent, commissioners or judges to constitute a court for hearing and determining the matter in question: but if they cannot agree, Congress shall name three persons out of each of the United States, and from the list of such persons each party shall alternately strike out one, the petitioners beginning, until the number shall be reduced to thirteen; and from that number not less than seven, nor more than nine names as Congress shall direct, shall in the presence of Congress be drawn out by lot, and the persons whose names shall be so drawn or any five of them, shall be commissioners or judges, to hear and finally determine the controversy, so always as a major part of the judges who shall hear the cause shall agree in the determination: and if either party shall neglect to attend at the day appointed, without showing reasons, which Congress shall judge sufficient, or being present shall re-

fuse to strike, the Congress shall proceed to nominate three
persons out of each State, and the secretary of Congress shall
strike in behalf of such party absent or refusing; and the judgement and sentence of the court to be appointed, in the manner
before prescribed, shall be final and conclusive; and if any of
the parties shall refuse to submit to the authority of such court,
or to appear or defend their claim or cause, the court shall nevertheless proceed to pronounce sentence, or judgement, which
shall in like manner be final and decisive, the judgement or
sentence and other proceedings being in either case transmitted to Congress, and lodged among the acts of Congress for
the security of the parties concerned: provided that every commissioner, before he sits in judgement, shall take an oath to be
administered by one of the judges of the supreme or superior
court of the State, where the cause shall be tried, 'well and truly
to hear and determine the matter in question, according to the
best of his judgement, without favor, affection or hope of reward': provided also, that no State shall be deprived of territory
for the benefit of the United States.

All controversies concerning the private right of soil
claimed under different grants of two or more States, whose
jurisdictions as they may respect such lands, and the States
which passed such grants are adjusted, the said grants or either
of them being at the same time claimed to have originated an-
tecedent to such settlement of jurisdiction, shall on the petition
of either party to the Congress of the United States, be finally
determined as near as may be in the same manner as is before
prescribed for deciding disputes respecting territorial jurisdiction between different States.

The United States in Congress assembled shall also have
the sole and exclusive right and power of regulating the alloy

and value of coin struck by their own authority, or by that of the respective States—fixing the standards of weights and measures throughout the United States—regulating the trade and managing all affairs with the Indians, not members of any of the States, provided that the legislative right of any State within its own limits be not infringed or violated—establishing or regulating post offices from one State to another, throughout all the United States, and exacting such postage on the papers passing through the same as may be requisite to defray the expenses of the said office—appointing all officers of the land forces, in the service of the United States, excepting regimental officers—appointing all the officers of the naval forces, and commissioning all officers whatever in the service of the United States—making rules for the government and regulation of the said land and naval forces, and directing their operations.

The United States in Congress assembled shall have authority to appoint a committee, to sit in the recess of Congress, to be denominated 'A Committee of the States,' and to consist of one delegate from each State; and to appoint such other committees and civil officers as may be necessary for managing the general affairs of the United States under their direction— to appoint one of their members to preside, provided that no person be allowed to serve in the office of president more than one year in any term of three years; to ascertain the necessary sums of money to be raised for the service of the United States, and to appropriate and apply the same for defraying the public expenses—to borrow money, or emit bills on the credit of the United States, transmitting every half-year to the respective States an account of the sums of money so borrowed or emitted—to build and equip a navy—to agree upon the number of land forces, and to make requisitions from each State for its quota, in proportion to the number of white inhabitants in such State; which requisition shall be binding, and thereupon the legislature of each State shall appoint the regimental officers, raise the men and cloath, arm and equip them in a solid-like manner, at the expense of the United States; and the officers and men so cloathed, armed and equipped shall march to the place appointed, and within the time agreed on by the United States in Congress assembled. But if the United States in Congress assembled shall, on consideration of circumstances judge proper that any State should not raise men, or should raise a smaller number of men than the quota thereof, such extra number shall be raised, officered, cloathed, armed and equipped in the same manner as the quota of each State, unless the legislature of such State shall judge that such extra number cannot be safely spread out in the same, in which case they shall raise, officer, cloath, arm and equip as many of such extra number as they judge can be safely spared. And the officers and men so cloathed, armed, and equipped, shall march to the place appointed, and within the time agreed on by the United States in Congress assembled.

The United States in Congress assembled shall never engage in a war, nor grant letters of marque or reprisal in time of peace, nor enter into any treaties or alliances, nor coin money, nor regulate the value thereof, nor ascertain the sums and expenses necessary for the defense and welfare of the United States, or any of them, nor emit bills, nor borrow money on the credit of the United States, nor appropriate money, nor agree upon the number of vessels of war, to be built or purchased, or the number of land or sea forces to be raised, nor appoint a commander in chief of the army or navy, unless nine States assent to the same: nor shall a question on any other point, ex-cept for adjourning from day to day be determined, unless by the votes of the majority of the United States in Congress assembled.

The Congress of the United States shall have power to ad-journ to any time within the year, and to any place within the United States, so that no period of adjournment be for a longer duration than the space of six months, and shall publish the journal of their proceedings monthly, except such parts thereof relating to treaties, alliances or military operations, as in their judgement require secrecy; and the yeas and nays of the dele-gates of each State on any question shall be entered on the journal, when it is desired by any delegates of a State, or any of them, at his or their request shall be furnished with a transcript of the said journal, except such parts as are above excepted, to lay before the legislatures of the several States.

## *Article X.*

The Committee of the States, or any nine of them, shall be au-thorized to execute, in the recess of Congress, such of the pow-ers of Congress as the United States in Congress assembled, by the consent of the nine States, shall from time to time think expedient to vest them with; provided that no power be dele-gated to the said Committee, for the exercise of which, by the Articles of Confederation, the voice of nine States in the Con-gress of the United States assembled be requisite.

## *Article XI.*

Canada acceding to this confederation, and adjoining in the measures of the United States, shall be admitted into, and entitled to all the advantages of this Union; but no other colony shall be admitted into the same, unless such admission be agreed to by nine States.

## *Article XII.*

All bills of credit emitted, monies borrowed, and debts contracted by, or under the authority of Congress, before the assembling of the United States, in pursuance of the present confederation, shall be deemed and considered as a charge against the United States, for payment and satisfaction whereof the said United States, and the public faith are hereby solemnly pledged.

## *Article XIII.*

Every State shall abide by the determination of the United States in Congress assembled, on all questions which by this confederation are submitted to them. And the Articles of this Confederation shall be inviolably observed by every State, and the Union shall be perpetual; nor shall any alteration at any time hereafter be made in any of them; unless such alteration be agreed to in a Congress of the United States, and be afterwards confirmed by the legislatures of every State.

AND WHEREAS it hath pleased the Great Governor of the World to incline the hearts of the legislatures we respectively represent in Congress, to approve of, and to authorize us to ratify the said Articles of Confederation and perpetual Union. Know Ye that we the undersigned delegates, by virtue of the power and authority to us given for that purpose, do by these presents, in the name and in behalf of our respective constituents, fully and entirely ratify and confirm each and every of the said Articles of Confederation and perpetual Union, and all and singular the matters and things therein contained: And we do further solemnly plight and engage the faith of our respective constituents, that they shall abide by the determinations of the United States in Congress assembled, on all questions, which by the said Confederation are submitted to them. And that the Articles thereof shall be inviolably observed by the States we respectively represent, and that the Union shall be perpetual.

In Witness whereof we have hereunto set our hands in Congress. Done at Philadelphia in the State of Pennsylvania the ninth day of July in the Year of our Lord One Thousand Seven Hundred and Seventy-Eight, and in the Third Year of the independence of America.

On the part and behalf of the State of New Hampshire:
Josiah Bartlett
John Wentworth Junr.
August 8th 1778

On the part and behalf of The State of Massachusetts Bay:
John Hancock
Francis Dana
Samuel Adams
James Lovell
Elbridge Gerry
Samuel Holten

On the part and behalf of the State of Rhode Island and Providence Plantations:
William Ellery

John Collins
Henry Marchant

On the part and behalf of the State of Connecticut:
Roger Sherman
Titus Hosmer
Samuel Huntington
Andrew Adams
Oliver Wolcott

On the Part and Behalf of the State of New York:
James Duane
Wm Duer
Francis Lewis
Gouv Morris

On the Part and in Behalf of the State of New Jersey, November 26, 1778.
Jno Witherspoon
Nathaniel Scudder

On the part and behalf of the State of Pennsylvania:
Robt Morris
William Clingan
Daniel Roberdeau
Joseph Reed
John Bayard Smith
22nd July 1778

On the part and behalf of the State of Delaware:
Tho Mckean February 12, 1779

John Dickinson May 5th 1779
Nicholas Van Dyke

On the part and behalf of the State of Maryland:
John Hanson March 1 1781
Daniel Carroll Do

On the Part and Behalf of the State of Virginia:
Richard Henry Lee
Jno Harvie
John Banister
Francis Lightfoot Lee
Thomas Adams

On the part and Behalf of the State of No Carolina:
John Penn July 21St 1778
Corns Harnett
Jno Williams

On the part and behalf of the State of South Carolina:
Henry Laurens
Richd Hutson
William Henry Drayton
Thos Heyward Junr
Jno Mathews

On the part and behalf of the State of Georgia:
Jno Walton 24th July 1778
Edwd Telfair
Edwd Langworthy

# The United States Constitution

W E THE PEOPLE OF THE UNITED STATES, in Order to form a more perfect Union, establish Justice, insure domestic Tranquility, provide for the common defence, promote the general Welfare, and secure the Blessings of Liberty to ourselves and our Posterity, do ordain and establish this Constitution for the United States of America.

## Article. I.

### SECTION. 1.

All legislative Powers herein granted shall be vested in a Congress of the United States, which shall consist of a Senate and House of Representatives.

### SECTION. 2.

Clause 1: The House of Representatives shall be composed of Members chosen every second Year by the People of the several States, and the Electors in each State shall have the Qualifications requisite for Electors of the most numerous Branch of the State Legislature.

Clause 2: No Person shall be a Representative who shall not have attained to the Age of twenty five Years, and been seven Years a Citizen of the United States, and who shall not, when elected, be an Inhabitant of that State in which he shall be chosen.

Clause 3: Representatives and direct Taxes shall be apportioned among the several States which may be included within this Union, according to their respective Numbers, which shall be determined by adding to the whole Number of free Persons, including those bound to Service for a Term of Years, and excluding Indians not taxed, three fifths of all other Persons. The actual Enumeration shall be made within three Years after the first Meeting of the Congress of the United States, and within every subsequent Term of ten Years, in such Manner as they shall by Law direct. The Number of Representatives shall not exceed one for every thirty Thousand, but each State shall have at Least one Representative; and until such enumeration shall be made, the State of New Hampshire shall be entitled to chuse three, Massachusetts eight, Rhode-Island and Providence Plantations one, Connecticut five, New-York six, New Jersey four, Pennsylvania eight, Delaware one, Maryland six, Virginia ten, North Carolina five, South Carolina five, and Georgia three.

Clause 4: When vacancies happen in the Representation from any State, the Executive Authority thereof shall issue Writs of Election to fill such Vacancies.

Clause 5: The House of Representatives shall chuse their

Speaker and other Officers; and shall have the sole Power of Impeachment.

SECTION. 3.

Clause 1: The Senate of the United States shall be composed of two Senators from each State, chosen by the Legislature thereof, for six Years; and each Senator shall have one Vote.

Clause 2: Immediately after they shall be assembled in Consequence of the first Election, they shall be divided as equally as may be into three Classes. The Seats of the Senators of the first Class shall be vacated at the Expiration of the second Year, of the second Class at the Expiration of the fourth Year, and of the third Class at the Expiration of the sixth Year, so that one third may be chosen every second Year; and if Vacancies happen by Resignation, or otherwise, during the Recess of the Legislature of any State, the Executive thereof may make temporary Appointments until the next Meeting of the Legislature, which shall then fill such Vacancies.

Clause 3: No Person shall be a Senator who shall not have attained to the Age of thirty Years, and been nine Years a Citizen of the United States, and who shall not, when elected, be an Inhabitant of that State for which he shall be chosen.

Clause 4: The Vice President of the United States shall be President of the Senate, but shall have no Vote, unless they be equally divided.

Clause 5: The Senate shall chuse their other Officers, and also a President pro tempore, in the Absence of the Vice President, or when he shall exercise the Office of President of the United States.

Clause 6: The Senate shall have the sole Power to try all Impeachments. When sitting for that Purpose, they shall be on Oath or Affirmation. When the President of the United States is tried, the Chief Justice shall preside: And no Person shall be convicted without the Concurrence of two thirds of the Members present.

Clause 7: Judgment in Cases of Impeachment shall not extend further than to removal from Office, and disqualification to hold and enjoy any Office of honor, Trust or Profit under the United States: but the Party convicted shall nevertheless be liable and subject to Indictment, Trial, Judgment and Punishment, according to Law.

### SECTION. 4.

Clause 1: The Times, Places and Manner of holding Elections for Senators and Representatives, shall be prescribed in each State by the Legislature thereof; but the Congress may at any time by Law make or alter such Regulations, except as to the Places of chusing Senators.

Clause 2: The Congress shall assemble at least once in every Year, and such Meeting shall be on the first Monday in December, unless they shall by Law appoint a different Day.

### SECTION. 5.

Clause 1: Each House shall be the Judge of the Elections, Returns and Qualifications of its own Members, and a Majority of each shall constitute a Quorum to do Business; but a smaller Number may adjourn from day to day, and may be authorized to compel the Attendance of absent Members, in such Manner, and under such Penalties as each House may provide.

Clause 2: Each House may determine the Rules of its Proceedings, punish its Members for disorderly Behaviour, and, with the Concurrence of two thirds, expel a Member.

Clause 3: Each House shall keep a Journal of its Proceedings, and from time to time publish the same, excepting such Parts as may in their Judgment require Secrecy; and the Yeas and Nays of the Members of either House on any question shall, at the Desire of one fifth of those Present, be entered on the Journal.

Clause 4: Neither House, during the Session of Congress, shall, without the Consent of the other, adjourn for more than three days, nor to any other Place than that in which the two Houses shall be sitting.

## SECTION. 6.

Clause 1: The Senators and Representatives shall receive a Compensation for their Services, to be ascertained by Law, and paid out of the Treasury of the United States. They shall in all Cases, except Treason, Felony and Breach of the Peace, be privileged from Arrest during their Attendance at the Session of their respective Houses, and in going to and returning from the same; and for any Speech or Debate in either House, they shall not be questioned in any other Place.

Clause 2: No Senator or Representative shall, during the Time for which he was elected, be appointed to any civil Office under the Authority of the United States, which shall have been created, or the Emoluments whereof shall have been encreased during such time; and no Person holding any Office under the United States, shall be a Member of either House during his Continuance in Office.

## Section. 7.

Clause 1: All Bills for raising Revenue shall originate in the House of Representatives; but the Senate may propose or concur with Amendments as on other Bills.

Clause 2: Every Bill which shall have passed the House of Representatives and the Senate, shall, before it become a Law, be presented to the President of the United States; If he approve he shall sign it, but if not he shall return it, with his Objections to that House in which it shall have originated, who shall enter the Objections at large on their Journal, and proceed to reconsider it. If after such Reconsideration two thirds of that House shall agree to pass the Bill, it shall be sent, together with the Objections, to the other House, by which it shall likewise be reconsidered, and if approved by two thirds of that House, it shall become a Law. But in all such Cases the Votes of both Houses shall be determined by yeas and Nays, and the Names of the Persons voting for and against the Bill shall be entered on the Journal of each House respectively. If any Bill shall not be returned by the President within ten Days (Sundays excepted) after it shall have been presented to him, the Same shall be a Law, in like Manner as if he had signed it, unless the Congress by their Adjournment prevent its Return, in which Case it shall not be a Law.

Clause 3: Every Order, Resolution, or Vote to which the Concurrence of the Senate and House of Representatives may be necessary (except on a question of Adjournment) shall be presented to the President of the United States; and before the Same shall take Effect, shall be approved by him, or being disapproved by him, shall be repassed by two thirds of the Senate and House of Representatives, according to the Rules and Limitations prescribed in the Case of a Bill.

SECTION. 8.

Clause 1: The Congress shall have Power to lay and collect Taxes, Duties, Imposts and Excises, to pay the Debts and provide for the common Defence and general Welfare of the United States; but all Duties, Imposts and Excises shall be uniform throughout the United States;

Clause 2: To borrow Money on the credit of the United States;

Clause 3: To regulate Commerce with foreign Nations, and among the several States, and with the Indian Tribes;

Clause 4: To establish an uniform Rule of Naturalization, and uniform Laws on the subject of Bankruptcies throughout the United States;

Clause 5: To coin Money, regulate the Value thereof, and of foreign Coin, and fix the Standard of Weights and Measures;

Clause 6: To provide for the Punishment of counterfeiting the Securities and current Coin of the United States;

Clause 7: To establish Post Offices and post Roads;

Clause 8: To promote the Progress of Science and useful Arts, by securing for limited Times to Authors and Inventors the exclusive Right to their respective Writings and Discoveries;

Clause 9: To constitute Tribunals inferior to the supreme Court;

Clause 10: To define and punish Piracies and Felonies committed on the high Seas, and Offences against the Law of Nations;

Clause 11: To declare War, grant Letters of Marque and Reprisal, and make Rules concerning Captures on Land and Water;

Clause 12: To raise and support Armies, but no Appropriation of Money to that Use shall be for a longer Term than two Years;

Clause 13: To provide and maintain a Navy;

Clause 14: To make Rules for the Government and Regulation of the land and naval Forces;

Clause 15: To provide for calling forth the Militia to execute the Laws of the Union, suppress Insurrections and repel Invasions;

Clause 16: To provide for organizing, arming, and disciplining, the Militia, and for governing such Part of them as may be employed in the Service of the United States, reserving to the States respectively, the Appointment of the Officers, and the Authority of training the Militia according to the discipline prescribed by Congress;

Clause 17: To exercise exclusive Legislation in all Cases whatsoever, over such District (not exceeding ten Miles square) as may, by Cession of particular States, and the Acceptance of Congress, become the Seat of the Government of the United

States, and to exercise like Authority over all Places purchased by the Consent of the Legislature of the State in which the Same shall be, for the Erection of Forts, Magazines, Arsenals, dock-Yards, and other needful Buildings;—And

Clause 18: To make all Laws which shall be necessary and proper for carrying into Execution the foregoing Powers, and all other Powers vested by this Constitution in the Government of the United States, or in any Department or Officer thereof.

Section. 9.

Clause 1: The Migration or Importation of such Persons as any of the States now existing shall think proper to admit, shall not be prohibited by the Congress prior to the Year one thousand eight hundred and eight, but a Tax or duty may be imposed on such Importation, not exceeding ten dollars for each Person.

Clause 2: The Privilege of the Writ of Habeas Corpus shall not be suspended, unless when in Cases of Rebellion or Invasion the public Safety may require it.

Clause 3: No Bill of Attainder or ex post facto Law shall be passed.

Clause 4: No Capitation, or other direct, Tax shall be laid, unless in Proportion to the Census or Enumeration herein before directed to be taken.

Clause 5: No Tax or Duty shall be laid on Articles exported from any State.

Clause 6: No Preference shall be given by any Regulation of Commerce or Revenue to the Ports of one State over those of another: nor shall Vessels bound to, or from, one State, be obliged to enter, clear, or pay Duties in another.

Clause 7: No Money shall be drawn from the Treasury, but in Consequence of Appropriations made by Law; and a regular Statement and Account of the Receipts and Expenditures of all public Money shall be published from time to time.

Clause 8: No Title of Nobility shall be granted by the United States: And no Person holding any Office of Profit or Trust under them, shall, without the Consent of the Congress, accept of any present, Emolument, Office, or Title, of any kind whatever, from any King, Prince, or foreign State.

SECTION. 10.

Clause 1: No State shall enter into any Treaty, Alliance, or Confederation; grant Letters of Marque and Reprisal; coin Money; emit Bills of Credit; make any Thing but gold and silver Coin a Tender in Payment of Debts; pass any Bill of Attainder, ex post facto Law, or Law impairing the Obligation of Contracts, or grant any Title of Nobility.

Clause 2: No State shall, without the Consent of the Congress, lay any Imposts or Duties on Imports or Exports, except what may be absolutely necessary for executing its inspection Laws: and the net Produce of all Duties and Imposts, laid by any State on Imports or Exports, shall be for the Use of the Treasury of the United States; and all such Laws shall be subject to the Revision and Controul of the Congress.

Clause 3: No State shall, without the Consent of Congress, lay any Duty of Tonnage, keep Troops, or Ships of War in time of

Peace, enter into any Agreement or Compact with another State, or with a foreign Power, or engage in War, unless actually invaded, or in such imminent Danger as will not admit of delay.

## Article. II.

### SECTION. 1.

Clause 1: The executive Power shall be vested in a President of the United States of America. He shall hold his Office during the Term of four Years, and, together with the Vice President, chosen for the same Term, be elected, as follows

Clause 2: Each State shall appoint, in such Manner as the Legislature thereof may direct, a Number of Electors, equal to the whole Number of Senators and Representatives to which the State may be entitled in the Congress: but no Senator or Representative, or Person holding an Office of Trust or Profit under the United States, shall be appointed an Elector.

Clause 3: The Electors shall meet in their respective States, and vote by Ballot for two Persons, of whom one at least shall not be an Inhabitant of the same State with themselves. And they shall make a List of all the Persons voted for, and of the Number of Votes for each; which List they shall sign and certify, and transmit sealed to the Seat of the Government of the United States, directed to the President of the Senate. The President of the Senate shall, in the Presence of the Senate and House of Representatives, open all the Certificates, and the Votes shall then be counted. The Person having the greatest Number of Votes shall be the President, if such Number be a Majority of the whole Number of Electors appointed; and if there be more than one who have such Majority, and have an equal Number of Votes, then the House of Representatives shall immediately chuse by Ballot one of them for President; and if no Person have a Majority, then from the five highest on the List the said House shall in like Manner chuse the President. But in chusing the President, the Votes shall be taken by States, the Representation from each State having one Vote; A quorum for this Purpose shall consist of a Member or Members from two thirds of the States, and a Majority of all the States shall be necessary to a Choice. In every Case, after the Choice of the President, the Person having the greatest Number of Votes of the Electors shall be the Vice President. But if there should remain two or more who have equal Votes, the Senate shall chuse from them by Ballot the Vice President.

Clause 4: The Congress may determine the Time of chusing the Electors, and the Day on which they shall give their Votes; which Day shall be the same throughout the United States.

Clause 5: No Person except a natural born Citizen, or a Citizen of the United States, at the time of the Adoption of this Constitution, shall be eligible to the Office of President; neither shall any Person be eligible to that Office who shall not have attained to the Age of thirty five Years, and been fourteen Years a Resident within the United States.

Clause 6: In Case of the Removal of the President from Office, or of his Death, Resignation, or Inability to discharge the Powers and Duties of the said Office, the Same shall devolve on the Vice President, and the Congress may by Law provide for the Case of Removal, Death, Resignation or Inability, both of the President and Vice President, declaring what Officer shall then act as President, and such Officer shall act accordingly, until the Disability be removed, or a President shall be elected.

Clause 7: The President shall, at stated Times, receive for his Services, a Compensation, which shall neither be encreased nor diminished during the Period for which he shall have been elected, and he shall not receive within that Period any other Emolument from the United States, or any of them.

Clause 8: Before he enter on the Execution of his Office, he shall take the following Oath or Affirmation:—"I do solemnly swear (or affirm) that I will faithfully execute the Office of President of the United States, and will to the best of my Ability, preserve, protect and defend the Constitution of the United States."

SECTION. 2.

Clause 1: The President shall be Commander in Chief of the Army and Navy of the United States, and of the Militia of the several States, when called into the actual Service of the United States; he may require the Opinion, in writing, of the principal Officer in each of the executive Departments, upon any Subject relating to the Duties of their respective Offices, and he shall have Power to grant Reprieves and Pardons for Offences against the United States, except in Cases of Impeachment.

Clause 2: He shall have Power, by and with the Advice and Consent of the Senate, to make Treaties, provided two thirds of the Senators present concur; and he shall nominate, and by and with the Advice and Consent of the Senate, shall appoint Ambassadors, other public Ministers and Consuls, Judges of the supreme Court, and all other Officers of the United States, whose Appointments are not herein otherwise provided for, and which shall be established by Law: but the Congress may by Law vest the Appointment of such inferior Officers, as they think proper, in the President alone, in the Courts of Law, or in the Heads of Departments.

Clause 3: The President shall have Power to fill up all Vacancies that may happen during the Recess of the Senate, by granting Commissions which shall expire at the End of their next Session.

## SECTION. 3.

He shall from time to time give to the Congress Information of the State of the Union, and recommend to their Consideration such Measures as he shall judge necessary and expedient; he may, on extraordinary Occasions, convene both Houses, or either of them, and in Case of Disagreement between them, with Respect to the Time of Adjournment, he may adjourn them to such Time as he shall think proper; he shall receive Ambassadors and other public Ministers; he shall take Care that the Laws be faithfully executed, and shall Commission all the Officers of the United States.

## SECTION. 4.

The President, Vice President and all civil Officers of the United States, shall be removed from Office on Impeachment for, and Conviction of, Treason, Bribery, or other high Crimes and Misdemeanors.

## *Article. III.*

### SECTION. 1.

The judicial Power of the United States, shall be vested in one supreme Court, and in such inferior Courts as the Congress may from time to time ordain and establish. The Judges, both of the supreme and inferior Courts, shall hold their Offices during good Behaviour, and shall, at stated Times, receive for their Services, a Compensation, which shall not be diminished during their Continuance in Office.

### SECTION. 2.

Clause 1: The judicial Power shall extend to all Cases, in Law and Equity, arising under this Constitution, the Laws of the United States, and Treaties made, or which shall be made, under their Authority;—to all Cases affecting Ambassadors, other public Ministers and Consuls;—to all Cases of admiralty and maritime Jurisdiction;—to Controversies to which the United States shall be a Party;—to Controversies between two or more States;—between a State and Citizens of another State;—between Citizens of different States,—between Citizens of the same State claiming Lands under Grants of different States, and between a State, or the Citizens thereof, and foreign States, Citizens or Subjects.

Clause 2: In all Cases affecting Ambassadors, other public

Ministers and Consuls, and those in which a State shall be Party, the supreme Court shall have original Jurisdiction. In all the other Cases before mentioned, the supreme Court shall have appellate Jurisdiction, both as to Law and Fact, with such Exceptions, and under such Regulations as the Congress shall make.

Clause 3: The Trial of all Crimes, except in Cases of Impeachment, shall be by Jury; and such Trial shall be held in the State where the said Crimes shall have been committed; but when not committed within any State, the Trial shall be at such Place or Places as the Congress may by Law have directed.

## SECTION. 3.

Clause 1: Treason against the United States, shall consist only in levying War against them, or in adhering to their Enemies, giving them Aid and Comfort. No Person shall be convicted of Treason unless on the Testimony of two Witnesses to the same overt Act, or on Confession in open Court.

Clause 2: The Congress shall have Power to declare the Punishment of Treason, but no Attainder of Treason shall work Corruption of Blood, or Forfeiture except during the Life of the Person attainted.

# Article. IV.

## SECTION. 1.

Full Faith and Credit shall be given in each State to the public Acts, Records, and judicial Proceedings of every other State. And the Congress may by general Laws prescribe the Manner in which such Acts, Records and Proceedings shall be proved, and the Effect thereof.

## SECTION. 2.

Clause 1: The Citizens of each State shall be entitled to all Privileges and Immunities of Citizens in the several States.

Clause 2: A Person charged in any State with Treason, Felony, or other Crime, who shall flee from Justice, and be found in another State, shall on Demand of the executive Authority of the State from which he fled, be delivered up, to be removed to the State having Jurisdiction of the Crime.

Clause 3: No Person held to Service or Labour in one State, under the Laws thereof, escaping into another, shall, in Consequence of any Law or Regulation therein, be discharged from such Service or Labour, but shall be delivered up on Claim of the Party to whom such Service or Labour may be due.

## SECTION. 3.

Clause 1: New States may be admitted by the Congress into this Union; but no new State shall be formed or erected within the Jurisdiction of any other State; nor any State be formed by the Junction of two or more States, or Parts of States, without the Consent of the Legislatures of the States concerned as well as of the Congress.

Clause 2: The Congress shall have Power to dispose of and make all needful Rules and Regulations respecting the Territory or other Property belonging to the United States; and nothing in this Constitution shall be so construed as to Prejudice any Claims of the United States, or of any particular State.

Section. 4.

The United States shall guarantee to every State in this Union a Republican Form of Government, and shall protect each of them against Invasion; and on Application of the Legislature, or of the Executive (when the Legislature cannot be convened) against domestic Violence.

## Article. V.

The Congress, whenever two thirds of both Houses shall deem it necessary, shall propose Amendments to this Constitution, or, on the Application of the Legislatures of two thirds of the several States, shall call a Convention for proposing Amendments, which, in either Case, shall be valid to all Intents and Purposes, as Part of this Constitution, when ratified by the Legislatures of three fourths of the several States, or by Conventions in three fourths thereof, as the one or the other Mode of Ratification may be proposed by the Congress; Provided that no Amendment which may be made prior to the Year one thousand eight hundred and eight shall in any Manner affect the first and fourth Clauses in the Ninth Section of the first Article; and that no State, without its Consent, shall be deprived of its equal Suffrage in the Senate.

## Article. VI.

Clause 1: All Debts contracted and Engagements entered into, before the Adoption of this Constitution, shall be as valid against the United States under this Constitution, as under the Confederation.

Clause 2: This Constitution, and the Laws of the United States which shall be made in Pursuance thereof; and all Treaties made, or which shall be made, under the Authority of the United States, shall be the supreme Law of the Land; and the Judges in every State shall be bound thereby, any Thing in the Constitution or Laws of any State to the Contrary notwithstanding.

Clause 3: The Senators and Representatives before mentioned, and the Members of the several State Legislatures, and all executive and judicial Officers, both of the United States and of the several States, shall be bound by Oath or Affirmation, to support this Constitution; but no religious Test shall ever be required as a Qualification to any Office or public Trust under the United States.

## Article. VII.

The Ratification of the Conventions of nine States, shall be sufficient for the Establishment of this Constitution between the States so ratifying the Same.

done in Convention by the Unanimous Consent of the States present the Seventeenth Day of September in the Year of our Lord one thousand seven hundred and eighty seven and of the Independence of the United States of America the Twelfth In witness whereof We have hereunto subscribed our Names,

GO WASHINGTON—Presidt. and deputy from Virginia

[Signed also by the deputies of twelve States.]

DELAWARE
Geo: Read
Gunning Bedford jun
John Dickinson
Richard Bassett
Jaco: Broom

MARYLAND
James MCHenry
Dan of ST ThoS. Jenifer
DanL Carroll.

VIRGINIA
John Blair—
James Madison Jr.

NORTH CAROLINA
WM Blount
RichD. Dobbs Spaight.
Hu Williamson

SOUTH CAROLINA
J. Rutledge
Charles Cotesworth Pinckney
Charles Pinckney
Pierce Butler.

GEORGIA
William Few
Abr Baldwin

NEW HAMPSHIRE
John Langdon
Nicholas Gilman

MASSACHUSETTS
Nathaniel Gorham
Rufus King

CONNECTICUT
WM. SamL. Johnson
Roger Sherman

NEW YORK
Alexander Hamilton

NEW JERSEY
Wil: Livingston
David Brearley.
WM. Paterson.
Jona: Dayton

PENNSYLVANIA
B Franklin
Thomas Mifflin
RobT Morris
Geo. Clymer
ThoS. FitzSimons
Jared Ingersoll
James Wilson.
Gouv Morris

Attest William Jackson Secretary

# A Note on Sources

THE CONSTITUTIONAL CONVENTION has always held a fascination for students of the Revolution and the Early Republic. Both popular historians and scholars have been drawn to the drama of that summer of debate, compromise, and conflict that brought together political leaders from twelve of the thirteen original states. If this book sparks a similar, insatiable interest in the birth of the Constitution and the battle over its ratification in its readers, they have a wealth of sources to profitably pursue.

Readers who want to follow the debates in the convention as they unfolded day by day can settle down for weeks with Max Farrand's four-volume edition of *The Records of the Federal Convention of 1787* [1937] or with Madison's personal record, which is now available on the Web through Yale University's ambitious and much welcomed Avalon Project. For the opinions and comments of members of the Confederation Congress and others during the deliberations of the convention and the battle over ratification, a reader can turn to the remarkable multivolume edition of the *Letters of Delegates to Congress, 1774–1789,* edited by Paul H. Smith and published by the Library of Congress.

Those who want to explore scholarly and popular interpretations of the Constitutional convention and its handiwork can turn to the polemics of Charles Beard, whose *An Economic Interpretation of the Constitution* raised a storm of controversy within the academy when it was published in 1913—and which has been stimulating students to debate the nature of the Constitution and the motives of its framers ever since. They can read Gordon Wood's *The Creation of the American Republic, 1776–1787* [1993] for a more positive, erudite critique, or turn to Jack Rakove's *Original Meanings: Politics and Ideas in the Making of the Constitution* [1997] and his *James Madison and the Creation of the American Republic* [1990] for an analysis of the political theory that guided the framers. Christopher and James Lincoln Collier celebrate the Constitution and its creators in their *Decision in Philadelphia: The Constitutional Convention of 1787* [1986], and Catherine Drinker Bowen provides her own well-written celebration of that summer of political inventiveness in her *Miracle at Philadelphia: The Story of the Constitution, May to September, 1787* [1966]. For accounts of the ratification struggle, readers can turn to Jackson Turner Main's classic *The Antifederalists: Critics of the Constitution, 1781–1788* [1961] and they can probe a modern scholar's interpretation of the economic motives of the framers in Forrest McDonald's *We The People: Economic Origins of the American Republic, 1776–1790* [1958] or his *E Pluribus Unum: The Formation of the American Republic, 1776–1790* [1965]. Primary sources on ratification have been collected by three prominent historians, Merrill Jensen, John P. Kaminski, and Gaspare

Saladino, who have undertaken a multivolume project, *The Documentary History of the Ratification of the Constitution* [1976]. For readers who want to delve further into the scholarship on the Constitution, its origins, its advocates, and opponents, they might look at the excellent bibliographic essay by Patrick T. Conley in *The Constitution and the States: The Role of the Original Thirteen in the Framing and Adoption of the Federal Constitution* [1988], which Conley coedited with John Kaminski.

Biographies of the convention delegates abound, and thus, if a particular delegate captures readers' interest or imagination, they are almost certain to find a book to satisfy their curiosity. Or, if they choose, readers can form their own views of many of the framers and their colleagues by reading their collected correspondence. The papers of James Madison, Alexander Hamilton, John Jay, George Washington, Benjamin Franklin, John Adams, and Thomas Jefferson, to name only the most notable, have been edited, annotated, and made available by the remarkable energies of historians working for decades on these major projects. Having worked on both the Hamilton Papers and the Papers of John Jay myself, I can assure readers that reading a man's daily letters to family, friends, political allies, and political enemies provides the most intimate knowledge of his character and personality possible.

# Acknowledgments

A LTHOUGH LATE AT NIGHT, hunched over the computer, a historian might feel that her work is a solitary enterprise, she knows it is not. Her work rests upon the labors of scholars and writers who came before her, and she is helped at every stage along the way by colleagues, students, and editors who patiently read the manuscript from its roughest, most tentative stages to its final version. To have the opportunity to thank these friends and critics is one of the genuine rewards of finishing a book. *A Brilliant Solution* is dedicated to three of my graduate students who took precious time during our biweekly meetings—which we dubbed our "Sunday Morning Dissertation Salon"—to critique their advisor's work in progress. I am proud to say they were fearless; they did not hesitate to tell me when something was poorly developed or poorly argued even though they knew quite well I held their futures in my hands. Their suggestions and criticisms were always right, and as I rewrote and revised, I consoled myself that I had, after all, trained these young scholars well.

My colleague at CUNY's Graduate Center, Professor Thomas Kessner, also read sections of the manuscript, offering sage advice on every occasion. Both Roberta McCutcheon and Norman Fainstein added their comments as well. When the task of turning a manuscript into a book began, Harcourt's Managing Editor David Hough lightened the task of reading the copyedited manuscript with his good humor and frequent words of praise, and Erin DeWitt, whose task it was to catch grammatical errors, monitor punctuation, correct spelling mistakes, and bring clarity to certain convoluted sentences, handled her duties with tact and skill. Through the entire process, Dan Green provided encouragement and politic prodding to insure I met deadlines. And my editor, Jane Isay, demonstrated the patience of Job and the tact of a seasoned diplomat; any academic hoping to write to a larger audience ought to seek out her guidance.

Finally, and as always, I offer my thanks to my two children, Hannah and Matthew, for tolerating the mess of papers and mountains of books spread out on the dining room table whenever their mom embarks on a project. Over the years, they have eaten more than their fair share of Chinese food and pizza, served up inelegantly in the original paper or plastic containers. They have endured their mother's moans and groans, her frantic search for her glasses, and her hysterical calls for help when the computer or the printer gobbled up the day's pages or refused to open up a file. Most of all, they have saved me from any fears that my temporary neglect has had bad consequences by growing into the most beautiful, the most handsome, the most talented, and the most delightful young people in the world.

# Index